W9-AQZ-234

The Air-Line to Seattle

THE AIR-LINE TO SEATTLE

Studies in Literary and Historical Writing about America

Kenneth S. Lynn

The University of Chicago Press
Chicago and London

KENNETH S. LYNN, currently professor of history at Johns Hopkins University, is a prolific and gifted writer. In addition to his many articles, essays, and reviews he is the author of *The Dream of Success, Mark Twain and Southwestern Humor, William Dean Howells, Visions of America,* and *A Divided People.*

The University of Chicago Press, Chicago 60637
The University of Chicago Press, Ltd., London

Printed in the United States of America

5 4 3 2 1   83 84 85 86 87 88 89

Library of Congress Cataloging in Publication Data

Lynn, Kenneth Schuyler.
The air-line to Seattle.

Includes index.
1. United States—Historiography—Addresses, essays, lectures. 2. American literature—History and criticism—Addresses, essays, lectures. 3. United States in literature—Addresses, essays, lectures. I. Title.
E175.L93 1983   973′.072   82-13459
ISBN 0-226-49832-8

**For
Joseph Epstein**

Contents

Acknowledgments

All of the essays herein first appeared in periodicals. Some of the essays, however, have been revised for publication in this book. For help in revising "The Regressive Historians," I am grateful to William W. Freehling, Jack P. Greene, and especially David Schuyler.

1

Prologue: The Air-Line to Seattle

The Harvard faculty of the 1890s thought of itself as made up of men of superbly independent mind. George Santayana, a prodigy of detachment, knew otherwise. For years he suppressed his irritation with a whole host of the attitudes that his colleagues uncritically held in common, from their sanctimonious and often disingenuous Protestantism to their snobbish assumption that the Irish Catholics who also lived in Cambridge were nothing more than muckers and their studied lack of interest in the spectacular achievements of American industrial enterprise. Only when America's appetite for global power was denounced as immoral at a gathering of the philosophy department did Santayana finally decide to let the entire university community know how he felt about it.

Because of his Spanish birth, and because his father, stepfather, and maternal grandfather had all lived in the Philippines for a time, Santayana might have been expected to object to the American annexation of the Islands at the conclusion of the war with Spain, and possibly to the installation of an American presence in Puerto Rico, Guam, and insurgent Cuba as well.

Reprinted by permission from *Commentary*, Volume 73, Number 5 (May 1982).

Yet while he was indeed resentful of "the school-master's manner of the American government, walking switch in hand into a neighbor's garden to settle the children's quarrel there," he also believed that Spain's weakness and America's strength made the fall of one empire and the rise of another inevitable—and he was reinforced in this conviction by the philosophical acceptance of loss by his friends and relatives in Spain. Therefore, when his colleague William James denounced the annexation of the Philippines as a "shameless betrayal of American principles" that reeked of "greed, ambition, corruption, and imperialism," Santayana asked himself, "Why was William James so much upset by an event that the victims of it could take so calmly?"

Santayana's answer to that question illustrated his overall opinion of the Harvard faculty. Although James thought of himself as a free man, he was not, because his mind was "held back by old instincts" and was "subject to old delusions." As a pragmatist and a physician, James ought to have realized that the entrance of the United States on to the world stage was a natural development in its "physiological history," but because the "overriding tradition" in him was a mixture of outmoded Transcendentalist idealism and even more outmoded Calvinistic guilt, he had instead given way to moralistic lamentations about the nation's failure to grant instant independence to the Filipinos in the name of Thomas Jefferson's immortal Declaration. James simply could not see that in the context of America's drive to acquire the far-flung bases for which Alfred Thayer Mahan had persuasively argued in his recent book on the influence of seapower upon history, the Declaration of Independence was nothing but "a piece of literature, a salad of illusions."

The forum that Santayana chose for his attack on his fellow professors was the Signet Society, the undergraduate literary club. He liked the company of students anyway, and on this occasion he especially wanted to be in their irreverent midst. Thus it was that on an October evening in 1900, as President McKinley's re-election campaign was entering its final month and the national debate on the Philippines question continued to intensify, Santayana arose amid the wine glasses of a club dinner and recited a satirical poem entitled "Young Sammy's First Wild Oats."

The poem's opening stanzas evoke a secluded glade, the learned inhabitants of which have only the dimmest sense of the hordes of immigrants and the whizzing, west-bound trains that characterize the world beyond its fenced-in limits. The audience at the Signet presumably had no difficulty in recognizing that the poet was talking about the Harvard Yard.

> Mid Uncle Sam's expanded acres
> There's an old, secluded glade
> Where grey Puritans and Quakers
> Still grow fervid in the shade;
> And the same great elms and beeches
> That once graced the ancestral farm,
> Bending to the old men's speeches,
> Lend their words an echo's charm.
> Laurel, clematis, and vine
> Weave green trellises about,
> And three maples and a pine
> Shut the mucker-village out.
> Yet the smoke of trade and battle
> Cannot quite be banished hence,
> And the air-line to Seattle
> Whizzes just behind the fence.

Hobbling across the glade comes an old man, who turns out not to be a professor, but—in poetic tribute to academic Cambridge's oldest intellectual tradition—the deacon of a church. Plaster is the deacon's name, and sanctimoniousness is the quality of his faith. A certain Pastor Wise is next introduced; as his name suggests, he is the spokesman for Santayana. Somewhat further on in the poem, another sort of contrast is set up through the characters of Uncle Sam ("that prim, pompous, pious man"), who stands for the older America for which William James nostalgically yearned, and impetuous, hot-blooded Young Sammy, who represents the ebullient spirit of a burgeoning empire.

Informed of the fact that Young Sammy has been sowing wild oats in various tropical locales with various dusky-skinned maidens, Deacon Plaster indignantly characterizes the youth's behavior as "a wicked sin." To this Puritanical judgment Pastor Wise replies that Americans of Sammy's generation should not be expected to submit to rules of conduct established in a vanished era and that the old men of the glade must not blame the young if they instead choose to be ruled by their proud belief in their own destiny. Although politely phrased, Wise's reply pours scorn on the men of the glade—in effect, on the members of the Harvard faculty—for the irrelevance of their teaching and the impotence of their leadership.

> Can we blame them we mistaught
> If now they seek another guide
> And, since our wisdom comes to naught,
> Take counsel of their proper pride?
> Nature beckons them inviting
> To a deeper draught of fate,
> And, the heart's desire inciting,
> Can we stop and bid them wait?

The wicked wit in "Young Sammy" must have brought down the house at the Signet, for a month later Santayana permitted the poem to be published in the undergraduate humor magazine, the *Lampoon.* Yet the act of making fun of his faculty colleagues only served to increase his sense of alienation from them. In the ensuing years Santayana spent as much time away from Cambridge as he possibly could without giving up his professorship. Even so, he continued to feel trapped by the place. His one consolation was the presence in the Boston area of his mother, to whom he was devoted.

In the summer of 1911, Santayana went on sabbatical leave. He spent most of July and August teaching at the University of California at Berkeley and then set off for Europe. Word reached him in England the following February that his mother had died. Not only did he at once resign his Harvard appointment, but he never again returned to the United States. The lecture he had delivered in August at the Philosophical Union at Berkeley, he later realized, had constituted his farewell address to America.

"The Genteel Tradition in American Philosophy," as the lecture was called, expanded the depiction of Deacon Plaster into a more inclusive portrait of moralizing intellectuals who had fenced themselves off from the mucker-village and the air-line to Seattle. The mentality of the American intelligentsia in general, like the mentality of the Harvard faculty in particular, was becalmed in a "backwater," whereas the mentality of men of affairs was "leaping down a sort of Niagara Rapids" of invention, industry, and social organization. Locked into the beliefs and practices of the past, the intelligentsia aped the Transcendentalists by dissolving the world around them into projections of mind, while the language in which it judged that world was borrowed from the agonized vocabulary of Calvinism.

At the outset of his analysis, Santayana told his listeners that there was no history of dissent from the stultified state of mind he was describing. The "American Intellect," he said grandly, "is all genteel tradition." As he continued speaking, though, he qualified his contention, making it clear that murmurings of revolt had been heard for a long time. Walt Whitman and Henry James, he further acknowledged, had entirely escaped the tradition, each in his own way, and the humorists of the Pacific Slope had half succeeded in doing so. Near the end of the lecture, he even went so far as to say that the tradition had recently "had its flanks turned." On one side, the revolt of the Bohemian temperament had broken out; on the other, an impassioned empiricism had come forward to declare that science was an instrument of success in action and that the universe was still wild and young. These amendments nevertheless left the central thesis of the lecture intact. The American intelligentsia was fatally cut off from "the variety, the unspeakable variety of possible life."

Eleven years separated "Young Sammy" from "The Genteel Tradition." Another eleven separated "The Genteel Tradition" from Santayana's review for the *Dial* of *Civilization in the United States,* a symposium edited by Harold Stearns and including contributions by such established luminaries and coming stars of the early 1920s as Lewis Mumford, H. L. Mencken, Van Wyck Brooks, George Jean Nathan, George Soule, and Ring Lardner. The assumption on which Stearns had set up the symposium was that American civilization was stewing in the juices of a vulgar architecture, idiotic politics, juvenile journalism, corrupt athletics, genteel "culture," hidebound morality, and bankrupt family life, among other poisons, and the contributors spelled out that assumption in unsparing detail. Through their essays there also ran a persistent complaint that American life was profoundly divided between theory and practice, ideals and experience, bookishness and business—a complaint that clearly derived, via Van Wyck

Brooks's intervening manifesto, *America's Coming-of-Age*, from "The Genteel Tradition." The editors of the *Dial* therefore asked Santayana to review the book in the expectation that he would say nice things about his brainchild.

The review that came back to them was a blast. Santayana began by characterizing the essays as "the plaints of superior and highly critical minds suffering from maladaptation." The symposium had taught him more, he said, about the contributors' "palpitating doubts than about America or about civilization." Things shock these authors, he continued, "and their compensatory ideals and plans of reform are fetched from abstract reflection or irrelevant enthusiasms. They are far from expressing the manly heart of America, emancipated from the genteel tradition. They seem to be morally underfed, and they are disaffected." The reviewer would not go so far as to say that *Civilization in the United States* was itself genteel, for "that would enrage its revolutionary authors," but having backed off from that judgment, he proceeded to sum up their work in a phrase that could easily have appeared in "The Genteel Tradition." "The spirit of these critics," he dismissively concluded, "is one of offended sensibility."

The reaction of Stearns and company can be imagined. All their lives, it seemed to them, they had gone out of their way to flout the genteel tradition. Most of them would not have been caught dead in a genteel academic job, nor would they have considered working for a genteel publishing house or a genteel magazine. Where they felt at home was in the city rooms of metropolitan newspapers, or in the editorial offices of journals specializing in avant-garde literature, left-liberal politics, or wholesale jeering. Iconoclasm was the banner under which these hard-drinking cynics, Nietzschean nay-sayers, gentle bookworms, would-be expatriates, and assorted mavericks marched. Santayana certainly had his nerve mentioning them in the same breath with the stifling tradition he had helped to teach them to despise!

After they recovered from their initial shock, however, the *Civilization* writers never gave another thought to what Santayana had said about them, nor did anyone else in the twenties who had admired his earlier work. Yet sixty years later we can see that Santayana's review for the *Dial* was as shrewd a piece of intellectual history as his lecture at Berkeley. To some extent, to be sure, and especially in the case of Mencken, the review had been unfair. Not only did Santayana refuse to concede that Mencken knew an enormous amount about American civilization, but he failed to understand that the Baltimorean's ferociously exaggerated denunciations of his homeland were at bottom an expression of love. But about the overwhelming majority of the *Civilization* symposiasts Santayana was brilliantly right. The intellectuals who turned against the genteel tradition were actually its sons, in the sense that they were as caught up in self-delusion about America as their predecessors had been. Indeed, as the twenties gave way to the thirties, the delusions of some of the sons took on an absurdity undreamed of in the fathers' philosophy. In 1936, for instance, Malcolm Cowley published a book entitled *After the Genteel Tradition*, in which he recapitulated the story of how the long reign of a theory-ridden mentality had at last been overthrown and of how a new generation of American intellectuals had rushed bravely forward to embrace reality. Yet at the very time that Cowley was working on the book he demonstrated how far removed from reality he himself was by turning out a series of columns for the *New Republic* in which he rebuked the condition of Franklin Roosevelt's America by paying glowing tribute to the state of Stalin's Russia.

The sons of the genteel tradition were too affronted by their native land to study it with care. Fortunately, this was not true of V. L. Parrington, Arthur M. Schlesinger, Sr., and a number of other academic authorities on American literature and American history who were at the height of their intellectual powers during the twenties, nor was it true of the procession of remarkable scholars who came to the fore in the thirties, forties, and fifties. Such men as Perry Miller, F. O. Matthiessen, Lionel Trilling, Oscar Handlin, David Herbert Donald, David Potter, T. Harry Williams, and Daniel J. Boorstin made it clear that university professors were indeed able to appreciate the reality of American life, in all its variety.

Yet professional scholarship in these decades was by no means free of the genteel tradition's self-pitying assumption that the American intellectual was morally superior to his countrymen. The literary historians of the twenties, thirties, and forties cherished the view that the American writer was the sensitive victim of a brutally uncaring society, while the so-called New Critics who came to dominate so many English departments in the fifties refused to make any sort of connection between literature and history lest it soil the experience of reading. As for the political and social historians, they beguiled themselves during the interwar decades with the notion that they were battlers in a Manichaean struggle between the forces of evil (the business community) and the forces of righteousness (the intellectuals plus the rest of society) for control of the nation's destiny. By the 1950s, however, many younger historians had come to the opposite but equally unrealistic conclusion that in a democracy characterized by cupidity and anti-intellectualism there was no side with which an intellectual would wish to identify himself.

When the professoriat that lived by such beliefs was finally confronted with the political turbulence of the 1960s, the language of Deacon Plaster was once again heard in the glades of academe. America's presence in Viet Nam was pronounced "a wicked sin." With that judgment ringing in its ears, the professoriat then proceeded to initiate a whole new scholarship about American civilization, in which it incorporated a host of dubious theories, old and new. In the 1980s, the fashioning of that scholarship continues. Seventy years after Santayana first pinned a brilliantly derogatory label upon the hermetic mentality of the nation's intelligentsia, the spirit of the genteel tradition is triumphantly alive in American thought.

2
Falsifying Jefferson

As Louis Hartz pointed out in *The Liberal Tradition in America* (1955), political theorists of the Left and the Right have always been frustrated by the fact that America skipped the feudal stage of history. The lack of a feudal experience means first of all that we lack a socialist tradition, for the hidden origin of socialist thought in Western societies, says Hartz, is to be found in the class consciousness of the feudal ethos. And the absence of a socialist tradition means in turn that we have never developed a tradition of reaction; lacking Robespierre, we also lack Maistre. What dominates our politics instead is a widely shared belief in the American Way of Life, which traces back through a series of transformations to revolutionary America's attachment to the liberalism of John Locke. Confronted by this maddeningly monolithic heritage, the disaffected analyst of modern American politics is hard put to discover home-grown precedents for an alternative philosophy of government. It therefore behooves him, says Hartz, to transcend the American past, rather than to attempt to recapture it. "As for a child who is leaving adolescence, there is no going home again for America."

The leftist (formerly rightist) writer Garry Wills, however,

Reprinted by permission from *Commentary*, Volume 66, Number 4 (October 1978).

refuses to believe that America can't go home again. In his startlingly inventive book, *Inventing America,* he sets out to recapture the Declaration of Independence by reinterpreting it. Wills's thesis is that the Declaration is not grounded in Lockean individualism, as we have been accustomed to think, but is a communitarian manifesto deriving from the common-sense philosophers of the Scottish Enlightenment—Kames, Hutcheson, Reid, Dugald Stewart, et al. It would have been a major accomplishment if Wills had succeeded in substantiating this bold proposition. At one stroke he would have altered our whole sense of the American experiment in self-government as Jefferson envisioned it. A new nation, conceived in liberty, would have been transmogrified into a new nation, conceived in communality.

But Wills does not build a credible case. Far from being a careful work of scholarship, *Inventing America* is the tendentious report of a highly political writer whose unannounced but nonetheless obvious aim is to supply the history of the Republic with as pink a dawn as possible. That his book has been prominently reviewed and lavishly praised—by academic authorities no less than by newspapermen—is a telling indication of the intellectual temper of the times. In an age of ideology, the inventions of ideologues have come to seem plausible, even though they are fantastic. *Inventing America* does not help us to understand Thomas Jefferson, but its totally unearned acclaim tells us a good deal about modern-day intellectuals and their terrible need for radical myths.

In the introduction he provided in the mid-1970s to Lillian Hellman's *Scoundrel Time,* Wills spewed out a wholesale contempt for the political spirit of post–World War II America. The same lack of discrimination marks his attitude in *Inventing America* toward previous commentators on Jefferson. From Abraham Lincoln to Erik Erikson, from Gilbert Chinard, Dumas Malone, Julian Boyd, and Howard Mumford Jones to Adrienne Koch, Daniel J. Boorstin, Merrill D. Peterson, and Fawn Brodie, no one is exempt from Wills's critical swipes. But his severest attacks are aimed at Carl Becker, for Becker's classic study, *The Declaration of Independence* (1922), is the principal obstacle in the path of his revisionism.

What has made Becker's book so conclusive, asks Wills, that even half a century later authorities on Jefferson have found nothing important to add to it? Merrill D. Peterson, he concedes, does express "misgivings" in *The Jefferson Image in the American Mind* (1960) about Becker's relativistic belief that the realities of the modern world have undermined the supposedly self-evident truths of the Declaration. Nevertheless, says Wills, Peterson agrees with every other well-known scholar in the field that Becker's book is a masterpiece—and the author of *Inventing America* is sure he knows why. "The secret of this universal acclaim lies in the inability of any later student to challenge Becker's basic thesis—that Jefferson found in *John Locke* [the emphasis is Wills's] 'the ideas which he put into the Declaration.'" Although Wills comes down very hard on what he refers to as the "misreadings" by other students of Jefferson, he himself is a spectacular misreader, surpassing even the redoubtable Fawn Brodie, as the foregoing quotations at least begin to make clear. Not only does Peterson not express misgivings about Becker's relativism, but it is not Becker's basic thesis that Jefferson found the ideas he put into the Declaration in the writings of John Locke. His thesis, rather, is that Jefferson found the Declaration's ideas in "the American mind," as Jefferson himself declared he did. The political philosophy of eighteenth-century Americans, Becker emphasized, was not only set forth in the works of Locke, but "was expounded from an early date in pamphlet and newspaper by many a Brutus, Cato, or Popliocola. An important, but less noticed, channel through which the fundamental ideas of that philosophy—God, Nature, Reason—were made familiar to the average man, was the church."

Becker's book begins with the important reminder that the document which we call the Declaration of Independence did not represent the formal act of separation from Great Britain—that step had already been taken by the Continental Congress on July 2, 1776—but was an argument designed to convince a "candid world" that the separation was necessary and right. According to Becker, the argument rests on two premises: (1) that all men have imprescriptible natural rights; (2) that the British empire is a voluntary federation of independent states. Jefferson did not dream up these premises for the occasion, Becker points out. The doctrine of natural rights had long been regarded as a commonplace. The theory that the British empire was a federal union and that Parliament had no authority over the colonies was more novel, having arisen out of the long dispute with Britain over colonial rights. Yet by the summer of 1776, this theory too was being taken for granted.

In later years, John Adams made the Declaration's lack of intellectual originality a ground for minimizing Jefferson's achievement. "There is not an idea in it," Adams wrote to Timothy Pickering, "but what had been hackneyed in Congress for two years before." Becker contends, however, that this criticism is wholly irrelevant, since the strength of the Declaration was precisely that it said what most colonists were thinking. Nothing would have been more futile than an attempt to justify a revolution on principles which no one had ever heard of before. As Jefferson patiently explained in 1825, the year before his death, his task in the Declaration had been

> not to find out new principles, or new arguments, never before thought of, not merely to say things which had never been said before, but to place before mankind the common sense of the subject, in terms so plain and firm as to command their assent. . . . Neither aiming at originality of principles or sentiments, nor yet copied from any particular and previous writing, it was intended to be an expression of the American mind. . . . All its authority rests then on the harmonizing sentiments of the day, whether expressed in conversation, in letters, printed essays, or the elementary books of public right, as Aristotle, Cicero, Locke, Sidney, etc.

It was not a path-breaking philosopher, or even the disciple of one, who was asked to draft the Declaration, but a writer who combined an extraordinary intellectual sensitivity with what John Adams called "a peculiar felicity of expression" and who could therefore be counted on to state the American case with uncommon clarity and eloquence.

Both in its form and in its phraseology, the Declaration so closely follows certain sentences in the second of Locke's *Two Treatises on Government* that Becker was convinced that Jefferson had not merely "absorbed" the idea of the *Treatise* secondhand, the way many other colonists had, but had read the text several times over. Yet while he found it "interesting" to establish this connection, Becker was more concerned with the question of why Jefferson and his contemporaries were ready to be impressed by the Whig apologist for the Revolution of 1688.

Unlike Garry Wills, who talks about Jefferson's mind as if it were a blob of hot sealing wax passively submitting to the imprint of European ideas, Becker believed that, "Generally speaking, men are influenced by books which clarify their own thought, which express their own notions well, or which suggest to them ideas which their minds are already predisposed to accept." Therefore, anyone interested in the origin of the Declaration's ideas must look for "the origin of those common underlying preconceptions that made the minds of many men, in different countries, run along the same track in their political thinking." In making that search, Becker found a congruence between the American rebellion against George the Third and the protracted parliamentary struggle with the monarchy in seventeenth-century England. A strong antipathy to kings predisposed the spokesman for the American mind, as it had predisposed Locke, to turn toward some new sanction for political authority. The Lockean philosophy in the Declaration expressed American notions well.

Because Becker's book adheres to Jefferson's own commentary on the Declaration, Wills has to explain away the latter in order to discredit the former. Thus he begins his critique with an attempt to minimize Jefferson's statement that the Declaration is an expression of the American mind. Jefferson was "probably referring," says Wills, only to the list of grievances which makes up the lengthiest part of the Declaration, and not to the preamble. There is not a shred of evidence—not even the slightest hint of ambiguity—to justify this notion. Jefferson's 1825 commentary (which Wills erroneously says was written in 1814) straightforwardly refers to the document as a whole. Nevertheless, Wills claims to see a distinction because he is determined to turn an argument based on the imprescriptible rights of individuals into an enunciation of brotherhood, and this effort requires him to do whatever he can to separate Jefferson's thinking from that of his more humdrum compatriots. Wills's reinterpretation of the Declaration consists in large part of an analysis of passages which precede the list of grievances; therefore, he cannot bring himself to admit that these passages merely express generally accepted sentiments of the day, rather than the very special vision of a very special man. All that one can say in defense of Wills in this matter is that at least he has the restraint to offer his novel idea as no more than probably true. Twenty-five pages later, alas, restraint vanishes: "Jefferson was expressing a common American mind on the concrete grievances that filled the practical debates at Philadelphia." That the rest of the document also expresses the American mind is a fact that no longer exists, as far as the author of *Inventing America* is concerned.

Another statement in Jefferson's commentary that Wills finds acutely embarrassing is the assertion that a portion of the Declaration's authority rests on ideas in "the elementary books of public right, as Aristotle, Cicero, Locke, Sidney, etc." Wills dearly wishes, of course, that Jefferson had not mentioned Locke's name, and he does his best to contain the damage by arguing that Jefferson "is deliberately citing works of general regard, rather than a set of specific influences on him." But the whole point of Jefferson's commentary is that the American mind was the specific influence on him and that that influence was compounded of conversation, letters, essays, and books, including Locke's.

Wills's main assault on Becker is on his literary criticism. Becker said that a number of phrases in the Declaration echoed phrases in Locke's second *Treatise on Government*, but he failed to single them out. To Wills, this means that they do not exist. There is no verbal echo of the *Treatise* in the Declaration, Wills flatly asserts. "There is, indeed, no demonstrable verbal echo of the *Treatise* in all of Jefferson's vast body of writings." With this statement Wills challenges Becker's scholarly authority in the teeth of his supposed strength, for throughout his career Becker was repeatedly praised for his sensitivity to other people's writings as well as for his own exceedingly graceful literary style. Yet if Becker were alive today, he would have no trouble defending himself, thanks to the fact that the Declaration contains many parallels to Locke, as two examples will suggest.

1. Jefferson says that "all experience hath shown, that mankind are more disposed to suffer, while evils are sufferable, than to right themselves by abolishing the forms to which they are accustomed." In the corresponding passage in his *Treatise*, Locke says that "the People, who are more disposed to suffer than right themselves by Resistance, are not apt to stir."

2. Jefferson says, "But when a long train of abuses and usur-

pations, pursuing invariably the same object, evinces a design to reduce them under absolute despotism . . ." Locke says, "But if a long train of Abuses, Prevarications, and Artifices, all tending the same way, make the design visible to the People . . ."

In the light of such comparisons, there can be little doubt that Becker was right when he said that Jefferson, "having read Locke's *Treatise*, was so taken with it that he read it again, and still again, so that afterwards its very phrases reappear in his own writing."

Having done his best to destroy Becker's reputation as an explicator of texts, Wills then proceeds to show us how competent he himself is in that line of work. Indeed, he is virtually compelled to do so, for external evidence of the ideas that were on Jefferson's mind at the time he wrote the Declaration is in extraordinarily short supply. On February 1, 1770, the twenty-six-year-old Jefferson suffered a catastrophe. His house in Albemarle burned to the ground, together with his books and papers. In the ensuing six years he not only failed to reconstruct a written record of his early life, but did not write enough letters to furnish us with an adequate record of his activities in the years immediately preceding his composition of the Declaration. This means that Wills, in order to convince us of the Scottish Enlightenment's formative influence on the mind of the Declaration's author, has to resort to an analysis of the document itself. Wills does his best to marshal other evidence in addition, but it is woefully thin, especially since Jefferson's retrospective commentary of 1825 is of no help to his interpretation.

In an attempt to extract some supporting facts from Jefferson's college days, Wills points out that William Small, Jefferson's favorite teacher at William and Mary, was a Scotsman who had studied with John Gregory, the center of a philosophical circle in Aberdeen in the 1750s. Small taught practically everything during Jefferson's years as an undergraduate. But Wills cannot pin down what, precisely, Small imparted to Jefferson. In Scotland, says Wills, men like Francis Hutcheson and Adam Smith used the ethics course to expound their central philosophical tenets, connecting them with the sciences through mathematics and with rhetoric through a philosophy of beauty. "This seems to be," says Wills—and the tentativeness of his language reveals that he does not really know—what Small attempted in his course on ethics, rhetoric, and belles-lettres. Yet even if it was, we do not know that the young Jefferson was impressed by what he learned about political science from the ideas of Hutcheson and Smith. In *The Commonplace Book,* which represents the notes taken by Jefferson on law, political science, and religion starting from the time when he was either a student of law or a young lawyer, there are no entries from the works of Hutcheson or Smith and no citation of either name. There is, on the other hand, an entry from Postlethwayt's *Universal Dictionary of Trade and Commerce* (1751), which Jefferson would trot out many years later in refutation of the theories of Adam Smith (see the letter to John W. Eppes, November 6, 1813). The fact that Jefferson copied Postlethwayt but not Smith into his *Commonplace Book* does not encourage belief in the idea that the mind of the man who wrote the Declaration was shaped by Scottish thinkers.

In 1764, the year of William Small's return to Scotland, Wills doggedly continues, the Scottish philosopher Thomas Reid, a figure on the Aberdeen scene, published his *Inquiry into the Human Mind.* Small was "bound to have met" Reid upon his return, and the gossip about Aberdeen philosophers that Small relayed to his former student in America (how Wills knows that he relayed such gossip, I have no idea) "must have made" Jefferson greet the publication of Reid's book with special interest. Once again, Wills's phrasing indicates he is just guessing. Jefferson's *Commonplace Book* has nothing in it from the *Inquiry,* or from any other book by Reid, and makes no reference to his name. The *Inquiry* does appear on a long list of books drawn up by Jefferson for his friend Robert Skipwith in 1771, but this scarcely justifies Wills's conclusion that Jefferson "came to know" Reid's book some time before the drawing up of the Skipwith list. Wills's further statement that Jefferson's knowledge of Reid grew through his friendship with Reid's student, Dugald Stewart, is irrelevant to the question of Reid's influence on the Declaration, because Jefferson did not come to know Stewart until many years later.

Wills mainly tries to persuade us of the truth of his thesis by the force of textual analysis. Unfortunately for him, he is neither sensitive to literature nor sensible about it. He first reveals his deficiencies as a literary critic in the prologue to *Inventing*

America. In the midst of criticizing Abraham Lincoln for what Wills regards as a romantic misreading of the Declaration, he pauses to pay tribute to the stylistic powers of the author of the Gettysburg Address. "Abraham Lincoln was a great and conscious verbal craftsman. The man who writes, 'The world will little note, nor long remember, what we do here,' has done his best—by mere ripple and interplay of liquids—to make sure the world will remember; as it has." But what the world remembers is that Lincoln said, "what we say here." The tin-eared critic then proceeds to mangle the music of the First Inaugural: "The mystic cords of memory, stretching from every battlefield and patriot grave to every living heart and hearthstone, all over this broad land, will yet swell the chorus of the Union . . ." How could any student of the American language not know that those were "chords" that would yet swell the chorus of the Union?

Hard upon the heels of misquotation comes critical absurdity. "Thomas Jefferson . . . was not, like Lincoln, a 19th-century romantic living in the full glow of transcendentalism." But the full glow of transcendentalism had faded by the time Lincoln became a national political figure, and in any event he had no interest in its doctrines.

Wills's literary criticism gets down to Jeffersonian cases in the chapter dealing with the Declaration's opening phrase: "When in the course of human events it becomes necessary . . ." This opening is "Newtonian," we are told. "It lays down the law. . . . In the flow of things there is perceivable necessity, a fixity within flux." With these words, Wills launches into an eighteen-page discussion of eighteenth-century science, strewing references to Diderot, Rittenhouse, Dr. Arbuthnot, Chastellux, Francis Hutcheson, Antoine Le Camus, J. L. Moreau de la Sarthe, Voltaire, Daniel Defoe, and Newton, among others, as he goes. Finally, in the closing paragraph, we return to the text of the Declaration. If Jefferson did not mean the opening phrase of the Declaration in a Newtonian sense, Wills astonishingly declares, then he has "seriously misled us," for he knew well "how large the claim was when he spoke of the separation of one people from another as 'necessary.'" At the last possible moment, in other words, Wills confronts the possibility that the flat statement with which he had begun the chapter may not be true after all. Driven into a corner by his inability to substantiate his claim, he responds to this threat to his intellectual reputation by impugning Jefferson's.

A less combative critic would have pointed out that in the *Oxford English Dictionary*'s definition of "necessary" in the modest sense of "needful to be done," two of the six examples given are from the seventeenth century and two are from the eighteenth. To the world of Jefferson, "necessary" had more than one meaning, and the opening of the Declaration is not prima facie Newtonian. Which meaning did the author and his audience have in mind? When we look at the accompanying verb, "becomes," we have our answer. Fixities within fluxes do not "become."

The aim of this opening exercise in textual analysis is to get us in an eighteenth-century mood for what is to follow. Becker had emphasized that a seventeenth-century inspiration lay behind the political theory and practice of revolutionary America. But Wills wants us to regard the Declaration as a thoroughly modern document, smacking of science and suffused with the communitarianism of the Scottish Enlightenment. According to Wills, the principal difference between Locke and the Scottish thinkers is that Locke conceived of man in a state of nature as an autonomous entity, whereas Kames, Hutcheson, Stewart, et al. believed that pregovernmental man was already bound to his fellows by ties of affection and instinctive benevolence. All men were born with a moral sense which enabled them to tell the difference between right and wrong. When men came together in society, they did so in order to guarantee, in Hutcheson's famous formula, "the greatest happiness of the greatest number."

Thus happiness had a public meaning for the Scottish thinkers, says Wills, a communitarian meaning. He also insists that they thought of equality in a different way than Locke did. In the Lockean system of natural rights, men were equal because they all were entitled to life, liberty, and property. But for the Scots, says Wills, equality was rooted in human nature; in spite of differences in intelligence, strength, cultural advantage, and wealth, all men had an innate moral faculty.

The reverse side of Wills's claim that there are no direct textual parallels between Locke's second *Treatise* and the Declaration is his assertion that parallels to the Declaration can be found everywhere in the writings of the Scottish school. The passages he offers by way of proof merely remind us that Wills has no feeling for the cadences of language. What his textual comparatism comes down to is a philosophical dissection of individual words in the Declaration in which Wills discerns a dominant Scottish influence. As in his chapter on "necessary," he wanders far afield in search of support for his interpretations. He also has no qualms about citing references from the older Jefferson in order to demonstrate what the thirty-three-year-old author of the Declaration had in mind.

For example, he backs up his contention that Jefferson in 1776 was a moral-sense egalitarian by quoting from the letter Jefferson wrote to his nephew, Peter Carr, in 1787: "The moral sense, or conscience, is . . . given to all human beings. . . . State a moral case to a plowman and a professor. The former will decide it as well and often better than the latter." What Wills neglects to tell us, however, is that when Jefferson wrote to Carr he was in Paris, his nephew in America. The spectacle of the idle, corrupt society of European courtiers disgusted Jefferson and aroused in him admiring thoughts of hardworking American farmers and of the harmony and dignity of Indian tribal life. The anti-intellectual egalitarianism he voiced in this letter was not a worked-out, consistently held philosophy, but a temporary means of identifying himself with the untainted life of simple people. It is a sign of Wills's lack of historical imagination, as well as of his relentless ideological bias, that he does not provide us with this context for the Carr letter.

Furthermore, even if Jefferson had been a consistent believer in moral-sense philosophy, this would not have made him an egalitarian, for Wills has magnified the extent to which the Scottish philosophers believed in the uniformity of human nature. Lord Kames, the one Scottish thinker whom the young Jefferson quoted at length in his *Commonplace Book*, explicitly denied that the moral sense was a fully formed and instinctively operating faculty in all men. The moral sense, said Kames, "improves gradually like our other powers and faculties." In the margin of one of Kames's *Essays on the Principles of Morality and Natural Religion*, Jefferson penned a note expressing his complete agreement with Kames's developmental conception, and even in the letter to Peter Carr he says at one point that moral sense is given to all human beings "in a stronger or weaker degree." All men, in sum, were not created equal, morally speaking. Some men had less well developed moral faculties than others, and while inferior faculties were susceptible of "refinement," as Jefferson noted in his marginal comment in Kames, the process required centuries of historical change. The claim that the author of the Declaration believed in the moral equality of eighteenth-century men (black as well as white, we are assured) represents Wills's most blatant effort to rewrite the Declaration in his own ideological terms.

In his *Treatise on Government* Locke defined man's fundamental rights in terms of "life, liberty, and property." Why did the author of the Declaration alter this familiar definition? Many interpreters believe that Jefferson merely hoped to give a rhetorically fresh twist to Locke's formulation, but did not intend to change its meaning. Wills thinks otherwise. "Property" connoted private selfishness to the eighteenth century; but to many thinkers, we are told, the alternative term employed by Jefferson referred to the common weal. Hutcheson, Chastellux, and other quantifying Scotsmen and Frenchmen believed that public happiness was a measurable phenomenon and could be augmented by conscious planning. Increased happiness was within the range of social possibility, and men pursued it.

Jefferson shared the quantifiers' faith, according to Wills. Chastellux in the early 1770s had proclaimed that one of the major indexes of happiness in any culture was population density; the higher the density, the happier the people. A decade later, in one of the chapters in *Notes on the State of Virginia* (1784–85), Jefferson also addressed himself to the problem of population growth. He opposed a large-scale immigration to Virginia because American society had not had much experience of self-rule and could not absorb many immigrants without endangering a precarious social harmony. "Suppose 20 millions of republican Americans thrown all of a sudden into France, what would be the condition of that kingdom? If it would be more turbulent, less happy, less strong, we may believe that the addition of half a million foreigners to our present number would produce a similar effect here." The passage would seem to indicate that Jefferson did not agree with Chastellux that large population was a key to public happiness, but Wills says that in fact the passage "implies" agreement. "Notice how, in that quote," says Wills—and the upcoming emphasis is his—"the amount of *happiness* is forecast *on the basis of numbers*."

Wills leaves out even more evidence than he distorts. As William Peden has pointed out, Jefferson wrote *Notes on Virginia* almost in spite of himself. The book was begun and all but completed during the darkest period of his life, in the final months of his governorship of an invaded Virginia and in the period of retirement that followed. The motivation behind the book was the urgent desire of the French government to acquire information about the American states. The French wanted facts and figures because they were becoming more involved with a political rebellion that was in deep trouble. At about the same time as the battle of Camden, in which demoralized Virginia soldiers were put to rout, François Marbois, the secretary of the French legation at Philadelphia, distributed a semiofficial questionnaire about the American states among members of the Continental Congress. Jefferson agreed to answer for Virginia.

He took up the question of Virginia's population because Marbois specifically asked him about it. He argued against the idea of rapidly populating the state with immigrants, on the grounds both of America's inexperience with self-rule and of the amount of unarable land in Virginia. Yet at the same time Jefferson sought to reassure the numbers-conscious French that eventually Virginia would achieve a "competent population" by natural propagation. That word, "competent," is significant. In effect, what Jefferson was saying in his chapter on population was that America was destined to become a viable nation and that the French need have no fears about an American alliance.

Notes on Virginia does not cast light on the meaning of "the pursuit of happiness." Indeed, happiness as a concept is not dealt with in the *Notes* in any form. In the quotation from the book that Wills himself cites, the word does not even appear. Jefferson uses three adjectives in sequence, "turbulent," "happy," and "strong." Wills converts the second into a noun, ignores the first and third, and bids us notice how Jefferson forecasts happiness on the basis of numbers—whereas Jefferson is really talking about social stability and how best to achieve it, as our conservative revolutionists were wont to do. It is on shell games like this that Wills builds his reinterpretation of the Declaration of Independence.

his motives for marrying her . . . , are not legitimately open to question."

Even more remarkable than the vehemence with which these sweeping statements are expressed is the absence of any substantive follow-up to them. Not a single detail of Emerson's pursuit of Ellen is adduced in support of the interpretation placed upon it.

"When I was young, I forgot how to laugh," a Danish contemporary of Emerson's once confessed. But "when I was older," he added, "I opened my eyes and beheld reality, at which I began to laugh, and since then I have not stopped laughing. I saw . . . that love's rich dream was marriage with an heiress . . . . This I saw, and I laughed." Was Emerson the sort of fortune-hunting hypocrite whom Kierkegaard had in mind when he wrote those sardonic words—and whom Henry James would depict some decades later in such novels as *The Portrait of a Lady* and *The Wings of the Dove*? The question is decidedly interesting, but like all his skittish predecessors, the author of *Representative Man* refused to explore it.

The failure of Porte and others to come to grips with the problem of Emerson's first marriage is only an example—to be sure, a particularly glaring example—of the larger deficiency in their work. Just as Emerson himself denied the inherent worth of sense experience and gloried instead in the vaporousness of an ideal world, so his biographers have traditionally underemphasized his life as a man and overemphasized his life as a thinker. Even Ralph L. Rusk, in his prodigiously scholarly *Life of Ralph Waldo Emerson* (1949), is extremely disappointing on the subject of what sort of a human being Emerson was and of how he got that way.

In giving his recent biography the private name by which Emerson was known to his family during his college days, Gay Wilson Allen has made clear his desire to bring Emersonian scholarship down to earth. As he goes on to say in the preface to *Waldo Emerson,* he undertook the book in the belief that Emerson's "intimate, personal life" deserved closer scrutiny than authorities like Rusk had accorded it.

On the very first page of the first chapter, Allen gets right down to business by presenting Emerson's resentful memories of being mistreated in early boyhood by his father. "I have no recollections of him that can serve me," the forty-seven-year-old essayist bitterly observed to his brother William in 1850. "I was eight years old when he died, & only remember a somewhat social gentleman, but severe to us children, who twice or thrice put me in mortal terror by forcing me into the salt water off some wharf or bathing house, and I still recall the fright with which, after some of this salt experience, I heard his voice one day, (as Adam that of the Lord in the garden,) summoning us to a new bath, and I vainly endeavouring to hide myself."

The severity of Emerson's mother took a different form. Every morning after breakfast, she retired to her room for an hour of Bible-reading, meditation, and soul-searching which her five sons (she lost three other children in their infancy) never once dared to interrupt. For in her husbandless household Ruth Haskins Emerson was no less absolute a sovereign than she believed God to be in the universe. If this deeply religious woman found it unnecessary to raise her voice to her offspring, it was because they were thoroughly intimidated by her reserve. So remote, indeed, was her manner that it makes one wonder whether she thought of motherhood as anything but a duty to be performed as efficiently as possible. Whenever, for instance, her sons were reunited with her after days or weeks of separation, she would embrace them briefly, but rarely touched them thereafter. As Allen notes, the lesson of emotional inhibition was learned early by the author of "Self-Reliance."

The Emerson boys also came under the care, from time to time, of their eccentric aunt, Mary Moody Emerson, whose fasts and other acts of self-denial were "masochistic" and "pathological," in the opinion of the author of *Waldo Emerson.* "It is an awful symptom," she confided to her diary one night, "if we cannot in the presence of God promise to renounce every indulgence of eating, sleep, dress, recreation, reading, study & friendship which appears *suspicious*!" In another entry, she reviled herself as "all animal—all eat and sleep," but three weeks later recorded a recovery of morale as she thought of the cleansing power of death. "Tomorrow," she ecstatically proclaimed, "we may be forever free from the grossness of a putrid carcase." Inasmuch as Aunt Mary did not keep such sentiments to herself, it is not suprising that her eventually famous nephew also became obsessed with the pursuit of moral purity.

A harsh father who suddenly died, an emotionally ungiving

mother, and an aunt whose eagerness for the immaculate embrace of eternity prompted her to make a shroud for herself long before her death and then wear it as a house dress—these were the principal adult figures in Emerson's childhood world. Allen's assessment of their personalities is superbly frank, as is his account of what Emerson was like as a boy. His physical health was not at all robust and he was often ill. Yet for all his frailness he was quarrelsome and aggressive toward other boys and was consequently disliked by them; as his uncle Samuel Ripley was said to have remarked, only grown people were fond of young Ralph. At the age of seventeen, however, by which time he was a senior at Harvard, Emerson did develop an attachment of sorts to a freshman named Martin Gay, although the two youths never exchanged "above a dozen words." For the most part, Emerson was content merely to stare at Martin or to write about him in his journal after they had parted. The possibility cannot be ruled out, Allen bluntly remarks, that Emerson at this point was "bordering on homosexuality."

Unfortunately, that kind of plain speaking does not last beyond the early chapters of *Waldo Emerson.* As the author follows Emerson out of adolescence into early manhood, he suddenly loses his biographical nerve. Instead of continuing his candid analysis of all the evidence available to him, Allen begins to explain away, ignore completely, or otherwise mishandle the most significant pieces of it.

The turning point in the book occurs on page 62, at the moment when the nineteen-year-old Emerson has decided to take a hard look at himself. "I have not the kind affections of a pigeon," Allen quotes Emerson as saying in his journal. This arrestingly phrased self-estimate would seem to be very much worth pondering, but the biographer urges us not to take it at face value. "Of course this severe judgment of Waldo Emerson on himself must be largely discounted—or at least modified. He was not so much selfish as unsociable, and this in turn was the result of his introversion, lack of confidence, and inability to take the initiative in meeting young people of his own age."

The disclaimer tells us more about Allen than about Emerson. In the first place, Emerson was not accusing himself of selfishness, but of a lack of human affection—a much more inclusive charge. Moreover, the charge cannot be reduced to unsociability simply by saying that Emerson was introverted and shy, for these qualities are often found in people who are fundamentally indifferent to their fellow men. And the two ensuing paragraphs in Emerson's journal which spell out his indictment of himself cannot be overlooked just because Allen finds it convenient not to quote them. I am "ungenerous & selfish, cautious & cold," Emerson wrote. "There is not in the whole wide Universe of God . . . one being to whom I am attached with warm & entire devotion,—not a being to whom I have joined fate for weal or woe, not one whose interests I have nearly & dearly at heart." These "frightful confessions," he concluded, are "a true picture of a barren & desolate soul."

In discussing the long-range psychological consequences of Emerson's relationship with his mother, Allen has no difficulty in making general reference to a legacy of emotional inhibition; but when confronted with the appalling specifics of that inhibition, he seeks to cover them up. Emerson, on the other hand, made no effort to conceal his coldness. At the age of nineteen, he identified himself as suffering from the same inability to feel warmly about people that would later make it impossible for him to find adequate satisfaction in his relations with Alcott, Carlyle, Thoreau, and Margaret Fuller and that would cause him to conclude his essay on "Friendship" with the austere assertion that we walk alone in this world.

At the same time that the young Emerson was unable to devote himself to anyone out of love, he was powerless to break free of a devotion based on fear. Thus when it came time for him to choose a profession, he elected to enter the Harvard Divinity School. He would become, like his father before him, a Unitarian minister.

Within a few weeks of making this counter-phobic identification with the authority figure who had terrorized his childhood, he began to be plagued by a series of health problems. First he came down with a painfully lame hip and then developed such serious eye trouble that he was unable to read. What part did unresolved psychological conflict play in these calamities? Even if ultimately unanswerable, that question needs to be addressed at length by anyone seriously interested in Emerson's intimate, personal life. Allen, alas, settles for a conjecture that is as cautious as it is brief. It "seems unlikely," he says, that Emerson's eye trouble was psychosomatic, because two operations completely restored his use of his eyes. The issue of whether there was a physical necessity for the operations is quietly sidestepped.

In the fall of 1826, just as the twenty-three-year-old Emerson was about to be licensed to preach by the Middlesex Association of Unitarian Ministers, calamity struck again. He felt a terrifying "constriction" in his lungs. Although all of Emerson's previous biographers have assumed he had developed tuberculosis, Allen, to his considerable credit, introduces a letter from Emerson to his brother William in which the invalid says that he had "no symptoms that any physician extant can recognize or understand. I have my maladies all to myself." Having made this important point, however, the author of *Waldo Emerson* is too reverential to do anything with it. "This does sound psychosomatic," he admits, but apparently no reason occurs to him why such a condition should have developed. "The pain in his chest could hardly have been caused by his fear of failing in the pulpit," Allen remarks in a tone of perplexity, as he hastily moves on to less confusing matters. In his desire to get away from the subject of Emerson's psychopathology, he does not even pause to point out that the ministerial career of Emerson's father had been interrupted by a bout of tuberculosis three years before his untimely demise, nor does he remind us about the child who had been frightened to death that he would drown, that is, that his lungs would fill up with water, when his father shoved him off a Boston wharf.

Assisted by a loan from his uncle, Samuel Ripley, Emerson spent the winter of 1826/27 convalescing in the South. Upon his return home, he considered abandoning his commitment to the ministry "on the score of health," but as the fear of tuberculosis faded he started accepting invitations to preach in the pulpits of other ministers. The inconsequential fees he earned in this way during the next two years did very little to diminish his concern about earning a living wage, reducing his considerable debts, and paying at least a part of the soaring medical bills being incurred by his brothers. Bulkeley, who was mentally retarded, had now become "perfectly deranged," and when servants could not cope with him, he had to be placed in McLean's Asylum. Edward was no sooner cured of tuberculosis than he began to suffer from fainting fits and descents into delirium; "in a state of violent derangement," he, too, was eventually sent to McLean's. Charles's health was also none too good, although

Emerson seems not to have noticed this, possibly because he was distracted by the news from New York that William had endangered his life by dint of too much work and too little food. "We are born to trouble," Emerson exclaimed in a letter to William.

It was in a time, then, of acute financial embarrassment for him that Emerson met and married a sheltered, innocent girl eight years his junior. Ellen Tucker was the daughter of a Boston merchant who upon his death had left a considerable fortune to his wife and children, and the stepdaughter of Colonel William Kent, one of the most prominent citizens of Concord, New Hampshire. Ellen's father and brother had died of tuberculosis; her mother and sister suffered from it as well; and she, too, had recently begun to "raise blood."

From the moment of her formal engagement in December, 1828, Ellen's expressions of love for Emerson were far more ardent than his for her. "I care not if he gives me a pint," she wrote in a letter, "I shall give him an ocean." Indeed, the excitement he aroused in her made her doctors wonder whether the experience of being with him was doing further damage to her health. In the early summer of 1829, their suspicions increased when she suffered another hemorrhage while Emerson was visiting her, and he was ordered to stay away from Concord until she had regained at least a portion of her lost strength. Not until early August was he permitted to see her again.

The only jarring note for Ellen during this blissful reunion was her fiancé's insistence that they discuss the making of her will. Perhaps all he said was that she ought to have one; perhaps he said a great deal more. The details of their conversation, says Allen, are "impossible to recover" from the "ambiguous references" in Ellen's subsequent letters to Emerson. As for Emerson's letters to Ellen, they "have not survived."

Why Emerson's letters no longer exist is the first issue Allen fails to confront. Did Ellen destroy them because they distressed her? Or did Emerson himself destroy them, after Ellen's death, because they did not conform with his image of himself as morally pure?

Allen also fails to make clear that Emerson's conversation with Ellen in Concord was but the opening gun of a considerable campaign—as Ellen's letters unmistakably demonstrate. She called her will "the ugly subject" and emphasized how reluctant she was to ask her mother to write to Pliny Cutler, the executor of her father's estate. She signalled her fervent desire to stop all the talk about the question of her will by referring to "that plan which has been convulsing the wise heads" as a dull and laughable topic. As tactfully as she could, she tried to persuade Emerson to cease meddling in the financial affairs of the Tucker family by telling him how glad she was that "you being a babe in such things will resign them to more experienced noddles and I thank you."

Another letter seems to have been written in response to an inquiry from Emerson as to whether she thought the executor of the estate would deem her humble fiancé worthy of being named the beneficiary of some sort of insurance policy, for she told him that if the "ugly *insurance* business" were mentioned to Mr. Cutler, "he would think you were doubting *yourself* and would be justified in doubting too." Whatever Mr. Cutler may have said to Ellen about these developments, there is no doubt that Colonel Kent, her stepfather, had come to hope that the impending wedding would not take place. That "disbeliever," Ellen informed Emerson, "told Margaret [Ellen's sister] that he was confident that we should not live together this winter."

Allen's hagiographical piety blocks his understanding of nearly all of this. "Almost any conjecture we might make on this mysterious debate would be unfavorable to Emerson," he says, and so he refuses to interpret it! In summing up what Ellen's letters reveal about the pressure that Emerson was exerting, he restricts himself to saying again that "possibly all he had done was to urge Ellen to make a will. If so, it was sound advice, though we might wish the lover had been less prudent." Unlike earlier Emerson biographies, *Waldo Emerson* makes it possible for readers to see for themselves how interested Emerson was in his future wife's money, and we must be grateful for that. Allen himself, however, has no wish to behold the Kierkegaardian reality of Emerson's romance.

Three months after Ellen's death in February, 1831, Emerson wrote an expansive note to his brother William. (The text is not included in *Waldo Emerson*, but it is quoted in a surprisingly candid discussion of Emerson's conduct as a widower in Porte's *Representative Man.*) Don't worry about our brother Bulkeley's expenses, Emerson told William, "I can pay for B. without difficulty, especially as it seems that Ellen is to continue to benefit her husband whenever hereafter the estate shall be settled . . . . I please myself that Ellen's work of mercy is not done on earth, but she shall continue to help Edward & B. & Charles." Emerson's equation of Ellen's mercy with financial benefits to his brothers was certainly an odd way to pay tribute to her sweet personality, but such a thrifty choice of words would not have elicited any expression of surprise from the executor of Ellen's estate, if he had chanced to hear of it. For while Pliny Cutler may have held his tongue while Ellen was alive, he no longer felt any need to do so. As he soon informed Emerson's lawyer, he had no intention of allowing Emerson to get his hands on any of Ellen's money as long as he was alive.

In the light of this information, Emerson submitted a petition to a court of law, which after some months of consideration ruled in his favor. Stocks and cash were to be turned over to him in the amount of $23,000. The bequest would provide him with an annual income of $1,200, a sum sufficient to live on in the 1830s.

The court's ruling was handed down in the summer of 1832. During that same season, Emerson announced to the parishioners of the Second Church of Boston, whose minister he had been for almost three and a half years, that he could no longer in good conscience administer communion. The announcement eventually compelled the Church, as Emerson knew it would, to get rid of him. Toward the end of October, having done nothing to halt the dismissal process, he was finally voted out, and by Christmas he was on his way to Europe for a gloriously extended tour. Historians of the American mind like to say that Emerson left the Second Church out of a spiritual dissatisfaction with organized Christianity and that in going to Europe he launched himself upon the seas of Transcendentalist rebellion; but what they do not even want to think about is the court ruling that made possible these bold steps. If Emerson had not been assured of financial independence for life, it is difficult to believe that he would have abandoned so quickly the profession he had spent years of psychological travail attempting to enter or that he would not have thought twice about the high cost of rebellious voyages.

The historians also like to tell of how Emerson returned from Europe to pioneer the new vocation of "the American scholar" and of how he was made famous by the address of that name which he delivered at Harvard in 1837. Young men of the fairest promise, Emerson told the students, who begin life upon our shores with all the stars of God shining upon them, are hindered from action by the disgust which the principles of business management inspire in them, and they turn into drudges, or die of their disgust, some of them by suicide. The trouble is that they do not see, "and thousands of young men as hopeful now crowding to the barriers for the career do not yet see, that if the single man plant himself indomitably on his instincts, and there abide, the huge world will come round to him." Although "Man Thinking," as Emerson called the brave figure of whom he was speaking, must be willing to relinquish "display and immediate fame," resist "the vulgar prosperity that retrogrades ever to barbarism," and accept if necessary "poverty and solitude," he will be solaced for his sacrifice by the knowledge that he has become the eye and heart of the world.

The story of that address has been told many times, but what the historians always leave out of their accounts of it is the fact that the speaker had a dirty little secret. Emerson called upon the students to avoid involvement in business, spurn material values, dedicate themselves to the life of the mind, and imitate the career of—he all but said it— Ralph Waldo Emerson. What the speaker neglected to add, however, was that Ralph Waldo Emerson was an American scholar who was living on a subsidy and that the source of that subsidy was the business fortune of a Boston merchant.

Ever since it was delivered, the "American Scholar" address has been a holy text for American intellectuals who like to believe that they are morally superior beings who have risen above their countrymen's worship of money. They thus have a vested interest in not learning anything about the author of the address that might tend to discredit him. American intellectuals in general, like Emerson's biographers in particular, have never wished to know that the cold young man who successfully sought the hand of Ellen Tucker was in no less hot pursuit of vulgar prosperity than the most barbaric businessman of the age.

4
Speaking for Whitman

The cult of the "naturalness" of homosexuality fools no one but those who need a rationalization of their own problems.
Edward Sapir

The best opportunity a biographer has for appreciating Walt Whitman's unfolding sense of himself lies in the careful examination of his successive revisions of, and additions to, *Leaves of Grass*. The comparative study of texts, however, is not a task that has much appeal to the author of the latest attempt to assess the poet's life, because in Justin Kaplan's view biography is something other than a "historical or scholarly form." Biographers ought to think of themselves, Kaplan told an interviewer from *Harvard Magazine* in 1980, as creative artists whose work has "a lot in common with the novel," rather than as mere historical observers or literary critics.

Thus in *Walt Whitman: A Life* the various versions of Whitman's poems have not been handled with care; they have been smashed into fragments and distributed through the text as thematic accompaniments to the telling of a highly unhistorical

Reprinted by permission from *Commentary*, Volume 71, Number 2 (February 1981).

tale. For although Kaplan's book is purportedly the story of a nineteenth-century writer, its hero has an astonishly modern mind. Particularly in his sexual and political attitudes, Kaplan's Whitman appears to be the product not of a Victorian world, but of the post–World War II period.

"In a way," Kaplan declares in his *Harvard* interview, "you have to speak for Whitman. Though he's a very eloquent fellow, sometimes you've got to give him a voice where he remains silent. You take that liberty. For example, I decided to face the issue of homosexuality in a worldly and sophisticated way. So what if he is homosexual? What is the big news? Where's the scandal? There simply isn't any."

What is most striking about this passage is its lack of perspective. Like many other self-described sophisticates of our time, Kaplan is apparently convinced that he is living in the age of ultimate truths, one of which is that homosexuality is not an illness. So committed is he to the current wisdom of the American Psychiatric Association and the gay-liberation ideologues that he finds it hard to imagine that any sensitive person could ever have subscribed to a harsher wisdom, particularly not anyone who was the author, as Whitman was, of a series of salutes to the pleasures of male companionship. As a result, Kaplan experiences not a tremor of historical doubt as he takes the liberty of endowing the hero of *Walt Whitman: A Life* with an assumption about the healthiness of homosexual preference that is in reality his own.

The psychological crisis that unarguably overtook Whitman in 1859, four years after the publication of the first edition of *Leaves of Grass*, the "slough" of melancholy into which he fell, the hours of dread that he endured, had three sources, Kaplan's biography would have us believe. The first was his awareness of being forty years old. As the poet "rounded the potently symbolic turn into his fifth decade, he entered a dark period." What makes this explanation immediately suspect is that Kaplan has a habit of finding psychological significance in birthday anniversaries. But far more damaging to the explanation is the biographer's failure to come up with any evidence in support of it—which is not surprising, because the only explicit response to his fortieth birthday that Whitman ever made was to say to himself in his notebook that the time had come for him "*to stir . . .* and get out of this *Slough*." Far from plunging him into despondency, Whitman's entrance into his fifth decade prompted him to try to surmount his gloomy feelings.

Kaplan also argues that the crisis of 1859 was partially precipitated by the decision of Whitman's beloved brother Jeff to get married. "His cherished and exclusive relationship with Jeff had been fractured.... Confronting his bare-stripped heart, the brave and joyous poet yielded to the profoundest melancholy." Once again, alas, resounding words conceal a factual void. In 1890, the aged Whitman recalled that he and Jeff had been "greatly attached to each other till he got married." But there is no indication in this reminiscence, or in any other autobiographical commentary, that at the time of the wedding Whitman's joy in his brother's happiness was shadowed by a sense of loss. As for the woman Jeff married, Whitman was not only not jealous of her but quickly came to love her as if she were a sister.

Finally, Kaplan associates Whitman's loss of morale in 1859 with the discovery that he was a homosexual. But in keeping with his blasé "Where's the scandal?" attitude, Kaplan downplays the importance of the discovery, first by giving house room to alternative explanations of the poet's despondency (the birthday anniversary and brother Jeff), and second by severely underestimating what Whitman was talking about when he spoke of the "sick, sick" feelings that accompanied his consciousness of the sort of sexual creature he was.

Whitman's special word for his homosexual thoughts was "perturbations," which his biographer takes as a synonym for the mental distresses attendant upon a sexual itch. Kaplan's poet knows the torment of physical longing, the humiliation of undignified pursuit, and the sense of inadequacy that unfulfillment breeds. But he most definitely does not know the agony of guilt or the hell of self-hatred. That "perturbations," in Victorian usage, referred not only to the distresses of desire, but to the agitations that were "characteristic of a bad conscience," as Cardinal Newman once put it, is not an etymological lesson one will learn from a biographer who does not like to have his creative artistry constricted by any form of scholarly inquiry.

Kaplan also misses the self-revulsion that is at work in some of the additions to the 1860 edition of *Leaves of Grass*. In the mid-1850s, the poet had joyously celebrated bodily contact. "I mind how once we lay such a transparent summer morning /

How you settled your head athwart my hips and gently turn'd over upon me . . ." Then suddenly the author of those lines came to perceive himself as a poetic dupe who had utterly failed to understand the significance of what he had been saying. In the poem "As I Ebb'd with the Ocean of Life," first published in the *Atlantic Monthly* in April, 1860, he confessed how oppressed with himself he felt for having "dared to open my mouth" and how bitter the realization was that "amid all that blab whose echoes recoil upon me / I have not once had the least idea who or what I am." Only a few years earlier he had looked down into the water and seen the haloed head of a poet-god ("the fine centrifugal spokes of light round the shape of my head in the sunlit water"); now he gazed again into the watery mirror and saw

> loose windrows, little corpses,
> Froth, snowy white, and bubbles,
> (See, from my dead lips the ooze
> exuding at last,
> See, the prismatic colors glistening
> and rolling,)
> Tufts of straw, sands, fragments.

Yet at the same time that Whitman expanded the 1860 edition of *Leaves of Grass* to include a number of poems in which images of vileness loom large, he defiantly added a series of exquisitely tender dramatizations of homosexual love. The pressure of desire as well as the pressure of disgust is felt in the 1860 edition, and the contradiction between them is so intense that one has to wonder whether the bedeviled writer was not headed for collapse.

With the coming of the Civil War, however, Whitman was able to transcend his emotional conflict by assuming the role of a wound dresser to the young men who came to recuperate, or to die, in the military hospitals around Washington, D.C. If he sponged, fed, caressed, and finally bestowed a kiss on a "darling boy" named Lewy that lasted fully half a minute, was he not simply doing his nursely duty? Sexual embraces in a hospital setting were not a sign of sickness, they were a part of the drama of trying to get men well, and in the light of that reassurance Whitman bloomed. "I am running over with health," he exclaimed to a friend in 1863, "fat, red & sunburnt in face &c. I tell thee I am just the one to go [to] our sick boys."

Whitman gained from his wound-dressing experiences the psychological stamina to write the poems he eventually collected in *Drum-Taps* (1865). But with the return of peace his own peace was soon lost. Without the moral sanction that had blessed his encounters with Lewy and other soldiers, a newly cultivated friendship with the Washington streetcar conductor Peter Doyle devolved into an "incessant enormous abnormal perturbation." By 1870, he was desperate. "Depress the adhesive nature," he finally commanded himself in his notebook. "It is in excess—making life a torment . . . diseased feverish disproportionate adhesiveness." Control of his sexual thoughts had become absolutely vital to the sense of personal well-being on which his future career as a poet depended. Yet how could this control be established?

In the only intelligent assessment of Kaplan's book that I have seen, Marcus Cunliffe complains about its failure to grapple with the great unsolved questions about Whitman's life. One of the questions that Cunliffe cites is, why did Whitman seem to welcome the onset of old age? If Kaplan's treatment of Whitman's homosexual problem had not been so casual, he would have been in a position, it seems to me, to propose a plausible, if admittedly speculative, answer to that conundrum.

Whitman in the early 1870s was a man in his early fifties who looked fifteen to twenty years older. He had reduced the intolerable pressure on his imagination by suddenly turning into an old man. For the Good Gray Poet, grayness was the guarantor of his goodness, or at least of his ability to deny that his relations with young men had ever been anything but fatherly. Thus in 1890, when the English cultural historian John Addington Symonds wrote to him and asked, in curiously urgent tones, whether the poems of male companionship that had first appeared in the 1860 edition of the *Leaves* had not been calculated to "encourage ardent and *physical* intimacies," Whitman was able to disavow the question as "damnable." Vastly disappointed by this reply, Symonds thereafter characterized Whitman as a poet whose feelings were "at least as hostile to sexual inversion as any law-abiding hum-drum Anglo-Saxon could desire." No more revealing words have ever been written about

Whitman's tortured inner conflict, but Kaplan, unfortunately, does not perceive their importance.

Another question about Whitman's life that still awaits a convincing answer is, how did Walter turn into Walt? What moved a hack journalist of the 1840s, whose principal contribution to American literature had been a fictional confection called *Franklin Evans, or the Inebriate,* to reappear before the reading public in 1855 as a Broadway swaggerer sounding a "barbaric yawp" for all the world to hear? In strictly personal terms, no explanation of this astonishing metamorphosis is possible, because of the paucity of evidence about Whitman's day-to-day development during his chrysalis years. Nevertheless, the question can be dealt with by discussing the political and cultural context within which the transformation took place.

Such a discussion, however, not only does not occur in *Walt Whitman: A Life,* but would be doomed to failure if it did, because of the author's time-bound inability to look at any large event in American history from the point of view of the participants. Thus in his prejudged account of Whitman's career as editor of the Brooklyn *Daily Eagle* in the 1840s, Kaplan speaks of the *Eagle*'s editorial support of Manifest Destiny and of the conflict with Mexico in the accents of a Viet Nam War critic condemning contemporary American "imperialism." "When Polk's war message came over the telegraph from Washington, Whitman, a Democratic regular writing for a Democratic paper in support of a Democratic President, took up the rant of the war party." This knee-jerk sentence betrays not the slightest awareness of why, for instance, the late historian of the American West, Frederick Merk, once called Manifest Destiny the greatest of all the reform movements of the reform-minded 1840s. Like many other youthful idealists of the period, Whitman took up the cause of American expansion into territories controlled by Mexico because he saw in it the means of renewing the Jeffersonian dream of a land-based egalitarianism.

Manifest Destiny also spoke to a cultural question. Americans in the 1840s were enormously excited about the nation's technological advancement. Yet within that excitement there festered a nagging anxiety—how widespread it actually was can never be established with certainty—that in subduing the wilderness we were losing our naturalness as a people and becoming like Europeans. Territorial gain at the expense of

Mexico represented one means of allaying that anxiety. And in the decade following the war with Mexico, a number of gifted writers conjured up memorable examples of an invincible American barbarism. The year before Walter Whitman's histrionic début as Walt, Thoreau recounted the story of his defiantly uncluttered life at Walden Pond, while in the very year that the first edition of the *Leaves* appeared, Melville pictured John Paul Jones in Paris: "Intrepid, unprincipled, reckless, predatory, with boundless ambition, civilized in externals but a savage at heart, America is, or may yet be, the Paul Jones of nations."

Yet if Whitman's barbaric yawp conceivably could have appealed to America's nostalgia for the vanishing world of the pioneer, he did not succeed in winning the attention of a general audience. His technical innovations were too radical, his sexuality too explicit, his barbarism too regressive (I wish, said Whitman, that I could "turn and live with the animals, they are so placid and self-contained"). Despite his presentation of himself as the prophet of the people, he never enjoyed a popular success in his own lifetime, while in our own time he is still not widely accepted in many of the occupational groups that his poetry so picturesquely describes. First and last, the would-be bard of democracy has primarily been the poetic companion of intellectuals.

5

Welcome Back from the Raft, Huck Honey!

The influence of *Adventures of Huckleberry Finn* on American culture has been enormous. Consider Hemingway's tribute: "All modern American literature comes from one book by Mark Twain called *Huckleberry Finn.*" The main reason, however, why this book has come to play such a major role in our cultural life is that students repeatedly run into it in the course of their formal education. They read it, usually for the first time, in a high school English class. Then they read it again during their freshman year in college, in a general education course entitled something like "The Hero in Western Thought." If, as sophomores, they elect to take the survey course in American literature, they unquestionably will be asked to read it once more. I know students who claim to have encountered the novel on half a dozen different reading lists, starting as far back as the ninth grade and extending into graduate school.

Yet if the novel is often taught it is not well taught. In March, 1885, the Library Committee of Concord, Massachusetts, banned *Huckleberry Finn* from its shelves on the grounds that

Reprinted from *The American Scholar*, Volume 46, Number 3 (Summer 1977).

the book was "trash and suitable only for the slums." Not quite a century later, I wish to state that the only trash contained in *Huckleberry Finn* has been put there by the teachers thereof. In the high school and college classrooms of this country students are being presented with a condemnation of American life that Mark Twain himself did not formulate.

The misinterpretation of the book originated thirty years ago, largely as a result of a persistent misreading of its famous final sentences: "But I reckon I got to light out for the Territory ahead of the rest, because Aunt Sally she's going to adopt me and sivilize me and I can't stand it. I been there before." In the early 1950s, a small but impressive group of literary critics took those words to mean that Huck felt so suffocated by American civilization that he had decided to turn his back on it forever. By 1958, the chorus of critical agreement had swelled to the point where the literary editor of the Mark Twain estate, Henry Nash Smith, was moved to write an essay pointing out how irresponsible this interpretation was. Smith's effort to make the critics pay attention to the facts of the matter is worth quoting at length:

> But when [in the last fifth of the book] the Evasion from the Phelps plantation under Tom Sawyer's leadership restores the mood of the opening chapters, Huck's desire to escape is stripped of the meaning it had acquired in the middle section of the book. We are brought back to the situation at the end of *Tom Sawyer*. Even the robber gang reappears, for Tom's imagination peoples the territory with robbers in his "nonnamous letters" of warning. It is Tom, again, who conceives the plan to "go for howling adventures amongst the Injuns, over in the Territory, for a couple of weeks or two." When Huck says he means to set out ahead of the others, there is nothing in the text to indicate that his intention is more serious than Tom's.
>
> This reading of Huck's last sentence contradicts a view that has been gaining in popularity among critics, a view which sees a portentous meaning in Huck's final escape on the theory that he has become disgusted with a society that tolerates slavery and is making a drastic, final gesture of alienation and rejection.

Smith's corrective essay never had a chance of carrying the day, for he was pitted against a crowd of clever writers that was growing by leaps and bounds. Soon their view was being accepted as gospel truth by high school and college teachers all across the country. Since the mid-1960s, what might be termed the "Dropoutsville" interpretation of *Huckleberry Finn* has reigned supreme in American classrooms.

Yet no honest reader can doubt that at the end of the novel Huck is most emphatically *not* planning to exile himself forever from organized society. In lighting out for the Oklahoma Territory he is merely going along with Tom Sawyer's latest disappearance-reappearance act. Upon their return from their adventures, Tom and Huck plan to take Nigger Jim—who has been freed in the will of his now-dead owner—"back up home on a steamboat, in style, and pay him for his lost time, and write word ahead and get out all the niggers around, and have them waltz him into town with a torchlight procession and a brass band, and then he would be a hero, and so would we." As Huck later tells us in the sequel called *Tom Sawyer Abroad*, the gaudy scheme was eventually carried out exactly the way Tom had wanted it to be: "You see, when we three came back up the river in glory, as you may say, from that long travel, and the village received us with a torchlight procession and speeches, and everybody hurrah'd and shouted, it made us heroes, and that was what Tom Sawyer had always been hankering to be."

For decades, students who have finished reading *Huckleberry Finn* have been encouraged by their teachers to entertain misleading fantasies about a young boy's continuing search for freedom and self-realization in the tabula rasa of the Territory. In more properly conducted classes, they would be encouraged to speculate about what sort of life Huck will lead when he returns to St. Petersburg. The question would seem to take us beyond the limits of the novel, yet in reality it leads us back into it, and into *Tom Sawyer* as well. Moreover, the question has the virtue of drawing attention to the curiously overlooked character of the Widow Douglas, and to the painful problems she created for her creator.

Potentially, the Widow Douglas, "fair, smart, and forty," is the most interesting female character Mark Twain ever introduced. We meet her for the first time in *Tom Sawyer*. The house she occupies atop beautiful Cardiff Hill, "the only palace in town," symbolizes her social position in the St. Petersburg community. As hospitable as she is intelligent, this aristocratic lady gives parties that are "the most lavish . . . that St. Petersburg could boast." Her generosities, furthermore, are not limited to her gentry friends or to people of her own age. So far as we know, the Widow herself is childless, but she likes and understands boys and girls all the same and encourages them to come see her. It is only natural that Tom Sawyer should suggest to Becky Thatcher that they "climb right up the hill and stop at the Widow Douglas'. She'll have ice-cream! She has it most every day—dead loads of it. And she'll be awful glad to have us." Even Huckleberry Finn, the juvenile pariah of the village, son of the town drunkard and of an illiterate woman long since dead, with whom the middle-class mothers of St. Petersburg have forbidden their children to associate, has "more than once" been befriended by the Widow. In all likelihood she has fed him when he was hungry, for Huck's principal complaint about the anarchic life he leads is that "I don't ever get enough to eat, gen'ally."

One dark night, on the edge of the Widow's estate, Huck overhears the dreaded Injun Joe vow to a criminal companion that before leaving St. Petersburg for good he is going to slit the Widow's nostrils and notch her ears like a sow, in revenge for being jugged as a vagrant and publicly horsewhipped by order of the Widow's late husband, who had been the town's justice of the peace. Although Huck fears he will be murdered if Injun Joe should discover who has informed on him, he immediately plunges down the hillside to warn a sturdy townsman and his sons that the Widow is in peril. All Huck asks for himself is that his own role in the affair be kept secret from everyone, including the Widow. "Please don't ever tell *I* told you," Huck begs the man. "Please don't—I'd be killed, sure—but the Widow's been good friends to me sometimes, and I want to tell—I *will* tell if you'll promise you won't ever say it was me." The man promises, and Huck spills out his story.

Thus it is out of no special feeling of gratitude to Huck that the Widow Douglas volunteers to nurse the homeless boy when, a short time later, he falls deliriously ill with fever. Her willingness to take charge of him possibly saves his life, because all the doctors in town, along with all the other able-bodied men, are off at McDougal's cave looking for Tom Sawyer and Becky Thatcher, who are lost in its uncharted depths. In contrast to the disdainful attitudes of the other women of St. Petersburg, the Widow's feeling about Huck is that "whether he was good, bad, or indifferent, he was the Lord's, and nothing that was the Lord's was a thing to be neglected." Her Christianity, in other words, is a living faith, not an ossified piety.

In towns the size of St. Petersburg, secrets do not keep for long. Eventually, the Widow learns who had saved her from the Indian's revenge. From this revelation flows her decision "to give Huck a home under her roof and have him educated; and . . . when she could spare the money she would start him in a business in a modest way." Huck accepts the Widow's offer—but with a deep sense of unease. After all, his only recollection of family life is an early childhood memory of the constant quarreling between his father and mother: "Fight! Why, they used to fight all the time." Since his mother's death, Huck's drunken father has simply let the boy run wild. He has worn the cast-off clothes of grown men, slept on doorsteps in fine weather and in empty hogsheads in wet, and avoided soap and water like the plague. He smokes and chews tobacco. He swears "wonderfully." He has never been to church or to school and cannot recognize the letters of the alphabet.

In the last episode of *Tom Sawyer*, we witness this child being "introduced . . . no, dragged" into society. The Widow's servants keep him neat and clean. He has to eat with a knife and fork. He has to sleep in "unsympathetic sheets that had not one little spot or stain which he could press to his heart and know for a friend." He is required to go to church and to cut out swearing. Plans are afoot to send him to school, as soon as the new term begins. "Whithersoever he turned, the bars and shackles of civilization shut him in and bound him hand and foot." After three weeks of misery, he runs off. Finally Tom Sawyer locates him, stretched at ease in an empty hogshead down behind an abandoned slaughterhouse, smoking a pipe, clad in rags, and superbly uncombed. Tom understands the feelings of his friend—and yet loves him enough to give him advice he knows Huck does not want to hear. Go back to the Widow's, Tom urges him: "if you'll try this thing for just a while longer you'll come to like it." Huck adamantly refuses.

In the long run, however, Huck is no match for the master manipulator who once had persuaded all the boys in St. Petersburg to whitewash a fence for him. Thinking fast, Tom tells Huck he is going to form a "high-toned" robber gang, of the sort that in most European countries is made up of "dukes and such." In order to keep up the tone of his gang, Tom will restrict its membership to respectable boys. Returning to the Widow is the price Huck will have to pay for belonging. Upon hearing this, Huck ceases to resist. "I'll stick to the widder till I rot," he declares, as *The Adventures of Tom Sawyer* draws to a close, "and if I git to be a reg'lar ripper of a robber, and everybody talking 'bout it, I reckon she'll be proud she snaked me in out of the wet."

With that sentence Mark Twain set the stage for a follow-up novel that could have become an extraordinarily interesting study of acculturation, centering on a contest of wills between an emotionally deprived juvenile outcast and a smart, attractive, still youthful woman. Somewhere along the line, though, Mark Twain decided he had a better idea. The sequel to *Tom Sawyer* became a story about a runaway boy and a runaway slave, rafting down the Mississippi on the June rise.

It was a marvelous idea. Yet by making Huck Finn his runaway hero, Mark Twain created certain problems for himself. The conventional wisdom about *Huckleberry Finn* is that the novel lets its readers down only in the long final episode at the Phelps plantation, when Tom Sawyer reenters the story and, with his romantic schemes, effectively destroys the emotional connnection between Huck and Jim. Hemingway, for example, qualified his tribute to the novel by adding, "If you read it you must stop where the Nigger Jim is stolen from the boys. That is the real end. The rest is just cheating." As bad as cheating, however, are the incidents that occur at the outset of the story, in the chapters dealing with Huck's life at the Widow's.

The first problem Mark Twain confronted was how to blur the awareness of readers who were familiar with *Tom Sawyer* that Huck and the Widow are bound together by mutual feelings of gratitude, that they both are warmhearted, and that their experiment in living as symbolic son and mother has a chance of succeeding. Since *Huckleberry Finn* was to be a story of rafting on the river, the author had to spring Huck free from his ties to the Widow. Mark Twain solved this problem—if one can call a travesty a solution—by introducing, on page 2, the cartoon character of Miss Watson. "A tolerable slim old maid with goggles on," Miss Watson is the Widow's sister, who has just recently—oh, yes, very recently!—come to live in the Douglas mansion. It is altogether incredible that the Widow would surrender the bulk of her parental responsibilities to this two-dimensional caricature of old-maid prissiness and henpecking tyranny, but that is exactly what Mark Twain was forced to ask us to believe. The richly interesting psychological conflict between Huck and the Widow that seemed to be promised to us at the end of *Tom Sawyer* is reduced in the first three chapters of *Huckleberry Finn* to a series of farcical confrontations between Huck and old Goggle Eyes, with the gentle, understanding Widow coming on stage only now and again.

As if embarrassed by the baldness of this stratagem, Mark Twain has Huck admit at the beginning of chapter 4 that after four months in the same household he and the Widow have grown somewhat closer together and that he is "getting sort of used" to her ways, albeit he still prefers his former habits. For her part, the Widow believes that Huck is coming along slowly but surely. Almost immediately, however, the reason why Mark Twain could afford this outburst of literary candor is revealed: he had hit upon a legalistic means of removing Huck from the Widow's jurisdiction, once and for all. No matter that in the course of executing this maneuver the author would have to resort to a few "stretchers," as Huck would say.

Pap Finn has been missing from town for more than a year. Now, suddenly, he returns. He has heard about Huck's and Tom's discovery (in *Tom Sawyer*) of a buried treasure of golden coins. Huck's share, which comes to six thousand dollars, has been banked for him by the Widow at 6 percent interest. Pap claims that as Huck's father he should be given control of the six thousand dollars and swears he will go to court about it. In the face of this threat, the Widow and the influential Judge Thatcher ask the court to take Huck away from his father and appoint one of them the boy's legal guardian. Confronted on one side of his courtroom by the Widow and Judge Thatcher, and on the other side by Pap Finn—"His hair was long and tangled and greasy, and hung down, and you could see his eyes shining through like he was behind vines . . . . There warn't no color in his face, where his face showed; it was white; not like another man's white, but a white to make a body sick, a white to make a body's flesh crawl"—what would any judge do?

Let us not ask the question only in moral terms. Let us also speak of political clout. St. Petersburg is a small southern town, whose power structure stands before the judge in the persons of the Widow and Judge Thatcher. The power structure's adversary is the trashiest white for miles around, a man totally without influence. How will the judge rule? Mark Twain knows damned well, yet he has no choice but to lie to us. "It was a new judge," the novel lamely explains, "that had just come, and he didn't know . . ." After ruling in favor of Huck's father, the judge invites Pap to his home and persuades him to take a temperance pledge. The presumably reformed drunkard then goes to bed in the judge's guest room. Sometime during the night he sneaks out, buys a jug of forty-rod, sneaks back in, kills the jug, "and towards daylight he crawled out again, drunk as a fiddler, and rolled off the porch and broke his left arm in two places and . . . when they come to look at that spare room, they had to take soundings before they could navigate it." Does the judge, first thing in the morning, grant the Widow a temporary injunction against the enforcement of his previous ruling, until a new trial on the guardianship question can be scheduled? Don't be silly.

Consequently, when Pap snatches Huck one day in the spring, takes him across the river to the Illinois shore, and locks him up in an old log hut, the Widow has no legal right to recover him. Some weeks later, Pap comes storming into the cabin on one of his irregular visits and reports that there are rumors floating around St. Petersburg that the Widow is about to make a second effort in the court. But thanks to her mysterious dilatoriness, Huck has had time to revert to his old ways, and as a result does not want to be "cramped up and sivilized" any more. He also has long since decided that he has no desire to go on living with his fearsome Pap. Thus, on the day he breaks out of the cabin and makes for the river, Huck is fleeing first of all from his father, which is understandable. It is, however, much less understandable that he is also fleeing from all his boyhood friends, including the woman who had befriended him off and on throughout his childhood, had nursed him through a dangerous illness, had invested his money for him rather than mulcting him out of it, had supplied him with bed and board and loving care for four months, and had sent him to school so that he could learn to read and write. Can it be that we have been wrong in thinking that Huck Finn is a warmhearted boy—that in fact he has been so deformed, psychologically speaking, by his nightmarish early years with his mother and father that he is incapable of caring about the people who care about him? Of course not. It is simply that Mark Twain had to turn Huck into a runaway, and he could not do so without temporarily violating the consistency of his hero's affectionate character.

The point of this analysis is not to downgrade Mark Twain's literary reputation by exposing the social and psychological implausibilities in the early chapters of his masterpiece. Implausibilities, after all, were Mark Twain's stock in trade, in every book he ever wrote. The point, rather, is that teachers of *Huckleberry Finn* read every detail in the early chapters with a deadly literal-mindedness. Partly this is because a lot of professional interpreters of literature lack a sense of humor. But mainly they interpret the early chapters of *Huckleberry Finn* with the utmost seriousness in order to build up an indictment of American life. Instead of showing students that the account of Huck's life at the Widow's simply consists of a series of chess moves designed to get Huck onto that raft with Nigger Jim as expeditiously as possible and that the account most certainly does not reflect Mark Twain's real opinion of the Widow Douglas, they take it at face value, in preparation for their misreading of the novel's final sentences.

Back in the 1950s, when all the trouble started, literary critics were moved to misread *Huckleberry Finn* for a variety of reasons. Americans in the postwar period were gradually coming to the conclusion—first in the area of sports, but raying out from there into other aspects of our national life—that the ancient pattern of discrimination against Negroes was morally indefensible. This conclusion precipitated numerous misinterpretations of *Huckleberry Finn*, including, I must admit, the one I set forth in *Mark Twain and Southwestern Humor* (1959). Critics like myself wanted to believe that Huck was renouncing membership in a society that condoned slavery because they themselves did not wish to live in a segregationist nation. A less palatable concomitant of this point of view was the distaste that some misreaders felt for southern whites. "Hatred of the South is the anti-Semitism of the liberals": that familiar observation was never more perfectly exemplified than in the attitude of those literary critics who were pleased to think that Huck Finn was seceding from society because he couldn't stand all those funny-talking white folks who lived in the southern part of the Mississippi Valley.

Another reason why the "Dropoutsville" interpretation became popular when it did had to do with the canonization of literary modernism that was taking place in English departments of the period. *Huckleberry Finn* would not have been included in their reading lists if a good many professors of the 1950s had not been able to think of it as a home-grown antecedent of *Portrait of the Artist as a Young Man*. Alienation, the great buzzword of fifties criticism, was recklessly applied to the hero's frame of mind in *Huckleberry Finn* as a means of gaining a place for the novel in a pre-Joycean pantheon.

The habitual tendency of American intellectuals to view family life as dreary, repressive, and conducive to the sickness, rather than the health, of husbands and wives, parents and children, has also figured in the critical distortion of the novel, as has the anti-Americanism that has been a part of campus life ever since the mid-1960s.

A few years ago, the Harvard undergraduate newspaper, the *Crimson*, ran a valedictory editorial by the first woman who had ever held the position of president of the paper. In the editorial she expressed her abiding hatred for American life. Never would she consent to settle down in such a sick society. Instead, she was going to drop out, take off, and never look back. Just the way Huck Finn did, she said. She had learned her classroom lesson well, that young woman.

6

The Masterpiece That Became a Hoax

In *Patriotic Gore* (1962), his sprawling study of the literature of the American Civil War, Edmund Wilson spoke of no other work with greater enthusiasm than he did of Mary Chesnut's Confederate diary, which Wilson had read in the edition published by Houghton Mifflin in 1949 under the title, *A Diary from Dixie*. Mrs. Chesnut's instincts as a writer were "uncanny," Wilson raved. Starting out with situations or relationships of which she could not possibly have known the outcome, she had developed and rounded out the daily turn of events "as if she were molding a novel." In following, for instance, the star-crossed love affair between the beautiful Southern belle "Buck" Preston and the crippled Confederate hero Colonel "Sam" Hood, the diarist had managed right from the start to infuse the story with a Chekhovian sense of doom that may also have been intended to symbolize the impotence and impending ruin of a whole society. By the end of Wilson's 21-page salute, he had persuaded himself that *A Diary from Dixie* was not only an "extraordinary document," but a "work of art," a "masterpiece" of its kind.

One wonders how many of these glowing words Wilson would have wanted to retract if he had lived long enough to learn that Mrs. Chesnut's achievement was not what it appeared to be. For the diary he had particularly admired for its prophetic qualities had actually been composed between 1881 and 1884, twenty years after the events presumed to have been recorded as they happened.

Of all the ironies, however, that attach to this surprising story, none is more poignant than the refusal of the eminent historian who has finally exposed Mrs. Chesnut's work as a hoax to bestow that label upon it. For C. Vann Woodward believes that Mrs. Chesnut's mind was illuminated by advanced ideas, and in Woodward's books the faults of forward-looking citizens are always explained away when they are not simply ignored.

Until recently, the most egregious instance of Woodward's special pleading for his favorites had been his biography of the Southern Populist Tom Watson, in which he insists on the basis of extremely shaky evidence that Watson's viciously xenophobic views were the aberrant product of the political disappointments he suffered in the early and middle 1890s and did not represent his real self. In Woodward's new edition of Mary Chesnut's diary, however, the defensiveness to which he and other liberal intellectuals from the South have always been given (especially those who, like Woodward, have moved to the North) is carried to new heights of implausibility. To begin with, he identifies the diarist in terms that tell us far more about his own eagerness to please present-day spokesmen for blacks and women than they do about Mrs. Chesnut. She was, he says, an abolitionist and a feminist—nay, a "militant feminist." Even more misleading, though, than his characterization of Mrs. Chesnut's politics is his endorsement of her diary as a historically reliable document. So anxious is he to embrace this nineteenth-century lady as a liberal Southern intellectual like himself that he cannot bear to admit that her diary represents one of the most audacious frauds in the history of American literature.

Because she was the wife of a highly placed Confederate government official, Mrs. Chesnut had the chance to be "in on the *real show*," as she once put it. Her home was a secluded plantation near Camden, South Carolina, but she managed to be in Montgomery, Alabama, as a witness to the founding of the

Confederacy, in Charleston, South Carolina, when Fort Sumter was fired on, in the Confederate capital in Richmond, Virginia, at various critical moments, and in Columbia, South Carolina, on the eve of its fall to Sherman. Her friends and acquaintances ranged across the political, military, and social élites of half a dozen secessionist states.

In February, 1861, shortly before her thirty-eighth birthday, she began to jot down notes about her increasingly interesting life; despite frequent lapses, she continued the practice until the Confederacy passed into history. These jottings were clearly never intended for publication, even though her omnivorous reading in English and French literature had already caused her to dream of devoting her life to writing books. For the pages of Mrs. Chesnut's Civil War diary were kept under lock and key. Not even her husband was permitted to read them.

Having been an ardent secessionist, Mrs. Chesnut took the defeat of the South very hard. Yet the postwar years were even more depressing for her, bringing little else, it seemed, besides the deaths of loved ones, severe financial stresses, crushing literary disappointments, and almost constant ill health. By 1881, she was suffering from a heart condition, lung trouble, and an assortment of other ailments, including, perhaps, a dependency on morphine. Her days were filled with the tedium of running a dairy farm, her nights with the annoyance of managing a household full of aging, ailing, and demanding relatives. As for her efforts to win recognition as a writer, the novels on which she had labored for the better part of fifteen years had not even been good enough to be published.

It was in the dark season of her fortunes, then, that she decided to gamble all her remaining energies on one more turn of the literary wheel. In the course of the next three years she wrote more words than she had in all the years of her fictional scribbling combined. A first and then a second draft of a book that purported to be a Civil War diary flowed from her pen.

While she carefully exploited the materials contained in the surviving volumes of her 1860s diary, she also took enormous liberties with them. "She omitted much," Woodward informs us, and then "usually added more than the amount omitted or condensed." Some of these expansions consisted of elaborations of brief original entries, but others were made up of new matter entirely. She dwelt upon the personalities of people to whom she had previously referred only briefly, plucked a host of bygone conversations from her brain, and interjected numerous authorial reflections on historical and personal events. Without hesitation, says Woodward, she also shifted dates around, changed the identities of speakers, and took ideas she had originally attributed to herself and put them in the mouths of other people.

Mrs. Chesnut went to her grave in 1886, still not satisfied that her manuscript was ready for submission to a publisher. Nineteen years later, however, D. Appleton—at the instigation of Isabella Martin, an old friend of the deceased diarist—published approximately a third of the manuscript. Mrs. Chesnut's fraudulent diary had at last become a part of American literature, wherein it would continue to serve as a trap for the unwary for an astonishingly long time to come. Houghton Mifflin's 1949 edition would print more than twice as much of the manuscript as the first edition did, but its editor, the New England novelist Ben Ames Williams, would no more understand the diary's false nature than had Isabella Martin. Indeed, Williams would blithely insert a few passages from the 1860s diary in his text without any announcement that they derived from a different source or any consciousness of scholarly irresponsibility.

Woodward's new edition is not only the fullest ever published, but by far the most careful. The annotations of Mrs. Chesnut's myriad references to South Carolina politicos, obscure English novels, and long-forgotten popular songs are admirably complete, and the complementary and supplementary passages from the 1860s diary that have been interpolated into the text are clearly marked off by brackets. On the other hand, it is highly regrettable that Woodward should have decided against including in *Mary Chesnut's Civil War* all the surviving elements of the 1860s diary. As Michael P. Johnson has pointed out in a thoughtful review in the *Journal of Southern History*, the reader who wishes to consult Woodward's edition as a source of the 1860s is restricted to those passages from the original diary that Woodward has arbitrarily elected to publish. The reader also cannot be sure, Johnson adds, that the material in the 1880s diary may be found in the analogous sections of the 1860s diary as well, nor can he conclude that if an account of a historical event is not in the 1880s diary it is not in the 1860s diary, either. In my opinion, though, the most exasperating consequence of Woodward's editorial decision is that he makes it impossible for the reader of *Mary Chesnut's Civil War* to make a full-scale test of the editor's contention that, for all the differences between them, the two diaries are essentially alike.

In support of this stupefying claim, Woodward repeatedly speaks of Mrs. Chesnut's "integrity" as a historian, of the "integrity" of her work, and of the "integrity" of her perceptions. The author of the 1880s diary, he asserts, showed "an unusual sense of responsibility" toward the past she was recreating, as well as a "reassuring faithfulness" to her sense of the period as she had first evoked it in the 1860s diary. Yet at the same time that he denies that the passage of twenty terrible years produced any significant alteration in the way she wished to write about the Civil War South, Woodward echoes Edmund Wilson's praise of the prophetic qualities of the 1880s diary, thereby contradicting his argument. For Mrs. Chesnut's Chekhovian sense of doom was unquestionably inspired by a historical knowledge that was not available to the 1860s diarist.

The simulated diary also contains a number of anachronistic allusions to events that have not yet happened, which again suggests that much of it was manufactured out of the whole cloth of hindsight. And many of the most vivid conversations in the 1880s diary simply ring false, especially those involving famous people. In an ecstatically favorable, defensive-aggressive assessment of *Mary Chesnut's Civil War* in the *New York Review of Books,* Woodward's fellow Southern liberal (and fellow Connecticut resident) William Styron states that Mrs. Chesnut's portraits of the leaders of the Confederacy are "as fascinating in their intimacy as they are invaluable." By way of illustration, Styron cites "a sketch of Jefferson Davis in June 1861":

> In Mrs. Davis's drawing room last night, the president took a seat beside me on the sofa where I sat. He talked for nearly an hour. He laughed at our faith in our own powers. We are like the British. We think every Southerner equal to three Yankees at least. We will have to be equivalent to a dozen now . . . . There was a sad refrain running through it all.

> For one thing, either way, he thinks it will be a long war. That floored me at once. It has been too long for me already. Then said: before the end came, we would have many a bitter experience. He said only fools doubted the courage of the Yankees or their willingness to fight when they saw fit. And now we have stung their pride—we have roused them till they will fight like devils.

With the sort of historical carelessness that characterizes his novels, Styron neglects to make mention of the fact that although the sketch is dated June 1861, it was actually written twenty years later. Nor does he pause to ask himself whether it is likely that the leader of the Confederacy would have unburdened himself in this way to an extremely talkative woman. The morale of the South depended to a tremendous degree on its faith that the war would be short. In the middle of the night, in the privacy of his own bedroom, Davis might have admitted to himself that that faith was unfounded. He might also have shared his pessimism with his most trusted military advisers. But to have spoken in public with such chilling candor would have been to subvert the cause he was attempting with every fiber of his being to sustain. The whole sketch reeks of fraud.

On the basis of the passages Woodward has printed from the earlier diary, it would also appear that Mrs. Chesnut's account of the institution of slavery is significantly less harsh in the 1880s diary than it is in the diary she composed twenty years earlier. In the 1860s diary we encounter the wife of a slave owner who is willing to acknowledge in quite powerful language that the slave system inflicted degradation on blacks and whites alike:

> I wonder if it be a sin to think slavery a curse in any land. [Senator Charles] Sumner said not one word of this hated institution which is not true. Men and women are punished when their masters and mistresses are brutes and not when they do wrong—and then we live surrounded by prostitutes. . . . Who thinks any worse of a negro or mulatto woman for being a thing we can't name? God forgive us, but ours is a *monstrous* system and wrong and iniquity. . . . Like the patriarchs of old our men live all in one house with their wives and their concubines, and the mulattoes one sees in every family exactly resemble the white children—and every

> lady tells you who is the father of all the mulatto children in everybody's household, but those in her own she seems to think drop from the clouds, or pretends so to think.

The 1860s diarist also relates a story she has heard from her husband. "With *dramatic* power of loathing and shame, he told that the day before he saw a poor negro woman in the last stages of pregnancy, sitting by the roadside in bitter wailing, her eyes smashed up, and frightfully punished in the face. He rode up and said: 'Poor soul what can I do for you? How have you hurt yourself so?' She answered: 'Ride on, Massa. You can do no good. My Missis has been beating me.' He asked the brute's name and was answered 'Mrs. Ferguson,' some woman we did not know, thank Heaven."

Both of those memorable passages were eliminated in toto from the 1880s diary. Michael P. Johnson, who has read the 1860s diary in its entirety (the original manuscript and a transcript are in the South Caroliniana Library and another transcript is in the Sterling Memorial Library at Yale), reports in his *Journal of Southern History* review that the account of a slave auction in the 1880s diary is much less forceful than the account in the 1860s diary on which it is based. And Johnson goes on to say that the author of the 1880s diary also eliminated the following passage from her original diary: "I have read in the journal Camden paper a Sumter man advertising a slave *so white* as to be mistaken for a citizen but on lifting his hat the *brand might* be seen—JC [James Chesnut, Jr., Mary Chesnut's husband] went to the editor Tom Warren & told him such an advertisement disgraced humanity and he would not touch the money if he were a decent Editor paid him for it by such a brute—so it was taken out—Christ died for us—In his blood I hope to be cleansed *only*—sinful I am—but such brutes give me agony—for my country."

The 1880s diary does not fail to acknowledge the brutality of the South's peculiar institution. Nevertheless, the overriding emphasis in the later diary is on "softhearted" slave owners who buy shoes for black miscreants and who keep slave families intact, even though two-thirds of the people in question are "too old or too young to be of any use," and on the overworked wives of slave owners who "strive to ameliorate the condition of these Africans in every particular." The Negroes for their part are retrospectively presented as paragons of loyalty speeding to help their white mistresses disarm Yankee soldiers who have lost their way, or as ungrateful "animals" scheming to murder their owners in their beds, or as "children" reveling in idleness and huddling together "promiscuously" in their dirty cabins. As she summoned up remembrances of things past, the aging Mrs. Chesnut's heart did not go out to the slaves, it went out to women like her mother, her grandmother, and her mother-in-law, who "were educated at Northern schools mostly—read the same books as their Northern contemners, the same daily newspapers, the same Bible—have the same ideas of right and wrong—are highbred, lovely, good, pious," but who were forced by fate to live amongst undeveloped savage Africans—"dirty, slatternly, idle, ill-smelling by nature (when otherwise, it is the exception). These women are more troubled by their duty to negroes, have less chance to live their own lives in peace than if they were African missionaries."

In its mixture of moods ranging from nostalgia to nightmare, Mrs. Chesnut's remembrance of slavery days is very much a work of its postbellum time and Southern place. From the short stories that Thomas Nelson Page began to publish in the eighties about kindhearted masters and mistresses and their childlike, adoring slaves to Thomas Dixon, Jr.'s *The Clansman* (1905), with its horrifying vision of savage blacks running amok, postbellum Southern writers endeavored in one way or another to explain and defend the history of the white South. Because Northerners were now in a mood to read what these writers had to say, a market for Southern apologias sprang into being. Mrs. Chesnut set out to crack that market with a book purporting to be a Civil War diary. Is it any wonder that she left out of her manuscript the most troubling material about the conduct of white masters and mistresses toward their slaves which she had recorded two decades earlier? The ambitious but frustrated author dearly wanted to get her manuscript published; therefore she tailored its content to fit the emerging literary fashion.

Did she have any qualms about doing so? I myself would doubt it. As a very young woman, Mrs. Chesnut had described herself as an abolitionist, and Woodward has eagerly seized on the word as proof that his heroine deserves a place in the pantheon of Southern liberalism. But while the young Mrs. Chesnut was often subject to twinges of Christian guilt about the iniquities of slavery, she did not really like black people, and the older she grew the more contemptuous of them she became. There is no reason, therefore, to believe that as a writer in the 1880s it was morally difficult for her to betray them by censoring her manuscript.

Woodward's further characterization of Mrs. Chesnut as a millitant feminist is sheer ideological fantasy. As both her diaries demonstrate, she was extremely dependent on the cold, controlling man who was her husband. The reverse of an autonomous, liberated woman, she lived in fear of his sharp-tongued reproofs of her, and she went to great lengths to keep his feathers smoothed. "All the comfort of my life," she said, "depends upon his being in a good humor." She also was constantly concerned about his wandering eye. Sometimes she directly and explicitly referred to her sense of insecurity about her marriage. On other occasions, she expressed her anxiety more obliquely, through lavish compliments to herself about how attractive she was ("I can make anybody love me if I choose"), or through nervous observations about the attentions that other married men were wont to pay to young women who were not their wives ("Wanted to stop and ask Governor Cobb who that beautiful Juliet was to whom he seemed to be playing Romeo on the balcony").

While she was sure that her father-in-law had slave mistresses, she did not think this was true of her husband. All the same, she had no difficulty in imagining how her mother-in-law felt. For whenever Mrs. Chesnut became convinced that her husband was having an affair with a white woman, she could barely contain her bitterness and despair:

> The first Sunday after we went in [to Richmond] last year—J. C. had been there without me all summer—as we turned a corner suddenly going to church, we met a very handsome woman—very handsomely dressed. She rushed up to J. C., both hands extended.
>
> "So glad! Did not know you had come. When did you come? And you have not been to see me!" &c&c.
>
> I expected him to introduce me, but he said not a word—only continued to shake her hands.
>
> "Who is it?" I asked as we walked.

"Don't know. Never saw the woman before in my life. She evidently took me for somebody else."

"Very odd!" The subject was renewed again and again until it became a screaming farce—but he stuck to his formula.

"Never saw the woman before in my life—took me for somebody else—explanations always a bore—so I let her have it all her own way."

"What a credulous fool you must take me to be." So on to the end of the chapter.

As a young woman, Mrs. Chesnut did not respond to her husband's deceptions either by leaving him or by becoming a crusader for women's rights. In her later years, though, she herself became a deceiver, albeit not in the realm of sexual infidelity. She wrote a novel about the South during the Civil War and called it a diary.

7
The Rebels of Greenwich Village

Who were the men and women who came to Greenwich Village in the era of the Armory Show, the Paterson pageant, and the Provincetown Players? Where did they come from? What were their families like? How old were the rebels when they veered off the main roads of American life into the quiet, twisting streets near Washington Square? Why did their deviation occur at this precise time? While the answers to such questions that have been given to us by Henry F. May, Christopher Lasch, June Sochen, Lillian Symes, Albert Parry, William L. O'Neill, Emily Hahn, Allen Churchill, Robert E. Humphrey, Arthur F. Wertheim, Travers Clement, Van Wyck Brooks, and Daniel Aaron are not identical, they are mutually reinforcing to a remarkable degree. The result is that the story of the Greenwich Village rebellion seems as if it had been written by one author.

We have been told repeatedly, for instance, that the rebellion expressed a dispute between the old and the young and that the insurgents were marvelously young. This contention is why

Reprinted by permission from *Perspectives in American History,* Volume 8 (1974).

Henry F. May begins his book *The End of American Innocence* with a description of the seventy-fifth birthday dinner for William Dean Howells which the house of Harper laid on in 1912. The old novelist clung to old-fashioned ways of thinking, as did all the intellectuals of his generation. Ranged against those old-fashioned ways of thinking, however, were the liberating ideas of Freud, Bergson, Wells, Matisse, Diaghilev, et al., which in the United States "directly affected only certain small groups of young people." American culture in 1912 was caught up in a battle between aging traditionalists and youthful modernists.

We have also been assured and reassured that the young nonconformists who descended upon New York, circa 1912, were refugees, by and large, from villages and small towns in the Middle West. (Henry May rather oddly insists that another important source of supply was Harvard, Yale, and Princeton, even though college affiliations tell us nothing about home towns.) But no matter where they came from, the story continues, the rebels hated nineteenth-century, middle-class culture, with its "single, old, traditional set of doctrines," to quote May once more. On a more personal level, they also hated the nineteenth-century, middle-class family, with its combination of what Christopher Lasch calls "patriarchal authority and . . . sentimental veneration of women." The rebels had grown up in such families and had been suffocated by the experience. Luckily, these wonderful young people had been able to escape to Greenwich Village, where art was modern, politics was radical, love was free, and life was insistently gay.

The story is as romantic as it is familiar, and it has become a significant part of a broad view of twentieth-century American life. But is it true?

Before reporting on my own investigation of the subject, let me stress the fact that I have tried to study not only the lives of the political radicals, avant-garde painters, and bohemian schoolteachers who come to mind almost automatically when one thinks of Greenwich Village in the teens, but of every newcomer I could find who had been drawn to the world of Washington Square in these years. The rebel population thus assembled contains approximately four hundred names. Unfortunately, biographical information concerning most of the rebels is far from complete, with the result that my statistics are generally based on about a quarter of the total population. I should also explain that some of the people who are referred to here as Greenwich Village rebels were actually residents of the Village for only a brief period, while others never lived there at all. Yet they deserve to be called Greenwich Village rebels because of their significant involvement in the activities of one or more of the Village's numerous coteries. Wallace Stevens, for example, occupied a room in a bachelors' hotel called the Benedick in Washington Square in the winter of 1908 and later an apartment at 117 West 11th Street, but after his marriage in the late summer of 1909 he moved north of the Village to 441 West 21st Street, where he remained until he took a job in Hartford, Connecticut, in 1916. Walter Lippmann, to cite another example, chose to live with his parents until his marriage in 1917 and was never a resident of Greenwich Village. Both Stevens and Lippman, however, were very much involved in Village life—Stevens with the poets who published in *Rogue* and *Others* and Lippmann with the group that frequented Mabel Dodge's salon at 23 Fifth Avenue.

A good place to start revising the story of the Greenwich Village rebellion is with the age of the rebels and the so-called battle of the generations. Floyd Dell, Louise Bryant, and John Reed were only twenty-five years old in 1912, and Albert Boni, Maxwell Bodenheim, Edna St. Vincent Millay, and Djuna Barnes had just turned twenty. Edna Kenton, on the other hand, was thirty-six, Mary Eleanor Fitzgerald thirty-five, and Elsa von Freytag von Loringhoven was forty-five if she was a day. Arthur B. Davies and Walt Kuhn, the two masterminds of the Armory Show, were fifty and thirty-two, respectively, while George Cram Cook, the future director of the Provincetown Players, was pushing forty, a milestone that John Sloan had already passed. To state the matter statistically, the average age in 1912 of the 131 rebels whose birth dates are known was thirty. Thirty-six men and women were thirty-five years old or more, while 44 were twenty-five years old or less. Some of the rebels were involved in Village life before 1912, but others would not be for another few years. Therefore the rebellion cannot usefully be described as the exclusive work of either the young *or* the old. For some rebels, Greenwich Village was a place for starting out in life; for others, it was a place for starting over. And the liberating ideas streaming in from Europe affected men and women of all ages.

As for their geographical background, 71 of the 141 Villagers whose birthplaces have been identified came from New York City, New York State, Massachusetts, New Jersey, Pennsylvania, and other eastern states, with New York City being by a considerable margin the biggest supplier. Twenty-nine came from foreign countries, the bulk of them from eastern Europe and the British Isles. The Middle West furnished 27 rebels to the Village, some of whom hailed not from the small towns of familiar legend, but from Chicago, Saint Louis, and other cities, while seven rebels came from the South and seven from the Far West. Thus the Greenwich Village rebels typically did not come from Gopher Prairie, U.S.A.; they came from older, more settled places, in the eastern United States and in Europe. As we shall see, it was more often a dissatisfaction with cities than with small towns that figured in the decision of the rebels to head for Washington Square.

Considerably more than half—59 out of 97—of the Villagers for whom there is economic information came from rich or well-to-do (today we would say, upper-middle-class) families. Gertrude Vanderbilt Whitney was by all odds the richest woman in Greenwich Village, but Helen Stokes and Dorothy Arnold were heiresses, too, while Ida Rauh, Margaret Anderson, Mabel Dodge, Mary Kingsbury Simkhovitch, Mary Heaton Vorse, Alyse Gregory, Theresa Helburn, Beatrice Hinkle, Frances Perkins, Inez Milholland, Nina Moise, Nina Wilcox, Mary Craig Kimbrough, Louise Norton, and Jean Starr grew up in extraordinarily comfortable circumstances. In some families, the Perkinses and the Heatons, for instance, the style of life was quiet; in the case of the Milhollands, it was pretentious. (Inez, complained Max Eastman, "for all her radical opinions, lived a high-geared, metropolitan, function-attending, opera-going, rich girl's life. Her time was full of meaningless appointments, and her house always full of male guests—a kaleidoscopic succession of men about town, millionaires, bounders, authors, opera singers, labor fakers, with now and then an earnest socialist or a real celebrity.") But behind the style, no matter what it was, lay the consciousness of parents and children alike that their status in life was vastly superior to the average American family's.

What was true of many women who came to the Village was also true of many men. Lincoln Steffens, Hutchins Hapgood, and George Cram Cook were brought up in the sort of style that Thorstein Veblen had in mind when he wrote *The Theory of the Leisure Class*; in time, the Steffens mansion became the official residence of the governors of California. The parents of Walter Lippmann, Louis Untermeyer, and Waldo Frank had the financial resources to lavish all kinds of special advantages upon their sons, including European travel, special schools, and countless tickets to cultural events. Wallace Stevens's father was a successful lawyer, Carl Van Vechten's a banker, Robert Carleton Brown's a financier, Eugen Boissevain's a wealthy publisher, Ernest Poole's a distinguished member of the Chicago Board of Trade. John Reed's parents knew occasional periods of financial embarrassment, but they also knew that behind them stood the wealth and social prestige of Reed's grandparents. ("I still remember my grandfather's house, where I was born," Reed once wrote, "a lordly gray mansion modeled on a French chateau, with its immense park, its formal gardens, lawns, stables, greenhouses and glass grape arbor, the tame deer among the trees.") For all his compulsive poor-mouthing, Eugene O'Neill's father also had money, some of which he used to purchase a sprawling summer place in Connecticut, not far from an estate of the Harkness family, and to send his gifted younger son to a series of fashionable boarding schools and then on to Princeton.

Six of the Villagers were born into families which, although not wealthy, had a distinguished social or intellectual lineage that also served to set them apart—in their own minds, at least—from the common run of the middle class. Having been raised in his parents' Southern-plantation-style mansion, George Cram Cook viewed Davenport, Iowa, from an aristocratic perspective—but so did his future wife, Susan Glaspell, even though her feed-dealer father was not particularly well-to-do. For the Glaspells were one of the oldest families in Iowa, as was Cook's mother's family, and the pride that they both took in their pioneer origins, coupled with the disdain they also shared for the commercialism of contemporary Davenport, was one of the things that drew "Jig" Cook and Susan Glaspell together. Max and Crystal Eastman were equally conscious of being part of a plain-living, high-thinking intellectual tradition which not only included their minister father, who was a "patriarch, a First Citizen of Elmira, New York," and their brilliant, charismatic mother, who was also an ordained minister of the Congregational Church, but generations of ancestors on both sides of the family.

Twenty of the Villagers, including Theodore Dreiser, Maurice Sterne, William Zorach, Maxwell Bodenheim, Robert Minor, William Gropper, Guy Pène du Bois, and Jerome Myers, grew up in poverty. In a good many cases, the radical political lessons taught them by their parents made the bitter fate of not having money in America seem even more unjust to the children. Robert Minor, for instance, was carefully indoctrinated by his father in Henry George's theories of how the poor in America are exploited by the rich, and Margaret Sanger's father did the same for her. But with or without the consciousness-heightening commentary of radical parents, poverty was a searing and alienating experience for the future rebels of Greenwich Village.

Dorothy Day, Harold Stearns, Stuart Davis, William J. Glackens, and eight other Villagers were the products of middle-class or lower-middle-class families of undistinguished lineage. While not insignificant, the number is certainly small enough to compel a more precise wording of the usual statement that the Greenwich Village rebellion was engineered by middle-class Americans. For of those rebels who have left us an indication of how they lived as children, more than 81 percent came from rich, well-to-do, or poor families. As in the late 1960s, when an affluent and educated élite joined with various spokesmen for the disadvantaged in ridiculing the manners, morals, and politics of middle-American "squares," the Greenwich Village attack on the "Puritanism" of middle-class culture was essentially a crossfire, laid down from opposite ends of the economic line.

Of the eighty-eight Villagers whose perceptions of their parents have been identified, twenty-four were raised in families in which the father was dead, or had been divorced by his wife, or had disappeared for some other reason, or was prolongedly and repeatedly absent from home. Sixteen were brought up in families in wihch the father was perceived by his children to be a business or professional failure. Twenty were brought up in families in which the father was perceived by his children as a professional success, but also as a social nonconformist of some sort. Twenty-two were brought up in families in which the father was perceived by his children as a professional success and a social conformist, but also as not opposed to their own nonconformism. Six were brought up in families in which the father was perceived as professionally successful, socially conformist, and actively opposed to his children's nonconformism.

The twenty-four Villagers whose fathers were either dead or missing were brought up, as we might expect, in female-dominated households. However, mothers were also perceived by their children to be the dominant personalities in almost all the households in which the fathers were perceived to have failed in their careers, as well as in those in which the fathers were perceived as professionally successful, socially conformist, and unopposed to their children's nonconformism. Contrary to Christopher Lasch's hypothesis that it was "patriarchal authority" which first taught the rebels of the early twentieth century to value freedom, two-thirds of the Greenwich Villagers were raised in households which they considered to be female-dominated. That domination, furthermore, was not the saccharine consequence of "a sentimental veneration of women"; it flowed, rather, from the personal force of the mothers and from the absence or startling weakness of the fathers.

Harold Stearns was one of the Villagers who grew up without a father, and his story is worth recounting in some detail, for it casts light on the psychology of other rebels. According to the tale his mother told him, Stearns's father was the proprietor of a jewelry store in Brockton, Massachusetts, who died of a heart attack three months before Harold's birth. Acutely affected by the demise of her husband, Mrs. Stearns temporarily lost her sanity. It was during her stay in a sanitarium that Harold was born. Having surrendered all claim to her husband's property during her period of insanity, Mrs. Stearns reentered the workaday world without any money but with two children to support. Conscious of his mother's love of the dramatic, Harold was never certain of the authenticity of this account of his birth, and his uneasiness was further intensified by his older brother's taunts that he did not know "the whole story."

There was no doubt, however, of the pennilessness which forced Mrs. Stearns to place her children in foster homes for a time until she was able to earn a decent income as a private nurse. Stearns's life with his mother, when it finally resumed, proved to be a more unsettling and alienating experience in certain ways than living with strangers had been, as she dragged her two sons into and out of a bewildering succession of Massachusetts towns—Taunton, Cambridgeport, Attleboro, Malden, Dorchester. These moves were made partly because of Mrs. Stearns's need to pursue employment, but mainly out of the grandiose habit of this forceful, determined, but thoroughly quixotic woman of renting houses she could not afford. Not even her remarriage, to an almost stone-deaf man whom Harold regarded as very odd and never got to know, could persuade his mother to settle down.

In spite, however, of his having been "supersensitive to her small faults" in his youth, Harold Stearns as a man paid homage to his mother's "indomitable spirit." Her lack of self-restraint, he was sure, had not scarred his childhood nearly so much as the lack of a father to talk to and to emulate. Driven in upon himself, beset by doubts about the circumstances of his birth, and tortured by sexual insecurities which he wanted to confess to an understanding older man but could not ("If only I had had a father!" he would cry out years later in his autobiography), he felt strange, lonely, and abnormal. Not knowing by example how a man was supposed to behave, he felt unsure of how to act as a boy, and when his peers in one of the many neighborhoods the Stearnses lived in became annoyed with his fumbling ways and excluded him from their gang, he retreated even further into a "protective shell of my own dreaming." Increasingly his mind became dominated by images of death—of the dead father he had never seen, and of his mother's dying patients, who made him feel that he was "the son of an executioner." Dead birds lying on a road could cause him to panic, and on a traumatic summer's day in Barre, Massachusetts, not far from the sanitarium where he had been born, he was unable to bring up the body of a suicide victim from the bottom of a river—which he had volunteered to do—when he was paralyzed with horror by the sight of the corpse's "old grey bloated face."

For all his psychological problems and his many changes of school, Stearns's grades were good enough to get him into Harvard, where in the ensuing years he did outstanding academic work and developed a Harvard *hauteur* (an "aristocratic impulse," Stearns termed it) that was proof against all questions about his sketchy family background. Graduating in the spring of 1913, he was drawn "instinctively," as if by a "magnet," to

New York City, although not to Greenwich Village, despite the national publicity the Village was receiving that year as a result of the Armory Show and the Paterson pageant. Buoyed up by his strong showing at Harvard, he floated without much effort into an interesting job with the *Dramatic Mirror* and then into a better-paying position as a theatrical feature writer for Frank Munsey's *Press*. Even though "lovely Mary Pyne and the dynamic, talented, curiously handsome Djuna Barnes"—two of the most notable young women in the Village—both worked for the *Press*, Stearns was still not interested in the life of Washington Square. The midtown "Main Stem," where successful newspapermen, publishers, composers, and Broadway playwrights congregated in ritzy saloons like Ike's, just two blocks around the corner from the Harvard Club on 44th Street—this was the world to which Stearns wished to belong. In the early summer of 1914, he felt so carelessly confident of the place he had made for himself in this world that he took a leave of absence from the *Press* and went to Europe. Despite the outbreak of war in August, the trip was a great success, especially his visit to London, where he encountered Somerset Maugham and Graham Wallas and looked up Walter Lippmann.

Upon his return to New York, he found that his old job was not waiting for him, and he was unable to land another. A sympathetic girl friend might have helped to ease the pain of these disappointments, but he was as short of female companionship that autumn as he was of cash. "What ought one to do in a melancholy situation like that? Something was demanded. I decided to become a Bohemian." The flippant, casual tone of this decisively important passage in Stearns's autobiography was designed by a broken but intermittently prideful man in his mid-forties to conceal the fact that at the age of twenty-three, long before his tragic marriage or any other event had given him an excuse for failure, his career had been short-circuited. With stunning suddenness, he had been shut out of the world he had come to love, and he was consumed with fear that he would never be readmitted to it. Just as he had once been excluded from a gang of boys, so now he found himself excluded from a fraternity of men, and as this fact sank into his consciousness, all of his childish feelings of alienation and inadequacy came over him again. In the Village, as at Harvard, he would temporarily recover his morale, yet in the long run Washington Square would prove to be an exile without an exit, except into other exiles.

He began by living, as so many recruits to the Village did, with a college friend, who helped to make a seedy rooming house on Greenwich Avenue seem like an undergraduate dormitory. The monthly rent that he and Walter Franzen paid was remarkably small, perhaps as low as fifteen dollars apiece, and in the Italian restaurants of the area a full meal could be commanded for sixty cents. The Village, however, was not only a place for saving money, it was a place for making money—out of thin air, as it seemed. Odd jobs in publicity, winning hands in poker at Polly Holladay's restaurant, and freelance assignments for high-brow magazines enabled Stearns to drink with Art Young and other regulars at a fly-specked but convivial saloon called the Hell Hole, to patronize the Boni brothers' bookshop, and every now and then to remember Paris with a meal at the Brevoort. But his talent for scrounging did not fully manifest itself until he met, or rather "acquired," a young woman referred to in his autobiography only as Felicia. The very same lack of purposefulness that had caused Stearns to lose his place in the harshly competitive league of big-city journalism rendered him—as it did Maurice Sterne, Andrew Dasburg, and other Villagers who had grown up without fathers—extraordinarily attractive to women with executive talents. On her income as a fashion artist, Felicia rented and furnished an apartment in the Village, where for two years she acted as Stearns's banker, housekeeper, seamstress, and mistress, even though she herself did not live in the apartment, preferring instead to maintain her residence in another part of New York. Like other women who were the talk of the Village in these years, Felicia apparently felt guilty about indulging her appetite for extramarital sex, for she seemed to welcome the punishments which Stearns meted out to her. Occasionally, but only occasionally, would he take her out to celebrate at Polly's or the Brevoort; mainly he repaid her for her financial, domestic, and sexual services with academic instruction. Professor Higgins to her Eliza, he assigned her extensive readings in history, English literature, and French, plus written exercises.

By the time Stearns had passed beyond his love affair with the young woman who was Felicia's successor, he had evolved for himself a new theory of morality. Morals, he concluded, "are concerned with action in its social significance—they are not, or at least ought not to be, concerned with personal sensations that have no general implications." In addition to excusing his own treatment of women, Stearns's theory excused the conduct of his father as well—whoever he may have been, whatever he may have done. Yet the self-exculpatory hedonism of the statement is not its only significant aspect, for Stearns's equation of morality with social significance indicated a shift in his interest from the theater to the factory and the mine and a gathering determination to place his literary talents at the service of liberal causes. Hired as a salaried contributor to the *New Republic*, he wrote some brilliant pieces for the magazine and for the first time since 1914 began to conceive of a career for himself inside an organization. The editors of the magazine seemed fond of him. Yet fondness was not the same thing as respect, and Stearns's sensitive antenna soon picked up the dreaded signals of secret derision: "I think all of them looked upon me at the time as something of the 'bad boy' of the office, and they refused—sometimes with a casualness that drove me to furious anger—to take my opinions seriously."

Discouraged by the situation at the *New Republic*, Stearns left New York in November 1917 and took over the editorship of the *Dial* in Chicago. But this excursion had no future in it either, and by the following summer he was back in the Village. Toward the end of 1918 he married, only to lose his wife in childbirth within a year. Stearns's fate was now fixed, if indeed it had not been long since. He would not become a vastly influential theater critic, or a magazine editor, or an author of books of vital consequence on social issues. Instead, he would go to Paris, turn out a racing column for the European edition of the Chicago *Tribune*, and drink until doctors warned him of impending blindness. By way of saying good-bye to his native land, he edited *Civilization in the United States: An Inquiry by Thirty Americans*. His own contribution to the volume expressed a total disdain for the petty regulations, grotesque regalia, and driving, drilling, regimenting discipline of the American social machine.

Though Stearns has a mythically tragic reputation, his personal problems were not at all unusual in Greenwich Village in the teens, especially among men who had grown up without strong male models. The belief that successful men found him ridiculous also haunted Donald Evans, who finally committed suicide, and Maxwell Bodenheim, whose life ended equally sordidly. Boyhood insecurities about sexual identity, which flowered in Stearns's manhood into an endless pursuit of women, hounded other men in the Village who had reputations as great lovers, including Floyd Dell and Max Eastman. As Dell once said, speaking from the heart, Greenwich Village was "a place where people came to solve some of their life problems. . . . A moral health resort—that was what it was." Stearns's admiration for his "indomitable" mother is also illustrative of a widespread attitude. Yet he was not really close to his mother, and in this sense his story is not representative of the rebellion. For almost all of the men and women raised in female-dominated households had remarkably intense relationships with their mothers, and these relationships strongly influenced their decisions to reject traditional social roles—as the following case histories will illustrate.

After his plans failed for manufacturing a smokeless furnace in a plant near his home in Kirkwood, Missouri, Marianne Moore's father suffered a nervous breakdown and permanently returned to the home of his parents in Portsmouth, Ohio. Therafter, Marianne and her older brother were raised exclusively by their mother, in a tightly-wound intimacy that soon shaped Marianne into a shy and bookish girl who avoided all social gatherings. When Mrs. Moore obtained a job as a teacher at the Metzger Institute in Carlisle, Pennsylvania, her daughter entered the Institute as a student, so that not even her schooling separated her from her mother. The college that Marianne chose to attend was Mrs. Moore's choice as well, just as the poems she began to write at Bryn Mawr were also marked by her mother's sensibility. In retrospect, Marianne Moore considered that the standards of aesthetics and behavior her mother had imposed upon her had been too rigorous, but she acknowledged that she had been "profoundly influenced" by them. In choosing to pursue a career as a poet, she also drew inspiration from her mother's career as a teacher, and Marianne further emulated Mary Moore in rejecting the old-fashioned idea that American women had to be married in order to be fulfilled. At the same time, she denied the new-fangled notion that single women at Greenwich Village parties could not conduct themselves by the Presbyterian precepts of their mothers. Mrs.

Moore, her daughter once said, by way of accounting for her own fiercely independent and self-disciplined personality, "always stood for the National Anthem, . . . even when it was on the radio."

Edna St. Vincent Millay, a very different person from Marianne Moore and a very different poet, was raised by a musically talented mother who had wanted to be a singer. Independent enough to have divorced her husband and to have found a way to earn her own living and support her daughters without aid from their father, Cora Millay lived the way she pleased. She called her most gifted child "Vincent," because she had wanted her to be a boy, and she challenged all her girls to be as imaginative as she was; without any guide but her own instincts, Cora Millay created a household atmosphere that prophesied what Provincetown would be like in 1915 as accurately as it reflected its location in the rural Maine of the 1890s. ("I am not being a Bohemian," Edna Millay would write to Arthur Ficke from New York in 1913. "I am not so Bohemian by half as I was when I came. You see, here one has to be one thing or the other, whereas at home one could be a little of both.") Thus the legendary entrance of a young Vassar graduate into the life of Greenwich Village in the teens in no sense represented a deviation from the direction of her earlier life. Edna Millay was an extraordinarily tough-minded as well as incorrigibly romantic woman who played a quite independent role in her famous love affairs ("Oh, think not I am faithful to a vow!") and was far more determined, as Max Eastman said, to be a poet than "some man's woman or even some child's mother." In all the respects that really counted, she was very much her mother's daughter.

Theresa Helburn's decision to give up the empty life of a society debutante and join the Washington Square Players also traced back to a "vital, dominant, ambitious" mother. An ex-teacher, Mrs. Helburn kept her daughter at home until she was ready to enter the fourth grade and poured into her her own passionate devotion to the arts. To move on to other examples, George Creel worked hard for the cause of equal rights for women during his Greenwich Village years because "I *knew* my mother had more character, brains, and competence than any man that ever lived"—including and especially Creel's alcoholic father, who had plunged his family into poverty by recklessly squandering his inheritance on a cattle-raising experiment in Missouri. Walter Lippmann's successful, kindly, but colorless and unforceful father almost certainly did not serve "as a model for Walter," in the opinion of Carl Binger, Lippmann's lifelong friend, whereas his unusually intelligent, cultivated, ambitious, imperious mother bulked very large in the slightly exophthalmic eyes of her only child. While Mr. Lippmann wanted his son to be a lawyer, Mrs. Lippmann encouraged him to believe that he could become anything he wanted to. In the boy's bedroom, there was a bust of Napoleon.

Margaret Anderson and Mabel Dodge also had intense relationships with their mothers, but of a much darker sort. These headstrong daughters and their dominating mothers were very much alike, psychologically speaking, yet they clashed bitterly and repeatedly. The more the mothers insisted upon the virtues of their own upper-class values, the more the daughters resisted them. The ultimate decision of the daughters to go to Greenwich Village thus represented a linear break with their childhoods, and in fact almost everything they did as adults was in some sense an act of revenge against their mothers.

Margaret Anderson regarded her mother as "one of those persons who gets an infinite pleasure out of making things disagreeable," and she spent much of her girlhood egging on her father to fight with his wife, in the hope that such fights would divert Mrs. Anderson's attention from her daughter. Much to Margaret's disgust, Mr. Anderson, a weak and indecisive man, was always more anxious to conciliate than to quarrel. At the end of her teens, Margaret escaped from the pretentious Indiana home that her mother had recently purchased and redecorated—Mrs. Anderson loved redecorating and consequently forced her family to change houses repeatedly—by enrolling at Western College in Oxford, Ohio. It was her mother's assumption that as soon as Margaret had finished her education she would "come home to the higher joys of country clubs and bridge." Instead, she fled to Chicago, San Francisco, Greenwich Village, and finally France. Wherever she went, she too showed that she had strong ideas about houses and interior decoration. After arriving in Chicago, she lived for six months in a tent on the shore of Lake Michigan. In her New York period, she fixed up an apartment by painting the floors dark plum, covering the walls of a bedroom with gold Chinese paper, and hanging a large divan from the ceiling by heavy black chains. Mrs. Anderson would have been appalled.

Pleasure for the young girl who was later known as Mabel Dodge also consisted in flouting, as outrageously as possible, the hypocritical respectability of her hateful mother. The first time that Mabel ever achieved an orgasm was when she tried sexual intercourse on the rug in her parents' parlor, where all through her unhappy childhood she had witnessed her father's "furious, impotent angers" at the wife whom he suspected of sexual infidelity, and her mother's "cold, merciless, expressionless contempt" for him. In time, Mabel Dodge would also be known for sexual escapades—with Jews, an American Indian, and other men who would have horrified her mother.

Such cases, however, are exceptional. Most of the intense mother-child relationships—between mothers and daughters as well as mothers and sons—were happy, not hateful. Max Eastman, to cite one more case, was so attached to his mother that he had, in his words, "a mother complex," and he never tired of singing her praises. She was the most noted woman preacher of her time. She was the friend of such unusual men as Mark Twain and the Reverend Thomas K. Beecher, and of Beecher's wife, Julia, who had bobbed her hair in 1857, thus "anticipating Irene Castle by about sixty years." She was one of the first, and certainly one of the oldest, women in the United States to be psychoanalyzed by A. A. Brill. (So much for the notion that Freud's ideas directly affected only young people in this period.) In the Eastman household, her strength was as proverbial as the weakness of her neurasthenic husband, and her steadfast presence was an enormous reassurance to the psychologically troubled Max in the years when he was growing up. As Eastman later remarked, "If there was anything in my childhood to account for my leaning toward revolution, it lay rather in the good than the bad luck of my birth. I grew up in a family where kindness and fair-dealing and sound logic prevailed to such a degree that, when I got out into the public world, it looked excessively unjust, irrational, a subject for indignation and extreme action." Although cast in strictly personal terms, the remark throws a bar of light across the early lives of most mother-dominated rebels.

Strong male parents mainly appear in two clusters, of which

the larger is composed of twenty fathers who were perceived by their children to be professionally successful but socially nonconformist in some way. Far from incarnating and authenticating conservative, middle-class values, these vivid, attractive men inspired their children to believe that all of the excitement of life consisted in deviating from the social norm.

John Jackson Cozad, for instance, was a great faro player—the "King of the Gamblers," he was called. Immaculately dressed in a Prince Albert coat, high silk hat, and kid gloves, he cut a wide swath through the casinos of the Mississippi Valley in the 1850s and 1860s. Switching to real estate promotion, he drifted westward to the high plains country, where in 1872, on the bank of the Platte River at the 100th meridian, he built his dream city: Cozad, Nebraska. By this time the promoter had a wife and two sons, John and Robert Henry. Since Robert Henry was a particularly talented boy, he was sent to a private school in Cincinnati, but each spring he returned to Cozad, where he spent his summers riding his horse over the prairies, looking for Indians. In 1882, when Robert Henry was seventeen, his father's growing difficulties with cattle ranchers in the area culminated in a fight with a man who drew a knife on Cozad. The ex-gambler killed his assailant with a single shot from his pistol and then left town, out of fear that he would be lynched. Fleeing from the law as well as the lynch mob, he changed his name to Richard H. Lee. Robert Henry Cozad now became Robert Henri and was passed off as a foundling whom his father had adopted. Within two years, the outlaw had created a new life for himself and his family in Atlantic City, New Jersey, and had launched another real estate bubble by purchasing a choice tract of land where Texas Avenue meets the beach.

Exactly when his son, Robert Henri, began reading Bakunin is not clear. Possibly it was in 1886, when he enrolled at the Pennsylvania Academy of the Fine Arts; possibly it was a few years later, when he was an art student in Paris. But the question does not really matter, for the anarchist philosophy of Bakunin merely confirmed a faith in untrammeled individualism that had been stamped upon Henri's imagination by the wildly romantic career of his father. Events in Cozad, Nebraska, had taught a seventeen-year-old boy to view conventional society as his enemy, and he spent a lifetime trying to create a counter culture inside the circle of his art students, first in Philadelphia and later in New York. John Jackson Cozad had a dream city; so did his son.

Inez Milholland, a young woman of Amazonian proportions, abounding energy, and considerable athletic skill—as a Vassar undergraduate she set a college record in the basketball throw—was the first of three children of John Elmer Milholland. An editorial writer for the New York *Tribune,* Milholland became a wealthy man by inventing and successfully marketing a pneumatic-tube system for sending short-distance mail. He also had definite ideas about reforming American life. Beginning as a mugwump Republican, he gradually broadened his field of operations until he was deeply involved in prison reform, pacifism, labor reform, woman's suffrage, federal aid to education, and Negro rights. He founded the Constitution League and later served as first treasurer of the National Association for the Advancement of Colored People. His oldest child, who adored her father, soon began to emulate him. As a high-school girl, she made a number of speeches in favor of woman's suffrage in London's Hyde Park and was twice arrested for her militancy. After graduating from Vassar, where she had enrolled two-thirds of the student body in the Votes for Women Club, she walked the picket lines in the shirtwaist and laundry workers' strikes in New York City, investigated prison conditions at Sing Sing, wrote a column on women for *McClure's,* and, after taking a law degree at New York University, worked as a lawyer for Elizabeth Gurley Flynn. Whereas John Elmer Milholland was a reform Republican, his daughter proclaimed herself a Socialist, but the difference was more seeming than real, for she worked for no movements other than those previously sanctioned as worthy causes by her father. Revolt, for Inez Milholland, was a means of offering homage to an icon, not of smashing it.

The Bohemian poet Scudder Middleton was "cast outside a certain pale" of social respectability by his gambler father, just as Robert Henri had been by his father. Like Inez Milholland, John Reed hero-worshipped the man who sat at the head of the family table ("a great fighter," Reed called him, "one of the first of the little band of insurgents . . . to give expression to the new social conscience of the middle class"), and Orrick Johns admired with corresponding fervor the elder Johns, a fighting

Pulitzer editor. Albert Boni and Hutchins Hapgood were decisively influenced by the advanced ideas of their fathers about religion and politics, as was Art Young. It was from listening to the sparkling conversation of a father who was quite unlike most Army officers that William Rose Benet first gained a sense of what it meant to be a thinker as well as a doer. Although Margaret Sanger had ambivalent feelings about the redheaded stone cutter who was her father, her career cannot possibly be understood without reference to his relish of sex or his championship of Henry George's single tax, Mrs. Bloomer's bloomers, free libraries, free education, and political equality for women. The father's improvidence kept his family in debt, and his equation of manliness with procreation helped send his wife to an early grave, but to Margaret he was not a failure in his career, he was a success, an artist, a genius, the most unforgettable man she would ever know.

The other cluster of strong male parents consists of the professionally successful fathers who actively discouraged the nonconformism of Hendrik Willem Van Loon, Edgard Varèse, Dorothy Day, Beatrice Hinkle, Inez Haynes, and Frederic C. Howe. The brutally tyrannical treatment of their sons by the Dutch and Franco-Italian fathers of Van Loon and Varèse may cast light on bourgeois family life in Europe, but it tells us nothing about family life in the United States. As for the paternal protectors who attempted to limit the independence of the three women rebels, they almost certainly would have behaved very differently if their gifted children had been boys. Mr. Day, for instance, had not minded at all when one of his sons had gone to work for E. W. Scripps's liberal and experimental *Day Book*; after all, he himself was a newspaperman. But when Dorothy also decided to follow in her father's footsteps by taking a job with the New York *Call*, he reacted violently. He had never kissed or embraced Dorothy during her childhood; he had been very strict with her about inviting boys to the house and about reading "trashy" books and magazines; and he had no intention of letting her work for a newspaper. Thus in order to emulate her father, she had to break with him—and once the break was made, she began to flout him in ways that he would have found incredible, had he known about them. By the summer of 1917, his nineteen-year-old daughter was sharing an apartment on Macdougal Street in platonic comradeship with

Floyd Dell, Merrill Rogers, and David Carb. She had also become involved, or was about to become involved, in a strange, three-cornered relationship with Agnes Boulton and Eugene O'Neill. Moreover, she was spending a good many of her nights buying shots of rye for unshaven, middle-aged men at the Hell Hole, singing revolutionary songs on piers and park benches with Mike Gold, and going down on her Episcopalian knees on the stone floors of Catholic churches. Though she continued to aver that "childhood was a happy time for me," she had completely rejected the world in which she had been brought up, and she never went back to it.

The only native-born male American in the entire group whose rebellious career may have arisen out of a youthful resentment of disapproving patriarchal authority was Frederic C. Howe—and even this case was not clear-cut. Despite Howe's disappointment at his father's refusal to help him through graduate school and law school, it is far from certain that Howe's feelings about the shortsightedness of one businessman had much to do with his subsequent career as a Progressive opponent of business interests in Cleveland, or with the surprising decision he made in his early forties to eschew the world of wheeling and dealing and settle among the Bohemians of Greenwich Village. But even if we count the Howe case, the successful fathers whose conservatism and authoritarianism aroused a rebellious ire in their sons and daughters were few. In the male-dominated families of future Villagers, as in the female-dominated families, children were encouraged to be nonconformist far more often than not.

Thus nineteenth-century, middle-class culture did not represent "a single, old, traditional set of doctrines." Nineteenth-century, middle-class culture, and its main instrumentality, the American family, were more complex than that. Some children were taught to accept conservative doctrines about laissez-faire capitalism, the Christian religion, the role of women in American and many other matters. America, though, was a big country and a free country, and other children were taught to question official values. For some of the men and women who came to Greenwich Village in the teens, rebellion necessitated a repudiation of a conservative heritage. But those men and women were in the minority. The majority of the Greenwich Village rebels had been readied for the revolutionary ideas of the twentieth century by the antitraditional ideas imbibed from their independent-minded parents in the nineteenth century.

Even more important than the specific ideas which the parents of the Villagers passed on to their children were the personal examples they set, and the expectations of adult life that were aroused by those examples. Strong fathers elicited in their gifted sons and daughters essentially the same expectation, that they would find American life a dull business unless they set themselves in opposition to it in some way. What their more passive mothers taught them is not recorded. Strong mothers taught their gifted daughters to believe that women in America could not be fulfilled unless they ignored restrictive definitions of their social role. In some cases, weak fathers appear to have engendered in their gifted daughters a wholesale contempt for men that reinforced the determination of these young women not to be dependent upon the opposite sex. Strong mothers taught their gifted sons to believe that they could do anything they wanted; indeed, they inflated their egos to the point where the sons were unprepared to accept the discipline of any organization not put together for their own benefit, or to be placed in a subordinate position of any kind. Yet their weak or absent fathers also left some of these men with a lurking self-distrust.

Long before they confronted it, the rebels had learned to feel superior to American society, or to feel superior to it and to fear it at one and the same time. Such feelings may have prompted some of them to delay their entrance into society as long as possible by going to college. In any event, of the 111 Villagers whose educational backgrounds are known, 72 went and 39 did not; a number of those who did not, attended finishing schools, or traveled in Europe, or studied painting. For all but a few of the rebels who enrolled, college was supremely enjoyable—the last and best chapter of childhood. But when the rebels finally entered the public world, they found it to be more restrictive than most of them had imagined it would be.

The rebels' sense of inadequacy no less than their sense of superiority required that their lives not be hampered by too many rules and regulations. Yet in the early years of their maturity they became convinced that the old-fashioned freedom of American life was waning. Between 1898 and 1902, a burst of merger activity never exceeded in importance in our history took place in the American economy. The numerous small- and medium-sized firms that had characterized many industries were absorbed into such giant enterprises as United States Steel, American Tobacco, International Harvester, Du Pont, Corn Products, Anaconda Copper, and American Smelting and Refining. In the year 1899 alone, more than a thousand firms disappeared into mergers. The human implications of the merger movement—as he saw them—were spelled out by Randolph Bourne in an article in the *Atlantic Monthly* in 1911. Still a student at Columbia, but already somewhat involved in the life of Greenwich Village, Bourne proclaimed that to him and his gifted friends, modern American society offered nothing but frustration because "the only choice for the vast majority of young men today is between being swallowed up in the routine of a big corporation, and experiencing the vicissitudes of a small business, which is now an uncertain, rickety affair, usually living by its wits, in the hands of men who are forced to subordinate everything to self-preservation, and in which the employee's livelihood is in constant jeopardy." The growing consciousness of this situation, he said, "explains many of the peculiar characteristics of our generation."

The universities, too, the rebels felt, were now great corporations, which not only swallowed up young men in their routines, but required them to have the Ph.D. Even in the arts there were diminished opportunities, in their opinion, for the eccentric individualist. The last of the old-time stock companies had disappeared, and in their place had arisen a theatrical syndicate which controlled theaters and bookings all over the country. When the grip of the syndicate was finally broken after a decade, it was not by the reestablishment of local theaters but by a rival chain of New York–controlled houses. The National Academy of Design similarly solidified its grip on American painting and sculpture in this period by cutting back exhibition outlets to nonmembers through its influence on the proprietors of New York art galleries and its domination of the channels of publicity.

Federal, state, and local laws, meanwhile, were encroaching more and more upon the autonomy of private lives. In the ironic words of George Santayana, whose Harvard classes had been attended by a number of the Greenwich Village rebels, "Liberalism had been supposed to advance liberty; but what the advanced parties that still call themselves liberal now advocate is control, control over property, trade, wages, hours of work, meat and drink, [and] amusements." The control of individual preferences by the democratic majority was also felt through means other than politics, for as the emergence of Hearst and Pulitzer signified, the United States in 1900 had entered a new era of mass culture, in which the lowest common denominator of taste quickly proved to be a frighteningly powerful arbiter. The triumph of mass culture had been made possible by the triumph of machine technology, and while the latter triumph elated many of the Greenwich Village rebels, it made others feel more hemmed in than ever—which is why Marcel Duchamp's transmogrification of a human being into something that looked like a robot as seen through a stroboscopic lens provoked more discussion in the Village than any other painting in the Armory Show of 1913. When William Carlos Williams walked into the show and saw *Nude Descending a Staircase,* he "laughed out loud . . . with relief." As far as he was concerned, the truth about modern civilization had at last been told.

The human dimensions of American cities were also being obliterated in this period by ever greater concentrations of tall buildings. By 1914, urban life in the United States had taken on an "impersonal quality" that Walter Lippmann, writing in *Drift and Mastery,* found "intolerable." "We live in great cities without knowing our neighbors," he exclaimed, "the loyalties of place have broken down, and our associations stretched over large territories, cemented by very little direct contact." Of all the threats to their sense of personal freedom, the depersonalization of urban life may have alarmed the Greenwich Village rebels more than any other.

Being intellectuals, the rebels discussed these developments on the level of abstraction. Yet behind their discussions lay their own experience. When Randolph Bourne, for instance, talked about how his generation felt caught between the anonymity of the big corporation and the rickety uncertainty of the small company, he was thinking first and foremost of his own life, especially of the five demoralizing years he spent in the job market before his enrollment at Columbia in 1909. At eighteen, Bourne had gone out into the world with more handicaps than most high-school graduates: a grotesquely hunched back, hideously torn ears, a scarred face, and haunting memories of a lost and defeated father. A failure in business, a failure in marriage, an incurable alcoholic, Charles Bourne had added to his son's woes sometime before the turn of the century by being careless about a flapping overcoat as he was descending from a New York trolley car. Caught and dragged, he suffered permanent back damage. His crippled eldest child almost inevitably identified himself with his crippled father, though Charles Bourne no longer lived with his family. For Mrs. Bourne's brother, a successful New Jersey lawyer, had agreed to support his sister and her children only if Charles Bourne promised to go away. Coddled by his mother and sister throughout his adolescence, young Randolph developed a tremendous sense of self-importance, at the same time that thoughts of his father filled him with foreboding. Suddenly catapulted out into the world when his uncle refused to pay for his college education, Bourne finally found employment with a company that turned out perforated music rolls for player pianos. In later years he said that the birth of his social awareness occurred in 1904, the year he went out in search of a job—and for all his intelligence was swallowed up in the dehumanizing routine of manufacturing mechanical music.

Other rebels suffered similiar defeats. Alfred Stieglitz, for example, came back to New York after ten delightful years of travel and study in Germany and with the financial backing of his wealthy father opened a photoengraving business. Distracted by his artistic interest in photography, and unprepared by a leisure-class upbringing to be a hard bargainer in the marketplace, Stieglitz found the rickety uncertainties of running a small business enterprise more burdensome than he was either able or willing to handle. The photoengraving firm soon went bankrupt.

Floyd Dell was so "cruelly disillusioned" with his financially ruined and broken-spirited father and so closely attached to the "all-powerful Goddess" who was his mother, that he grew up without "any identification with the masculine world." For such a boy, Dell retrospectively observed in his autobiography, "one would be inclined to predict trouble," especially with regard to "ultimate success in love and work." In a career start that foreshadowed a lifelong dissatisfaction with large organizations, Dell was fired for insolence from a newspaper in

Davenport, Iowa, and subsequently resigned from an excellent position with one of the major dailies in Chicago.

Dell's good friend, George Cram Cook, was the son of a highly successful corporation lawyer and of a mystical mother who taught her son to believe that life had cast him for a role as a man of genius. Surveying the American scene after college, Cook found it unthinkable that he should place his "Promethean" abilities at the service of any of the business firms that were his father's clients. Cook even found teaching English at Iowa State University a bore and took to playing his violin in the classroom. Before long, he returned to Davenport, exiled himself upon a truck farm, and began a long battle with drunkenness.

Hutchins Hapgood was the son of a well-educated, intellectually sophisticated businessman who had made money manufacturing plows in Alton, Illinois, but who otherwise held himself aloof from the town. The son grew up feeling that he, too, was "a stranger to everything around me." Persisting throughout his boyhood, these feelings finally climaxed in a nervous breakdown when he was about nineteen. Upon his recovery, he entered Harvard, did brilliantly, and could easily have gone on to an academic career—or so it seemed. But after discovering that graduate school was a more confining routine than undergraduate life, Hapgood left Harvard for a lengthy stay in Europe. It was during this period that he became the ardent womanizer whose exploits he would later record in *A Victorian in the Modern World.* When he finally returned home, he assisted in George Pierce Baker's drama course at Harvard, taught school in Chicago, and worked as a reporter for the New York *Commercial Advertiser.* In none of these positions, however, did he last very long. As the new century dawned, Hapgood was thirty-one years old and still had not found himself.

The rebels who were temperamentally unsuited to business, big-time journalism, university life, and other corporate pursuits eventually decided to try their luck in Greenwich Village. The decision of other rebels to join them was mainly prompted by private difficulties with parents and lovers. But whether their paramount problems had to do with work or love, the rebels were united in their disillusionment with life in big cities. As we have already seen, a substantial number of the 141 rebels whose birthplaces are known were born in big cities, more than 20 in New York City alone. But in the period immediately prior to their coming to the Village, most of the rebels who had been born in smaller cities and towns were also living in big cities. Like the heroines of the novels which reflected Theodore Dreiser's adventures in Chicago, New York, and Cleveland, these rebels found the modern American metropolis a fascinating but profoundly alienating environment. Although they would never have dreamed of going back where they came from, they acutely missed the personal associations of small-town life, and they turned to the Village in the hope of finding them again. As for the rebels who had been born and brought up in big cities, they lamented with Walter Lippmann the disappearance of the more intimate urban world they remembered from childhood. Though some of these rebels would continue to maintain their residences and to hold jobs in other parts of New York, they would come to the Village in search of friendship and a neighborhood atmosphere. Those rebels who came directly to the Village from smaller cities and towns were also disturbed by the changes in urban America that they had heard or read about, or had noticed during visits to metropolitan centers. From the perspective of Elmira, New York, Max Eastman announced that he "hated all cities and mortally dreaded their noise, tensity, and cold commotion." New York City, in particular, he regarded as a "purgatory." Historians of American culture have repeatedly stated that the Greenwich Village rebellion was one of several manifestations of a larger movement in twentieth-century American life called "the revolt from the village." But this statement is no more true than the statement that most rebels moved to the Village from small towns in the Middle West. The fact is that most rebels set out for Washington Square from urban addresses and that most rebels, no matter where they came from, were attracted to Greenwich Village because it was in some sense still a village.

Down to about 1890, the Village had a timeless quality that made it remarkable among New York neighborhoods. Its narrow, winding streets and lanes, running diagonally for the most part from the north-south axis of Manhattan Island, were not only the area's most distinctive characteristic, but its protective shield. For when the checkerboard street pattern had been adopted citywide in 1811, the planners had been unable to impose the pattern upon the tangled byways of the Village, thus sparing it from becoming a traffic corridor between midtown and lower Manhattan. Not until Seventh Avenue and the West Side subway were cut through in 1917 did the Village cease to be an island within an island. The charming row houses and stately mansions that had arisen by 1850 were also saved from the wrecking ball of office builders later in the century by the relative inaccessibility of the Village to the commercial life of New York, and by the sandy subsoil south of Fourteenth Street, which seemingly precluded the construction of high-rise buildings. As a result of its continuing residential attractiveness, the Village did not, like the lower East Side, become a slum predominantly peopled by newly arrived immigrants, but instead maintained a heterogeneous balance of ethnic and economic groups, including a very substantial representation of the native-born middle class, as well as a nucleus of wealthy families. In a city that was highly conscious of the ethnic makeup of its political wards, Greenwich Village was known as the "American Ward."

In the years after 1890, however, the stability of the area was at last disrupted when tenements sprang up on its western and southern edges and were largely filled by Italian immigrants. By 1900, tenements were being built in the center of the Village as well. With the sudden upsurge in the number of poor people, the middle class began to abandon the field. Although the discontinuation of tenement construction in 1910 succeeded in slowing the increase in the immigrant population, and World War I temporarily shut down the source of supply, these events did nothing to staunch the outward flow of middle-class families. Between 1910 and 1920, the residents of the area decreased by 19.3 percent. In 1890, the Village had finally been touched by history, and in the thirty years thereafter it declined very rapidly, both in per capita income and in population.

To the arriving rebels, the decline of the place was as important as its village charm. For most of them were not only looking for a more personal world, they were looking for the opportunity to build more congenial careers, and they therefore were interested to discover that rapidly changing conditions had endowed this old-fashioned neighborhood with some of the openness of a raw frontier, where cheap rents, if not free land, abounded. In the early twentieth century, everyone knew that the West had long since been won, that the frontier was firmly in the hands of the historians, and that safety valves had disappeared from American life; yet in Greenwich Village in the teens, a group of disaffected men and women—in full flight from American civilization—opened up a new territory, Bohemian style. Appropriately enough, Willa Cather lived at 5 Bank Street from 1913 onwards, conjuring up visions of Nebraska pioneers amid the "frontier" excitement of the Village. As other settlers had done before them, the rebels founded their own institutions and went into business for themselves. They created the Washington Square Players and the Provincetown Players. They started *The Masses, The Pagan, The Seven Arts, Others, Glebe, The Chimera, The Quill, The Liberator,* and *Bruno's Greenwich Village,* among other magazines. They opened restaurants, tea rooms, book shops, publishing businesses, art galleries, and settlement houses. In the jack-of-all-trades spirit of pioneer communities, they made a cult of the versatile amateur. Max Eastman had never worked for a magazine until he was made editor of *The Masses*. The founders of the Provincetown Players had no professional experience in the theater. The only large groups that John Reed had handled before taking charge of the Paterson pageant were the crowds he had led in cheers at Harvard football games. Edna Millay insisted on being an actress as well as a poet. Alfred Stieglitz not only worked as a photographer, but presided over a magazine and an art gallery. Wallace Steven's double career as a businessman and a poet—a source of amazement to his friends of later years in Hartford—was standard behavior in the Village; Louis Untermeyer, Lawrence Langner, and other rebels were equally ambidextrous.

Gifted amateurs were soon joined by a scattering of clever frauds. For as in the Old West, personal assertion counted very heavily in the evolving society of the Greenwich Village rebellion and masquerades were easy. Although Marie Marchand was in reality a Roumanian Jewish anarchist, in the Village she blossomed forth in a gaudy shawl as Romany Marie, the Roumanian gypsy, and her restaurants were extremely successful. A decade and a half earlier, Bobby Edwards had been a Harvard clubman, but by the time Maxwell Bodenheim caught up with him in the basement of the Purple Pup in 1916, Edwards had taken on a very different *persona*. "He was carrying a ukelele," Bodenheim remembered,

> made of a cigar box painted in vermilion, mauve, ochre, pink, and orange, with a handle like a small totem pole. He sold these instruments and advertised them by singing to their accompaniment. He wrote the songs and rendered them in a hard, nasal voice.
>
> I do not care for women who are fat, fat, fat.
> They always knock my indiscretions flat, flat, flat.
> And when they lock the door, dear,
> I whisper, "What a bore, dear.
> I simply couldn't think of doing that, that, that."
> (But lots of times I can't refuse.)

The sense that they had stumbled upon a wide-open world, where they could do or say anything they wanted to, or turn into anyone they wanted to, was tremendously exhilarating to the rebels. "We are free who live in Washington Square," John Reed exulted in a poem in 1913. Although "Puritanism" quickly became their favorite swear word, what the rebels were really lashing out against when they attacked moral inhibitions was the whole apparatus of the modern world which had placed such frightening pressures upon their individual freedom. "Puritanism" became the prime target of the rebels not because it was the enemy they most feared, but because it was the easiest to defy. Thus they asserted their personal autonomy by wearing outlandish and revealing costumes to "pagan routs" and masked balls. The same spirit marked their everyday appearance. In conscious defiance of business custom, Floyd Dell affected rough, checked, workingmen's shirts in his office at *The Masses*. Henrietta Rodman and her friends bobbed their hair, walked around in sandals and shapeless, meal-sack shifts, and smoked cigarettes. Elsa von Freytag von Loringhoven was apt to appear for dinner at Christine's restaurant wearing—among other scandalous items—a postage stamp on her cheek, a bright-yellow face powder, and a coal bucket on her head, strapped under her chin like a helmet.

A preoccupation with primitive vitality progressively encompassed the minds of many European and American intellectuals in the early years of the twentieth century, including the Greenwich Village rebels. They hung batik curtains in the windows of their apartments, in tribute to the exotic islands of the South Seas that most of them had never seen, except in the paintings of Paul Gauguin, and they splashed their walls with the wild colors Bakst had employed in his stage sets for the Russian ballet. Extramarital love affairs were announced as if they were health bulletins, and nude bathing at the Village's summer capital at Provincetown was hailed as the only way to swim. Once in the water, the rebels exclaimed at how free they felt. They also talked of bathing in the currents of Bergson's vitalistic flood, and with A. A. Brill, Beatrice Hinkle, and Smith Ely Jelliffe as guides they explored the labyrinths of their own psyches. Visions of violence and destruction appealed to them almost as powerfully as sex. They loved the violence that John Reed packed into his reporting of war in Mexico, that Emma Goldman communicated in her oratory, and that Robert Minor delineated in his cartoons of the class struggle. They thrilled, too, to the sham smashing of Shavian humor and Nietzschean philosophy, while modern art's destruction of the traditional visual forms in which human emotion had expressed itself was as intoxicating as wine. On the last night of the Armory Show, a celebrant raised his glass of champagne and offered an ironic toast to academic art. In mock protest, John Quinn shouted back above the din, "No, no! Don't you remember Captain John Philip of the *Texas*? When his guns sank a Spanish ship at Santiago, he said, 'Don't cheer, boys, the poor devils are dying!'"

By no means all of the rebels accepted all of these enthusiasms; a few of them, in fact, accepted none of them at all. Yet while tastes varied, there was one primitivistic longing which served to bring all factions of the rebellion together: the aesthetic love of poverty.

As a social worker, Mary Simkhovitch, the head of the Greenwich House settlement, was actively committed to ameliorating the lot of the poor, while Robert Henri and his circle of artists were philosophically committed to the same ideal. Nevertheless, these social idealists really did not wish to see the poverty that had come to Greenwich Village go away again, for such a change would have cost them an enormous pleasure. Some years before, when Mary Simkhovitch had come face to face for the first time with the squalor of the lower East Side, she had been overcome by a "vivid sense of new and overpowering vitality"; the sun had poured down on the crowded, noisome streets, and "welded [them] together into one impress of fetid fertility." At Greenwich House, she augmented such excitements with concatenations of sound and color organized under her direction. She began by hiring a summer orchestra and turning it loose in the slum area of Jones Street. Dancers had come crowding after, onlookers had filled the open windows to tenements, "and so the first little street pageant was given in New York." Thereafter, she used the talents of the immigrant poor to stage bigger and more elaborate pageants, as well as festivals, carnivals, fairs, and even baby-carriage parades.

As Meyer Schapiro has pointed out, Robert Henri and the ash-can artists were similarly caught up in the pure spectacle of teeming streets. In spite of their idealistic faith in political and social reform, their paintings portrayed the life of New York as having no meaning beyond the sheer phenomenon of animation. They loved parades, circuses, prize fights, and merry-go-rounds, as well as gypsies, foreigners, slum kids, and other people whose oddity of dress and appearance embodied a freedom from sober American conventions. The art of Henri and his circle was "no searching or epic realism of American life," says Schapiro, "but an enjoyment of impressions of vitality and movement."

Mary Simkhovitch (née Kingsbury) and Robert Henri both came from well-to-do families, and both became involved in the life of Greenwich Village about 1900. Their fascination with the culture of poverty foreshadowed the attitudes of other rebels from middle-class, upper-middle-class, and wealthy backgrounds who trickled into the Village in the course of the next ten years and flooded in after 1912. Having exchanged the cushioned comforts of home for the ruder joys of rooming houses and cold-water flats, the new arrivals were play-acting at being poor themselves and were delighted with their performances. They took satisfaction in eating in hole-in-the wall Italian restaurants, in shopping for bargains at the Jefferson Market, where vendors cried their wares in broken English, and in being known at dilapidated saloons like the Hell Hole and the Working Girls' Home, where the attractions included—as the name of the latter emporium indicated—a generous representation of prostitutes. With their jaded aura of knowing what "real life" was all about, the prostitutes of the Village were an endless source of interest to the rebels. Stuart Davis painted them, John Reed wrote stories about them, and Eugene O'Neill scattered them broadcast through his plays. Always searching for new thrills, the rebels also sought out the lower depths of the lower East Side, duly recording their experiences in such paeans to poverty as Lola Ridge's *The Ghetto and Other Poems* and Hutchins Hapgood's *The Spirit of the Ghetto*.

The fact that the poor and the foreign-born excited affluent rebels like Hutchins Hapgood is one of the principal reasons why the Greenwich Village rebellion included so many men and women who had been born in eastern Europe or came from indigent families in the United States. For if they had talent and were personally attractive, the poor and the foreign-born were apt to be taken up by wealthy Villagers, invited to parties, given jobs, and even married by them. In New York society in the 1890s the pinnacle of chic had been reached in the marriage of Consuelo Vanderbilt to the Duke of Marlborough. After the turn of the century, however, chic became more radical. Mrs. Belmont, who was Consuelo Vanderbilt's aggressive mother, now wrote checks to keep *The Masses* going, while the wealthy William English Walling, formerly of Louisville, Kentucky, married Anna Strunsky, formerly of Babinotz, Russia, and the millionaire Yale man J. G. Phelps Stokes was united with Rose Pastor—"Rose of the Ghetto," the newspapers called her. Greenwich Village blessed these events, as it did the newlyweds who set up housekeeping at 56 Grove Street, for E. J. Ballantine was a well-liked Scottish actor with the Provincetown Players and his bride, Stella Comminsky, was a relative of the redoubtable Emma Goldman. There was also a good deal of local interest in the Mike Gold–Dorothy Day friendship, and in the liaisons of Mabel Dodge with Maurice Sterne and Andrew Dasburg, while countless stories were told about the stormy affair between Polly Holladay, of Evanston, Illinois, and Hippolyte Havel, of obscure origin in Central Europe.

In such an atmosphere, it was easy for an ambitious young Latvian like Barney Gallant to make influential friends and thus to get a leg up on his subsequent career as a restaurateur; or for the talented and fast rising Jo Davidson, who had been born in the ghetto on New York's East Side, to make contacts among the intelligentsia at Mabel Dodge's salon that would help him to become the most celebrated "head hunter" in modern sculpture; or for radicals like Big Bill Haywood to find financial angels for their causes; or for the aging Terry Carlin to sponge off Eugene O'Neill and Hutchins Hapgood for long periods, because a seamy life had given Carlin a thousand stories to tell his fascinated hosts about drugs, sexual depravity, and violent death.

The presence of battle-scarred old-timers like one-eyed Bill Haywood and trembling-handed Terry Carlin, and of vigorous newcomers like Barney Gallant, contributed enormously to the Village's collective sense of itself as the most open and most vital community in America. The cartoonist Art Young declared that in the Village "a man felt something like his raw self, though he knew well that he had been cooked to a turn by the world's conventions." Yet the Village's obsessive pride in its own vitality was a sign of the precariousness of its health. The brilliant versatility that many rebels displayed in the early years of the rebellion gradually turned into a debilitating indecisiveness. The gaiety that historians have claimed to be the dominant tone of Village life was the product of an emotional release from pressure that was soon spent, and could only be aroused again by other sorts of stimulants—which is why so many rebels were so well known to Village bartenders. As for the Bohemian manners and morals that had symbolized the rebels' declaration of freedom from American life, they only succeeded in bringing American life to the Village with a vengeance, in the form of national publicity, flocks of tourists, and blatant commercialism. To Guido Bruno, who by the end of the teens was selling tickets to the curious who wanted to see "poets" at work in a Washington Square garret, Bohemianism was hucksterism, nothing more. It is no wonder that a number of rebels who still had serious work to do forswore further association with the Village.

At the same time, however, that Greenwich Village was being overrun by American life, the Village in turn was penetrating the nation. For in effect the rebels had served as the research and development wing of American society, and in the 1920s a middle-class culture co-opted, at least in part, its counter culture. *The New Yorker* had no use for the revolutionary rhetoric of *The Masses*, but adopted the earlier magazine's idea of natural-sounding, one-line captions for cartoons, and Howard Brubaker, who had worked as a humorist for Max Eastman, was hired by Harold Ross. The Washington Square Players, fancily reorganized as the Theatre Guild, sold its subscription-list idea to midtown audiences, while the experimental plays of Eugene O'Neill, the boy wonder of the Provincetown Players, also became box office on Broadway. Margaret Sanger's militant appeals to working-class mothers to save their unborn children from capitalistic exploitation by not having them in the first place were rewritten as lectures to middle-class matrons who wanted to know how to stop after having two. Short-haired, sexually liberated women like Henrietta Rodman were emulated all across the nation in the postwar period by short-haired, semiliberated flappers like Scott Fitzgerald's Gloria Gilbert. The studio apartments of Greenwich Village artists, which had emphasized large windows, clean-lined furniture, and bold uses of color, inspired a new openness and simplicity in the interior decoration of middle-class homes, while in the mansions of the wealthy one could find, fifteen years after the Armory Show, the world's most stunning collections of modern art. By adopting the tastes, manners, morals, and ideas of a small group of rebels in the teens, many Americans in the 1920s also sought to feel like their raw selves again, even though they too knew they were cooked.

8

The Strange Unhappy Life of Max Perkins

In 1927, the Communist "authority" on American literature, Joseph Freeman, attacked the novelists of the period for their failure to contribute to the coming destruction of capitalism. Instead of depicting the class struggle in America, they wrote stories about sensitive individuals who were alienated from the philistine bourgeoisie but who could not even imagine its overthrow. Because the novelists themselves were politically dormant, Freeman charged, their books portrayed the intelligentsia as utterly helpless in the face of modern industrial civilization. Not long after the appearance of this much discussed diatribe, Malcolm Cowley presented a more romantic and self-pitying version of the same ideas in a series of essays in *Hound and Horn* and the *New Republic*. Toward the end of 1932, Cowley co-authored the pamphlet, "Culture and the Crisis," which explained why the Communist William Z. Foster was the presidential candidate of recently awakened writers like himself. As his next contribution to political consciousness,

Reprinted by permission from *Commentary*, Volume 66, Number 6 (December 1978).

he collected his *Hound and Horn* and *New Republic* pieces into a book.

Exile's Return (1934) is a beautifully written but substantively self-indulgent study of American literary expatriates in the 1920s. Self-indulgent because Cowley completely ignores such important older writers as Edith Wharton and Bernard Berenson, while devoting nearly forty pages to the microscopically minor figure of Harry Crosby, who happened to have been born in the same year, 1898, that Cowley was. "A generation is usually computed at thirty years," observes the *Oxford English Dictionary*, but in the narcissistic perspective of *Exile's Return* the concept is computed in terms of writers who turned twenty-one years of age between 1915 and 1921. They had had common adventures and had formed common attitudes, Cowley argues, "that made it possible to describe them as a generation." And what, precisely, were those adventures and attitudes? "They had always rebelled," reads the clearest of Cowley's efforts to answer this question,

> if only by running away. First it was against the conventionality of their elders and the gentility of American letters; then it was against the high phrases that justified the slaughter of millions in the First World War; then it was against the philistinism and the scramble for money of the Harding years (although that rebellion took the form of flight).

The trouble with this statement—apart from its exaggeration of the rebels' feelings about the conventionality of their elders—is that most of the literary notables of the period who came of age before 1915 or after 1921 shared the attitudes that supposedly set the lost-generation writers apart, and so did countless other Americans who never published a novel or read a radical magazine. If Cowley and company felt let down by Woodrow Wilson's wartime performance or were repulsed by the materialism of the twenties, many of their incorrigibly "bourgeois" countrymen reacted in the same way. The literary exiles' feelings of disillusionment and disgust defined a spiritual kinship with American society in the postwar years, as well as an alienation from it.

Cowley, however, has no interest in the complexities of cultural analysis; black-and-white contrasts are his stock in trade.

Old versus young. Prewar versus postwar. Sacred versus profane. Artist versus philistine. Departure versus return. Alienation versus integration. The crudity of Cowley's thinking about an era that he himself lived through is astonishing, but what is even harder to credit is the long shadow that *Exile's Return* has cast on the thinking of other readers for half a century. No other interpretation of American literature has more engaged the national mind, or more thoroughly stultified it, than the legend of the lost generation that Cowley wove from the warp of the Communist line and the woof of his own romanticism. One of the principal reasons why we still do not possess a satisfactory account of one of the most fascinating decades in American literary history is that Cowley's polarities leave no room for paradoxes, and without an appreciation of paradoxes there can be no understanding of the twenties. Numerous biographies, too, have fallen drastically short of what they might have been because of their author's inability to break free of *Exile's Return.* A case in point is A. Scott Berg's life of Max Perkins, the editor of F. Scott Fitzgerald, Ernest Hemingway, and Thomas Wolfe.

In the course of almost eight years of work, which began while he was still an undergraduate at Princeton, Berg went through tens of thousands of letters, interviewed scores of people—and rarely paused to think. Why was Perkins such an unhappy man? Did the tensions and contradictions in his personality make him peculiarly receptive to certain authors? What does his career tell us about the decade in which he scored his greatest successes? Berg is so insensitive to psychology that he hardly touches the first two questions, but with the third he at least gets far enough to acknowledge that the study of an editor's life can be a means to larger ends. For an editor is a cultural middleman. If he is any good, he understands authors and he understands audiences. The biographer of an editor is therefore in a position to write cultural history of the broadest significance. Through the consideration of Perkins, a reconsideration of the twenties might have been launched. Unfortunately, Berg was unaware of any need for fresh discussion. Throughout his book he happily works within Cowley's clichés, automatically shaping his painstaking researches to fit an all too familiar pattern. *Max Perkins: Editor of Genius* is a compendium of lost opportunities.

It is Berg's black-and-white belief that the publishing business in the twenties was made up of good guys and bad guys, and that the peerless leader of the good guys was Max Perkins. The subtitle of Berg's biography hails Perkins as an editorial genius, while the Shelley sonnet which serves as epigraph to the text bids us think of him as a lonely prophet moving through the unheeding many. "A splendor among shadows, a bright blot / Upon this gloomy scene . . ." He was "a kind of hero," we are told in chapter 1, who not only "discovered" Fitzgerald, Hemingway, and Wolfe, but "staked his career" on them, "defying the established tastes of the earlier generation and revolutionizing American literature." Now, no one would deny that Perkins had many admirable qualities. He was what people used to call a real gentleman, which in his case meant more than manners. His unflagging loyalty and kindness brought him many friends, and he was a responsible father to the five daughters he had clearly wanted to be sons. His in-house evaluations of the manuscripts of Fitzgerald and Hemingway were remarkably perceptive, while the thousands of hours he devoted to cutting and rearranging the paper avalanches that Wolfe called novels set a record for editorial patience that still endures. The brassy fanfares of biographer Berg, however, grossly exaggerate Perkins's achievement and drown out the lessons we can learn from its limitations.

Predictably, the first person to present Perkins as a romantic hero taking on the suffocating orthodoxies of the publishing world single-handedly was the author of *Exile's Return*, writing in the *New Yorker* in 1944. In a two-part profile, Cowley described Scribners at the time that Perkins went to work there as a "fantastic" publishing house, "with an atmosphere like Queen Victoria's parlor." Perkins, however, put through sweeping changes, and the house "took a sudden leap from the age of innocence into the midst of the lost generation." Berg not only quotes this piece of rubbish with approval, but embroiders it with enthusiasm. Following up on Cowley's words about Queen Victoria, he says that at the end of the second decade of the twentieth century the three pillars of the House of Scribner were "long-established writers steeped in the English tradition," Galsworthy, Henry James, and Edith Wharton. There was a "Dickensian atmosphere" about the offices, and curmudgeonly Anglophiliacs held the reins of power. At age sixty-six,

Charles Scribner II, old CS, whose face "usually wore a severe expression," still ran the business, as he had for forty years. The editor-in-chief was William Crary Brownell, a white-bearded, walrus-mustached epitome of the genteel tradition, who had a habit of falling asleep in his office after lunch.

One would never be able to guess from this caricature of Victorian mustiness that old CS was a veritable dynamo of a man, "a born publisher with a great flair," as John Hall Wheelock has testified, "who truly loved getting books into print." Scribner had made a lot of money publishing such thoroughly un-English books as John Fox, Jr.'s novel of Kentucky, *The Little Shepherd of Kingdom Come* (1903), and intended to go on making more until he died, which is why he carefully listened to Perkins's recommendation that the firm publish the first novel of an unknown writer named Fitzgerald and then decisively supported it. When *This Side of Paradise* (1920) proved to be a bestseller, Scribner was delighted and sent a letter of thanks to the Irish poet and journalist Shane Leslie for discovering Fitzgerald. After reading Fitzgerald's manuscript, Leslie had sent it to Scribners, with a covering letter to the head of the firm. "Your introduction of Scott Fitzgerald," Scribner wrote to Leslie, "proved to be an important one for us; *This Side of Paradise* has been our best seller this season and is still going strong." Because he also was determined not to publish vulgarities, CS occasionally opposed Perkins's recommendations. Thus in 1925 he refused to publish Bruce Barton's portrayal of Christ as a supersalesman. But after *The Man Nobody Knows* began coining money for Bobbs-Merrill, Scribner was sorry he had not made an exception for this particular example of vulgarity. When Perkins reminded him that he had said it might sell, Scribner replied, "But you didn't tell me, Mr. Perkins, that it would sell four hundred thousand copies."

Berg grudgingly describes the publisher as making this remark with a "faint twinkle" in his eye, just as he says that "even" the severe-faced CS laughed at a manuscript of Ring Lardner's stories, but these are the linguistic games of an instinctively antibusiness biographer who is determined to distort the meaning of the materials he himself is presenting. In fact, CS had a zestful wit, which was not at all surprising in a man with his appetite for life. When he died in 1930, a lot of the firm's vitality went with him. Perkins was at the peak of his editorial influence in the thirties, yet Scribners in this period was not nearly the house it had been in the final ten years under CS. Neither Faulkner nor Steinbeck came to grace the Scribners list—Perkins thought Faulkner was "crazy"—while blockbusters like *Anthony Adverse* and *Gone with the Wind* made the stockholders of other companies happy. In a caustic letter to Perkins in 1938, Edmund Wilson spoke of the "general apathy and morbidity into which Scribners seems to have sunk. You people haven't shown any sign of life since old man Scribner died."

Berg is equally misleading about Brownell and the much-maligned literary standards for which he stood. Critics like Brander Matthews, James G. Huneker, and Brownell had no desire to keep American literature tied to Queen Victoria's skirts; they urged, rather, that American writers help to create a truly cosmopolitan culture. Brownell, the author of admiring books about French literature and art, felt that the greatest deficiency in American writing was its want of craftsmanship, its lack of form. If our writers would only submit their native energies to French discipline, they might become masters. Henry James and Edith Wharton exemplified the cultural amalgamation of which he dreamed. Thus Berg's reference to these writers as "steeped in the English tradition" completely misses the point of Brownell's fascination with them. They represented a cultural phenomenon that was neither English nor traditional.

Although Brownell was a conservative critic, he was not an opponent of change, in the manner of the neohumanists Irving Babbitt and Paul Elmer More. Brownell voted against the publication of *This Side of Paradise* because its frivolousness offended him. But on the day that the manuscript of *The Great Gatsby* came across his desk, he was as ready to bless the wedding of imaginative abundance and formal control as when he first read *The Golden Bowl* and *The Custom of the Country*. Emerging from his office, Fitzgerald's manuscript in hand, Brownell called to his colleagues, "May I read you something beautiful?" In a letter to Fitzgerald, T. S. Eliot praised *Gatsby* by mentioning it in the same breath with the work of Henry James. One wonders if Brownell was also thinking of that literary progression, as he stood outside his office reading aloud from the novel, and of the important role he himself had played in the internationalization of modern American literature.

Just as Brownell was not a literary reactionary, so Perkins was not a revolutionary. One of the most significant omissions in Berg's biography is his failure to describe Perkins's editorial role in the publication of Edmund Wilson's *Axel's Castle.* The book is one of the three or four most distinguished that Scribners published during Perkins's long tenure. Yet Berg reproduces not a word from Perkins to Wilson concerning it and gives us no indication that Perkins was conscious of the book's importance or even that he was proud to have it on the Scribners list. Berg tells us far more than we want to know about Perkins's encouragement and approval of the work of Marjorie Kinnan Rawlings and Marcia Davenport, but on the subject of his opinion of *Axel's Castle* silence prevails. The fact that Perkins was woefully unfamiliar—and in all likelihood quite unsympathetic—with the Symbolist writers whom Wilson was discussing almost certainly explains Berg's evasiveness. But while his biographer is anxious to minimize Perkins's intellectual shortcomings, Perkins himself was quite candid about the inadequacy of his literary knowledge. "How frightfully ignorant I am in literature," he once exclaimed to Hemingway, "where a literary man ought not to be."

Not surprisingly, his ignorance frequently led to lapses in taste and displays of naiveté. One of his favorite house authors in the thirties and forties was Taylor Caldwell, and he would become furious whenever literary critics or other Scribners editors ("pedantic editors," Berg loyally calls them) attacked her as a pulp writer, which is precisely what she was. He touted the third-rate Maxwell Geismar as "the best of the up-and-coming literary essayists." And he was so impressed by the superficial scholarship of Alden Brooks's *Will Shakespeare and the Dyer's Hand* as to be completely convinced that "the man Shakespeare was not the author of what we consider Shakespeare's works."

To his enduring credit, Perkins at once saw the importance of Fitzgerald, Hemingway, and Wolfe, but despite what Berg says, he discovered none of them. Shane Leslie, as we have seen, brought Fitzgerald to Scribners; Hemingway was an established author when he signed on with the firm; and it was the literary agent Madeleine Boyd who aroused Perkins's interest in Wolfe by telling him that unless he promised to read "every word" of Wolfe's "extraordinary" first novel, she would not show it to him. Furthermore, Perkins did not stake his whole career on these writers, as Berg maintains. The only episode that even comes close to vindicating this romantic claim was when Perkins argued with CS and the other members of the editorial board that the firm ought to publish *This Side of Paradise*. "If we're going to turn down the likes of Fitzgerald, I will lose all interest in publishing books," Perkins declared. Berg seems to believe that Perkins would have resigned if he had not had his way, but nothing in Perkins's carefully plotted career suggests that he would have carried out this threat, if indeed it was a threat. As Wolfe knew, Perkins was an extremely clever bargainer—which is why Wolfe gave him the name of Fox when he portrayed him in his fiction:

> O, guileful Fox, how innocent in guilefulness and in innocence how full of guile, in all directions how strange-devious, in all strange-deviousness how direct! Too straight for crookedness, and for envy too serene, too fair for blind intolerance, too just and seeing and too strong for hate, too honest for base dealing, too high for low suspiciousness, too innocent for the scheming tricks of swarming villainy—yet never had been taken in a horse trade yet!

In the discussion of *This Side of Paradise*, Perkins knew that he could not win a strictly literary argument with the formidable Brownell, so he chose instead to talk about the folly of turning away fresh talent. This was exactly the kind of practical argument that made sense to CS. In the end, it was not Brownell's high standards but Perkins's canny appeal to his boss's business instincts that carried the day. Berg's quixotic interpretation of his hero's words obscures appreciation of Perkins's resourcefulness as a bureaucratic infighter.

Yet Perkins went to bat for *This Side of Paradise* not only because he thought it was smart to invest in youth, but because he genuinely liked the novel. Fitzgerald's work spoke to him, as did Hemingway's and Wolfe's. Berg ascribes his instantaneous appreciation of their writings to editorial genius, but Perkins misjudged so many other important books in the course of his career that the explanation is unsatisfactory. Somehow, his sensibility had been conditioned to respond to these three particular authors. It is therefore to the events of Perkins's private life and to the nature of his personality that we must turn for an explanation of the editorial discernments that made him famous.

One of the most glaring faults of the Berg biography is that it pays almost no attention to Perkins's early relationship with his parents. Thus the biography is more than half over before we learn from a passing phrase that Perkins's mother regarded literature as "mental candy." Whether this grossly unsympathetic attitude was in any way symbolic of the way she had treated her bookish son during his formative years, Berg does not say, but if it was, then it helps to explain why Perkins as a grown man felt throttled by women, as Alice Roosevelt Longworth observed. Indeed, a number of people believe that he hated women, and certainly his persistent refusal to allow his wife, Louise, to pursue her career in the theater, even though her failure to achieve artistic fulfillment was manifestly damaging her personality, lends substance to the charge.

No less an authority than the dramatist Edward Sheldon assured the Perkinses that Louise had "talent galore for a career on the stage," but Max, having extracted a promise from Louise before they were married that she would not become a professional actress, would not budge. The quarrels that marked their marriage from the first increased in bitterness with the years. Eventually Louise converted to Catholicism, much to Max's disgust, and laid her histrionic talent on the altar of Jesus Christ with a fervor that came to seem like madness. Not satisfied with going to mass every day and cloistering herself on week-long retreats, she sprinkled holy water all over the house, dousing Max's pillow several times a week. After his death her deterioration accelerated. In the last half-decade of her life she was drunk every night, and finally died as horribly as Zelda Fitzgerald did, after falling asleep while smoking. Instead of acknowledging his own complicity in what was happening to her, Max simply scorned Louise for her bizarre behavior and sought excuses for spending the night away from home. To this highly frustrated husband, the stories of men without women that Hemingway submitted to Scribners must have seemed like balm in Gilead, while misogynistic outbursts like "The Short Happy Life of Francis Macomber" and "The Snows of Kilimanjaro" offered more savage satisfactions, as did Wolfe's evisceration of his mother in *Look Homeward, Angel.*

Intertwined with Perkins's feelings about women was an irremediable sadness about all of life. In Van Wyck Brooks's opinion, Perkins was engaged in a "perpetual war with himself that made him in the end 'a prey to sadness.'" Caught in a "despairing refusal" to be himself, he did not give "the consent of his will to his own being." In the face of such a terrible inhibition, one wishes more than ever that Berg had had an interest in tracing patterns of childhood experience. Alas, all that can be gleaned from his book about the early evidences of Perkins's psychic conflict is his reaction to the loss of his father, who died when Max was seventeen. As the oldest male child still living at home, Max felt it incumbent upon himself to smother his grief, sit at the head of the table, and become the surrogate father of his younger siblings. At an age when he might still have been involved in an uncompleted Oedipal struggle, he also in effect claimed his mother. If indeed she had treated him insensitively, his ensuing resentment did not represent the sum total of his feelings about her. He was not entitled, however, to the claim he now staked, and he may very well have incurred a sense of guilt about what he had done to his dead father. In any event, when he blurted out to one of his daughters a generation later that "Every good deed a man does is to please his father," he unconsciously revealed some sort of expiation.

The son who forever sought to please his father fiercely wanted to father a son of his own. After Louise presented him with his fifth daughter, he gave up trying. Consequently, Perkins's wish for a son would have gone unfulfilled if he had not met an enormously gifted, desperately flawed young man from North Carolina who himself had lost his father and needed paternal guidance. The incredible editorial effort that Perkins brought to bear upon the chaos of Wolfe's manuscripts and his unending willingness to put up with Wolfe's egomania, foul temper, and treachery had nothing to do with the publishing business, in the final analysis. Perkins did not merely collaborate with the author of *Look Homeward, Angel* and *Of Time and the River*, as Bernard De Voto charged in a famous critique; he adopted him. Together, Wolfe and Perkins roamed the nighttime streets of Manhattan and Brooklyn or sat drinking and talking in bars. The hungry author also became a fixture at the Perkinses' dinner table. As Wolfe's literary agent, Elizabeth Nowell, recalled, "He all but lived there as a member of the family—or as Perkins's son, which to all intents and purposes he was. Perkins never seemed to see enough of him." The obsessions of Wolfe's fiction—the death of a father, the loneliness of youth, the search for "an unfound door"—formed an accompaniment to a real-life drama of extraordinary intensity.

That Wolfe ultimately dissociated himself from Scribners is very much in the punitive pattern of what Perkins was always doing to himself. All his adult life, Perkins lived within the bounds of self-denial. His marriage was a nightmare, but he never considered divorce. The furniture in his office was old and scarred, the floor rugless. His white shirts—what other color was there?—peeked through the thinning fabric at the elbows of his suitcoats. At Cherio's, his favorite restaurant, he ate the same meal day after day, until the waiter took the initiative to bring him something different. Hand in hand with asceticism went prudishness. No "real lady" drinks beer or seasons her food with Worcestershire sauce, he announced. "In our family," he warned his daughters, "we say underclothes, not underwear."

His devotion to his work was abnormal. It was as if he were trying to drown himself in fatigue. Weekends and holidays he considered an abomination and did his best to survive them by reading through the bulging briefcases he lugged home from the office. At the same time, his imagination was flooded with fantasies of escape and transformation. When the time was ripe, he would run away. In the past he may have had a far more important identity than he did now, and he might assume another in the not too distant future. Somewhere there was a perfect woman who lived apart from modern life and knew the secret of how to make him happy. "I have a vision of taking to the road at sixty," Perkins confessed to his Harvard classmate, Waldo Pierce. Friends familiar with Perkins's doodlings were aware of a far gaudier dream. For years he obsessively sketched portraits of Napoleon, always in left profile, on any piece of paper that came to hand, and the more he sketched, the more the Emperor of the French came to resemble Max Perkins. The futuristic counterpart of this breathtaking communion with the past was the thought that some day he would become president of the United States. He would retire to Vermont and edit a country gazette—which soon would be read by millions, as the brilliance of his opinions brought him to the attention of the entire nation. Not long thereafter, a grateful people would ask him to assume the presidency. "Of course, Max never *really* wanted to be president," John Hall Wheelock has said. Nevertheless, Perkins held himself in secret readiness, outlining his positions on issues to whoever would listen and maintaining a perpetual concern for the country's welfare. Only his fantasy about the love of a perfect woman meant more to Perkins than his dream of taking power.

Elizabeth Lemmon was eight years younger than Perkins and stunningly beautiful. When he met her in the spring of 1922, he felt she was unlike any other woman he had ever known. The daughter of a large old family with roots in Middleburg, Virginia, and Baltimore, she seemed to have stepped from the pages of a nineteenth-century romantic novel. Franklin D. Roosevelt also found such a woman in Lucy Mercer, and the Prince of Wales discovered another in Mrs. Simpson. But Perkins neither married his Southern dream girl nor made love to her. Sitting together in the Ritz bar in New York in 1943, Perkins reached for Elizabeth's hand, but then pulled back. "Oh, Elizabeth," he exclaimed, "it's hopeless." "I know," she replied. That is the closest they ever came to physical contact, and the only time they ever explicitly discussed the true nature of their relationship.

Only occasionally in the long years of their love were they together. Letters were what held them close. For twenty-five years he wrote to her at her estate at Middleburg and she wrote back, addressing him at the office. Perkins's wife was aware that they corresponded, but had no idea how often, or what her husband said to this beautiful younger woman who never married. Although Perkins's letters suppressed the full truth of his feelings, he indirectly told Elizabeth everything. He spoke of his recurring bouts of depression. He told her that for him she had always represented the thought that life could be "wonderfully happy and good." In a particularly poignant variation on the same motif, he declared that "after I have been with you I always feel again that those things that now generally seem to be an illusion really do exist." Through Elizabeth, Perkins sustained a dream that was commensurate with his capacity for wonder.

Can there be any doubt why Perkins was attracted to Fitzgerald's fiction? A beautiful Southern girl was Fitzgerald's symbol, too, of the possibilities of perfect happiness. Yet his moral pessimism, no less deeply ingrained than Perkins's, caused him to believe that if dreams were ever realized they would die; when you get too close, things go glimmering, the author's spokesman warns in the story called "Absolution." Perkinsian themes can be found throughout Fitzgerald's fiction, but it is in *Gatsby* that they are most prominent. The transformation of James Gatz into the rich and mysterious Jay Gatsby is a literary acting-out of Perkins's Napoleonic doodlings and secret preparations for the presidency. The description of Gatsby standing in the darkness, his arms outstretched toward the green light which marks the property where the Southern-born Daisy Buchanan lives, is only the most memorable of a dozen passages in the novel in which Perkins must have recognized a parallel to his own relationship with Elizabeth. And Nick Carraway's simultaneous attraction to conservatism and experimentalism—as typified by his confession that whereas he "wanted the world to be in uniform and at a sort of moral attention forever," Gatsby was "exempt" from the requirement—was the story of Perkins's double life as well. "I think I'm peculiarly cursed in almost always knowing what I ought to do," Perkins once told Elizabeth, forgetting for the moment that even an epistolary love affair was a departure from the rules.

A paradoxical combination of conservative and experimental ideas dominated the minds of many Americans in the twenties. Middletown, Robert and Helen Lynd noted in 1929, in their famous "Study in American Culture," "tends to be at once . . . conservative and . . . experimental in those regions where its children are concerned." On the one hand, parents insisted that their offspring go to Sunday school, just as they had; on the other hand, they supported a group dental and medical program in the public schools that was unprecedented in their Republican philosophy. Caught between conflicting viewpoints, Middletown parents often felt torn apart by the effort to raise their children. Other citizens, not just in Middletown but across the nation, experienced the same sensation of inner division and uncertainty, as they attempted to cope with the problems of work and marriage in an era of bewilderingly rapid change. Fitzgerald remarked that "the test of a first-rate intelligence is the ability to hold two opposed ideas in the mind at the same time, and still retain the ability to function," but in the twenties that test was administered to Americans regardless of their intelligence level.

At times, it became bafflingly difficult to decide whether an idea was old or new. Prominent architects and critics of architecture, for instance, were influenced by Henry David Thoreau's ascetic insistence that less is more. Did their Thoreauvianism represent a throwback to the nineteenth century, or was it avant-garde? Lewis Mumford's inability either to accept the soaring skyscrapers of the modern city or to stop writing about them was a function of his larger inability to answer this question. Perkins, too, could not decide whether his asceticism was backward-looking or up-to-date. The descendant of Vermonters, he had a fondness for the laconic prose of Calvin Coolidge, and in the twenties he edited a collection of Coolidge's speeches. Yet his pleasure in linguistic economy also made him an admirer of the stripped-down modernism of Hemingway's style. Moreover, the personal friendship between Hemingway and Perkins developed more rapidly than it otherwise might have because Hemingway kept presenting himself to Perkins as a fellow ascetic. Always rivalrous, Hemingway very much wanted to displace Fitzgerald in Perkins's affection. To that end, he took every opportunity to remind Perkins that Fitzgerald squandered both his money and his talent on riotous living, whereas he himself worked assiduously and lived frugally.

In the course of the thirties, however, Hemingway's self-discipline went slack. His letters to Perkins continued to speak scornfully of Fitzgerald's drinking problem, but it was his own that secretly frightened him. Ironically, the alcoholism he did not wish to talk about probably bound Hemingway more closely to Perkins than the asceticism he formerly had advertised. For Perkins, in his quiet way, was also turning into a relentless boozer. Even in the twenties, he sometimes had shown an astonishing capacity to go the distance with heavy sluggers like Ring Lardner. But as his fantasies of political power failed to materialize and the House of Scribner slid further downhill, the aging editor began instructing the bartenders who mixed his martinis to make them doubles. "Daddy, don't you drink too much?" one of his daughters asked in 1942. "Churchill drinks too much," replied Perkins in an advertently revealing comparison; "all great men drink too much." James

Jones, his last important writer, recalled that Perkins displayed an "iron control" during their meetings. "From the steady way he walked, you could never tell that he was drunk." Even in his cups, Perkins was unable to give the consent of his will to his own being.

Americans in the 1920s lived in a state of tension between conservatism and experimentalism. While this tension generated a nervous excitement that we have come to think of as typical of the era, it also led to a terrible sense of defeat, when it proved to be unresolvable. Some of the era's finest works of fiction testify to those feelings of defeat. So does the strange unhappy life of Max Perkins.

9
Hemingway's Private War

In the summer of 1924, Ernest Hemingway wrote to Gertrude Stein and Alice B. Toklas to report on the progress he was making with a long short story in which he was "trying to do the country like Cézanne and having a hell of a time and sometimes getting it a little bit. It is about 100 pages long and nothing happens and the country is swell, I made it all up, so I see it all and part of it comes out the way it ought to, it is swell about the fish, but isn't writing a hard job though?" The story in question was "Big Two-Hearted River," which in addition to being swell about the fish and as visually powerful as a Cézanne landscape, turned out to be a nice little masterpiece of psychological indeterminacy.

As he walks into the Michigan woods, the solitary Nick Adams feels a sense of release. "He felt he had left everything behind, the need for thinking, the need to write, other needs. It was all back of him." Toward the end of the day, he pitches his tent and crawls inside, noting with pleasure how "homelike" the space seems. At last, he thinks, "he was settled. Nothing could touch him. It was a good place to camp. He was there, in

Reprinted by permission from *Commentary*, Volume 72, Number 1 (July 1981).

the good place. He was in his home where he had made it."

From this point forward the story abounds in details of how splendid the fishing is and what a good time Nick is having. Yet some sort of problem is lurking on the margins of his mind. Thus while he is finishing his supper the first night, he suddenly becomes aware that his mind is "starting to work," but because he is tired he is able to "choke it." The next day his happiness is again interrupted. An arduous battle with the biggest trout Nick has ever seen ends with the trout's escape, and as the fisherman is reeling in his line, he feels, vaguely, "a little sick." In the manipulative manner of a Watsonian behaviorist, he thereupon modifies his behavior so as to avoid the negative stimulus of a second defeat in one day. Instead of plunging into the armpit-deep water of a tree-filled swamp, wherein he might hook big trout in places impossible to land them, he decides to postpone the experience. "There were plenty of days coming when he could fish the swamp," he says to himself, as the story ends.

What are the "other needs" Nick feels he has put behind him on entering the woods? Why does he call the tent his home? What is the thought that he manages to choke off? Why is he so upset by defeat? Hemingway does not explain any of these puzzles. The angler on the bank of the Big Two-Hearted River is clearly a man with a divided heart, but the unhappiness underlying his predominant happiness is never specified.

For a decade and a half after its appearance as the concluding episode of *In Our Time* (1925), "Big Two-Hearted River" was admired by literary critics for its undefined tension. Then in the late 1930s this situation changed, when Edmund Wilson took it upon himself to improve the story by making it more explicit. The experience that has given Nick Adams "a touch of panic," Wilson asserted in 1939, is "the wholesale shattering of human beings in which he has taken part." The statement has no basis in fact. World War I is neither mentioned nor alluded to in "Big Two-Hearted River," and there is no reference in the story to feelings of panic.

That Wilson nevertheless described Hemingway's hero as the psychological victim of a brutal war was a measure of the extent to which his literary sensibility was ruled by political nausea. In the early thirties, Wilson's nausea had led him to the Marxist faith, because Marxism called for the total rejection of the entire existing society. With visions of destruction dancing in his head, Wilson had dedicated himself to writing an ambitious book on European radical thought. *To the Finland Station* was completed in 1939, but by that time the author had come to the realization that the Marxist cure for social disease was no solution. The Bolsheviks, he admitted, had not erected a "classless society out of the old illiterate feudal Russia," but rather had "encouraged the rise and domination of a new controlling and privileged class, who were . . . exploiting the workers almost as callously as the Czarist industrialists had done."

The recognition of Stalin's reign of terror, however, did not reconcile Wilson to the imperfections of capitalism; it merely caused him to include the Soviet Union among the governments of the world that he despised. Turning away from the study of radical political thought, he reread Hemingway—and promptly found in "Big Two-Hearted River" the vision of a sensitive writer whose suffering has been caused not by mistakes he himself has made, but by the belligerency of great powers. The commentators have been wrong in accusing Hemingway of an indifference to society, Wilson proclaimed at the end of his essay, for in fact "his whole work is a criticism of society."

When, in 1940, Malcolm Cowley finally ceased apologizing for Stalinism, he, too, began to cast about for non-Marxist modes of continuing his assault on the moral credentials of capitalist society. America's entrance into the war against Hitler made this problem particularly difficult for him, but Wilson's overinterpretation of Hemingway seems to have showed him how to solve it. In addition to shoveling much more war-victim material into "Big Two-Hearted River" than Wilson had done, Cowley insisted in the introduction to the Viking Portable *Hemingway* (1944) that a haunted, hypnagogic quality characterizes all of Hemingway's work. His stories are told against the background of the countries he has seen, Cowley said, but

> these countries are presented in a strangely mortuary light. In no other writer of our time can you find such a profusion of corpses: dead women in the rain; dead soldiers bloated in their uniforms and surrounded by torn papers; sunken liners full of bodies that float past the closed portholes. In no other writer can you find so many suffering animals: mules with their forelegs broken drowning in shallow water off the quay

at Smyrna; gored horses in the bull ring; wounded hyenas first snapping at their own entrails and then eating them with relish.

In a strangely mortuary light. To a critic who had argued all through the 1930s that the difference between the Soviet Union and other countries was the difference between life and death, it must have felt like vindication to write those words and to append to them that long list of fearsome illustrations. For while history had revealed that the critic might have been a bit incautious in his praise of the Soviet Union, Hemingway's stories certainly seemed to confirm Cowley's judgment of the rest of the world.

Was it really accurate, though, to say that Hemingway had presented France, Spain, Switzerland, the United States, and the other countries he knew as a series of hypnagogic visions? Convincing proof of this proposition would have required a great many demonstrations across the whole range of his work. The Portable *Hemingway*'s editor, however, stuck to a strikingly limited number of stories; indeed, there was one story he kept coming back to again and again. In the end, all the credibility of his "nightmares at noonday" interpretation was invested in his comments on "Big Two-Hearted River."

Cowley's Nick Adams is in far worse psychological shape than Edmund Wilson's. The evidence of his condition is not to be found in the story, to be sure, but that was nothing to worry about because "Hemingway's stories are most of them continued," and in a somewhat later book than *In Our Time* there is a story called "Now I Lay Me" that "casts a retrospective light" on "Big Two-Hearted River." The later story is concerned with "an American volunteer in the Italian army who isn't named but who might easily be Nick Adams." (The critic is in error. The volunteer is named, and his name is Nick.) As a result of being wounded in action, the young man is afraid to go to sleep at night. "I had been living for a long time," he confesses, "with the knowledge that if I ever shut my eyes in the dark and let myself go, my soul would go out of my body." This confession, we are assured, enables us to appreciate the psychological fragility of the man who is fishing the Big Two-Hearted River.

Among the things that Cowley neglects to tell us about "Now I Lay Me" is that the frightened American soldier is lying in a room a scant seven kilometers behind the lines. Moreover, the soldier knows that, as surely as autumn follows summer, he will have to return to the fighting—and in fact at the end of the story we learn of his later participation in the "October offensive." The story, in short, is very much like another Hemingway story called "In Another Country," in which a recuperating American soldier lies in bed at night in Milan, "afraid to die and wondering how I would be when I went back to the front again."

In "Big Two-Hearted River" we are in a very different world. Nick is a civilian, safely back in the United States. Now that he no longer has any worries about coming under fire again, has his psyche healed as rapidly as his body has, or is he still afraid to close his eyes at night, lest his soul take flight? Hemingway's answer is clear. "Nick lay down . . . under the blankets. He turned on his side and shut his eyes. He was sleepy. He felt sleep coming. He curled up under the blanket and went to sleep." So much for the retrospective light cast by "Now I Lay Me."

Cowley's essay on Hemingway is not a work that can bear careful scrutiny; it does not even give the correct year of Hemingway's birth; it exemplifies John Dos Passos's exasperated remark that Cowley never got anything right. Yet no sooner was the essay published than it began to influence critics everywhere. A young man named Philip Young, for instance, "ported a Portable *Hemingway* . . . half way across Europe during World War II," and after the war he wrote a book that carried Cowley's critical extravagances even further. The wound Hemingway suffered in World War I, Young contended, had so deeply traumatized him that he spent his entire life as a writer composing variations on the story of the psychically crippled "sick man" who fishes the Big Two-Hearted River. Alas, Young never thought to ask himself whether reading the Viking Portable *Hemingway* against the dramatic backdrop of World War II had not made it all too easy for him to believe in the obsessive importance to Hemingway of World War I. Nor did Young ever suspect that Cowley's conversion of a sun-drenched, Cézannesque picture of a predominantly happy fishing trip into a tale as spooky as any of Poe's or Hawthorne's was governed by an ideological purpose, which was to bathe American life in a strangely mortuary light.

Naiveté, however, was not the only reason Cowley's introduction slew the minds of so many critics. In the wake of the triumph of American power in World War II, the tendency of guilt-stricken intellectuals to equate goodness with powerlessness and heroism with victimization increased steadily, and so, accordingly, did their susceptibility to a "lost-generation" interpretation of Hemingway. In 1962, Mark Schorer spoke for an emerging critical consensus when he characterized the author of "Big Two-Hearted River" as the lifelong victim of a war wound. On July 8, 1918, Schorer wrote, Hemingway was "severely wounded by the explosion of a mortar shell and the next three months he spent in a hospital in Milan. Nothing more important than this wounding was ever to happen to him. A wound was to become the central symbol of nearly everything he was to write, and the consequences of a wound his persistent thematic preoccupation."

Carlos Baker had a golden opportunity to overturn such clichés when he undertook to write his massive *Ernest Hemingway: A Life Story* (1969). But the accumulated weight of thirty years of critical insistence was too much for Baker, and the opportunity was lost. Two events in early 1981 finally presented another opportunity. The first event was President Reagan's reminder to the nation in March that, despite the awful pain, human beings are sometimes able to respond to the experience of being wounded with an amazing gaiety. The second was the appearance in April of Carlos Baker's totally unstructured, badly underannotated, unhelpfully indexed, but marvelously rich edition of Hemingway letters, which among other things reveals that the young man who was struck down on July 8, 1918 reacted to the event with humorous equivalents of Reagan's "Honey, I forgot to duck."

The youth's first letter to his family, written from the hospital in Milan on his nineteenth birthday, not quite two weeks after he was hit, was adorned with a reassuringly funny cartoon he had drawn of himself lying on his back, a heavily bandaged leg thrust straight out. The balloon coming out of this comic figure's mouth reads, "gimme a drink!" The text of the letter is equally high-spirited. "This is a peach of a hospital," he began. "Everything is fine," he continued, "and I'm very comfortable and one of the best surgeons in Milan is looking after my wounds."

The wounds in his left leg were "healing finely"; the bullet in his right knee would be removed "by the time you get this letter."

A month later, he recounted to his family the whole story of how he had been "struck by a trench mortar and a machine gun while advancing toward the rear, as the Irish say." In spite of his wounds, he had carried an injured Italian soldier to a dugout, where "I kind of collapsed." When an ambulance finally came for Hemingway, he "ordered it down the road to get the soldiers that had been wounded first." Back at the dressing station at last, the officers "gave me a shot of morphine and an anti-tetanus injection and shaved my legs and took out about Twenty 8 shell fragments .... They did a fine job of bandaging and all shook hands with me and would have kissed me but I kidded them along."

In mid-September, he announced to his father that "my legs are coming on wonderfully and will both eventually be O.K. absolutely," and on October 18 he finished off another health report to his family by declaring that "it does give you an awfully satisfactory feeling to be wounded."

Mixed in, though, with the enormous pleasure it gave him to know that he had behaved heroically and was healing splendidly were some chillier thoughts he was not talking about. A quarter of a century would pass before he would admit in a letter that in World War I he not only had been "really scared" when he was hit, but that in the ensuing months his continuing fear of death had prompted him to become "very devout." For like the wounded American soldiers in "Now I Lay Me" and "In Another Country," Hemingway knew that once he had recuperated he was slated to return to the front. On the eve of being discharged from the hospital, he sought to quiet his family's anxieties by saying that "it has been fairly conclusively proved that I can't be bumped off," but as he nervously chattered on about what a "very simple thing" it was to die, and about how preferable it was "to die in . . . the happy period of undisillusioned youth, to go out in a blaze of light, than to have your body worn out and old," it became clear that, like Tom Sawyer, he was whistling to keep up his courage as he walked past the graveyard at midnight.

A day or so after rejoining his unit, Hemingway was felled by an attack of jaundice, and by the time he was healthy again the armistice had been signed. The knowledge that he was no longer in danger of being killed was immediately reflected in the tone and content of his letters. Self-deprecatory humor gave way to bragging, and an inadvertent revelation of deadly fear was replaced by an inadvertent revelation of how little he knew about liquor and women. "Lately I've been hitting it up," he boasted to his old friend Bill Smith in December, shortly before leaving Italy, "about 18 martinis a day." The letter to Smith also asserted that, in spite of the writer's "brutal" personality, a nurse he had met in the hospital had fallen madly in love with him and they were planning to get married and "have a wonderful time being poor together." This estimate of things was no more accurate than his report on his martini intake. Not long after Hemingway's return to the States, the nurse sent him a "Dear Ernest" letter. The recipient was so overcome with anger that he ran a fever and was obliged to take to his bed.

Between the time he arrived at his parents' home in Oak Park, Illinois, in January, 1919, and his reembarkation for Europe in the late fall of 1921, the returned war veteran wrote many letters to many people. In none of them is there either an explicit or an implicit indication of the sort of psychic malaise that literary criticism would subsequently assign to the autobiographical hero who fishes the Big Two-Hearted River. An emotion of startling intensity does surge to the surface of the correspondence in the middle of this postwar period, but the name of that emotion is not panic, or hypnagogic horror, or anything like. It is anger, an all-consuming anger, of the sort he manifested when he was jilted by the nurse. And what would trigger it would be a contest of wills with his mother.

Grace Hall Hemingway was an ardent Congregationalist, a frustrated opera singer, and the dominant personality in the Hemingway household. While her doctor-husband resented his wife's bossiness, he fully shared her moral values and as a parent was a considerably stricter disciplinarian. Where Grace occasionally used a hair brush on an erring child, Ed Hemingway was quick to employ a razor strop. Conflict between the parents and Ernest, their headstrong second child (but first son), thus became inevitable, even though the boy worshipped his father for his knowledge of nature and his extraordinary prowess as a hunter and fisherman. According to Carlos Baker's biography, young Ernest sometimes became so angered by the punishments meted out to him by his father that he would sit in the open door of a shed behind their house drawing beads on his father's head with a shotgun, as Dr. Hemingway worked among his tomato vines.

But the struggle with his mother was finally much more bitter. In the opening pages of *Ernest Hemingway: Selected Letters, 1917–1961*, we pick up the struggle at the point at which Mrs. Hemingway was attempting to maintain control of her son's life even though he had left home and taken a job with the Kansas City *Star*. It was an attempt which in some ways the eighteen-year-old Ernest welcomed. Thus he was very grateful for the food she regularly prepared and sent to him. "The box came tonight and we just opened it at the Press room," he informed her on March 2, 1918. With the help of some friends he had polished off the cake right there in the office. "Mother Hemingstein," he said, using one of his two favorite nicknames for her (the other was, more simply, "Mrs. Stein"), you are "some cook."

Yet if he was glad to reap the rewards of his continuing dependency, he refused to be bound by its obligations. As he would with all the women he would marry, the young Hemingway wanted to eat his cake and have it too. When his mother remonstrated with him for not attending church, he replied with a patently hypocritical excuse. "The reason I don't go to church on Sunday is because always I have to work till 1 A.M. getting out the Sunday *Star* . . . and I never open my eyes Sunday morning until 12:30 noon." Modulating into outright lying, he added, "so you see it isn't because I don't want to. You know I don't rave about religion but am as sincere a Christian as I can be."

The war hero who came back to Oak Park in January, 1919, felt it necessary to conceal from his parents not only that he had learned to smoke and drink, but that he had no intention of remaining for long in the United States. To one of his army buddies he revealed that he was keeping a bottle of booze in a "camouflaged bookcase in my room"; to another he grumbled that "My Family . . . are wolfing at me to go to college. They want me to settle down for a while and the place that they are pulling for is Wisconsin." Toward the end of the summer of 1919, he briefly escaped the constraints on his freedom by going on a fishing trip with two friends to the Big Fox and Little

Fox rivers in the northern peninsula of Michigan. Below an old dam, Hemingway hooked the "biggest trout I've ever seen," only to lose it after a long effort. Nevertheless, the fishing had been "priceless."

On his return home, the fisherman and his mother inexorably moved toward a confrontation, and in the summer of 1920, shortly after his twenty-first birthday, it occurred. One moonlit night at the Hemingways' summer place in Michigan, Ernest and some other young people in the neighborhood sneaked out after midnight and held a party on a sandbar that went on until 3 A.M. When the deception was discovered, the mother of one of the girls blamed Ernest, because he was older, and thereafter refused to speak to him. Mrs. Hemingway punished her son by coldly ordering him out of the house. In reprisal, Hemingway refused to communicate with either of his parents and left their letters to him unopened. "Am so darn disgusted," he wrote to his fifteen-year-old friend Grace Quinlan, "I don't care to have anything more to do with them for a year at least." In the first of a series of cruelly unfair allegations, Hemingway also told Grace Quinlan that his mother had been "glad of an excuse to oust me," because she had "more or less hated me" ever since he had told her—or so he claimed—that she was spending money on herself that should have been reserved for the younger Hemingway children in college.

By the fall of 1920, he was once again in touch with his father, but not with his mother. In an effort to comfort his wife, Dr. Hemingway wrote her a letter—the text is in Carlos Baker's biography—which left no doubt where his sympathies lay. "Ernest's last letter to me," he told her, "was written in anger and filled with expressions that were untrue to a gentleman and a son who has had everything done for him . . . . He must get busy and make his own way, and suffering alone will be the means of softening his Iron Heart of selfishness."

Eventually, a reconciliation took place. The senior Hemingways were present at Ernest's marriage to Hadley Richardson in September, 1921, and they did not protest the decision of the bride and groom to make their home in Paris. Yet for all the polite gestures back and forth, Hemingway was never able to come to terms with his mother. As the Baker edition of his letters makes clear, Hemingway in the course of his life was angry at politicians, churchmen, fellow writers, literary critics, and assorted sports figures. But above all, he was angry at his mother. Not until his suicide—that act of supreme anger—would his epistolary vilification of her cease.

Upon learning from her in 1926 that she considered *The Sun Also Rises* to be a filthy book, he was so furious that for a time he could not reply. "I did not answer when you wrote about the Sun etc. book," he finally explained to her on February 5, 1927, "as I could not help being angry and it is very foolish to write angry letters; and more than foolish to do so to one's mother. It is quite natural for you not to like the book and I regret your reading any book that causes you pain or disgust." Of course the book is unpleasant, he conceded with seeming good temper, as he prepared to counterattack, "but it is not *all* unpleasant and I am sure is no more unpleasant than the real inner lives of some of our best Oak Park families. You must remember that in such a book all the worst of the people's lives is displayed while at home there is a very lovely side for the public and the sort of thing of which I have had some experience in observing behind closed doors."

At times, his astonishing vulnerability to his mother's moral judgments caused him to respond not with insults, but with flights of self-justification and prevarication, as in his adolescent letters from Kansas City. On the day, for instance, when he sought to explain to his parents why he had divorced Hadley and married Pauline Pfeiffer, he began by apologizing to them for having caused them "so much shame and suffering," and then went on to declare, in a flagrant departure from the truth, that although he had been in love with both women for over a year, he had been "absolutely faithful to Hadley." Moreover, he claimed, he had been leading a very clean life in other respects. "I remember Mother saying once that she would rather see me in my grave than something—I forget what—smoking cigarettes perhaps. If it's of any interest I don't smoke. Haven't for almost 3 years altho you probably will hear stories that I smoke like a furnace." As for the nature of his fiction, he admitted that while he was "upset about Mother accusing me of pandering to the lowest tastes," his conscience was clear. "I *know* that I am not disgracing you in my writing but rather doing something that some day you will be proud of." You cannot know, he cried out, his voice rising in anguish, "how it makes me feel for Mother to be ashamed of what I know as sure as you know that there is a God in heaven is *not to be ashamed of.*"

A year after receiving that letter, Dr. Hemingway committed suicide by shooting himself in the head. Angina pectoris, diabetes, and the inability to sleep because of pain were the reasons behind the tragedy, according to the letter that Hemingway dispatched to his editor, Max Perkins. Physiological explanations, however, did not satisfy the letter writer for long. Whether because there simply was no limit to his desire to degrade his mother, or because he was trying to cover up his own guilty sense of having caused his father a great deal of unhappiness, Hemingway soon persuaded himself that a henpecking wife had "forced my father to suicide." Thenceforward he was wont to refer to her in correspondence as "my bitch of a mother." He refused to invite her to visit him at his home in Cuba, and he would not go to Oak Park, because "I can't stand to see her." Even after her death in 1951, he continued to rail at her as a husband killer.

Right from the start of his career as a creative writer, Hemingway also sought to pursue his war with his mother by fictional means. From the vantage point of Paris's Left Bank in 1924, he looked back upon Oak Park in anger, as he worked on the stories that became the book called *In Our Time*. "The Doctor and the Doctor's Wife," the second of the stories in the book, presents a sanctimonious wife, her henpecked husband, and their little boy. Instead of obeying his mother's request that he come up to the bedroom where she is lying with the blinds drawn and a Bible beside her, the boy goes off for a walk in the woods with his father. In "Soldier's Home," the seventh story, we meet a mother who willingly cooks breakfast for her war-veteran son, but who doesn't allow him to "muss up" the morning newspaper—it is the Kansas City *Star*, we learn—which he wants to read while eating. She then completes the young man's annoyance by asking him if he loves her, to which he replies, "I don't love anybody," and by urging him to kneel and pray with her, to which he replies, "I can't." In both of these stories, the need to comply with a mother's demands is defied by a rebellious son. The final story in *In Our Time*, as we have seen, centers on a fisherman who feels, as he enters the woods, that he has left everything behind, "the need for thinking, the need to write, other needs." Whether the "other needs" he has escaped include the need to please his mother is never made clear.

Yet if the fisherman's dark thoughts in "Big Two-Hearted River" are choked off before they reach the level of consciousness, Grace Hall Hemingway was surely on the storyteller's mind. The satisfaction Nick takes in referring to his tent as his home, for instance, derives from the author's inability either to forget or forgive his mother's banishment of him four years before from their home in Michigan. As Nick sets up the tent, he is defiantly establishing his own domicile—and as he proceeds to hang his pack from a nail that he has "gently" driven into a pine tree, to prepare a delicious meal of beans and spaghetti, to brew his coffee by a carefully described method, and to clean up after himself with scrupulous thoroughness, he is demonstrating that he, too, has domestic discipline. Hemingway may have rebelled against the values of his mother and father, but he was also marked by them; in the woods, Nick Adams apes the cooking skills and the careful housekeeping habits that Hemingway had observed in his father on fishing and hunting trips and in his mother at home.

Happiness for the hero of "Big Two-Hearted River" is an inordinate concern with small details. On the one hand, his obsessiveness keeps dark thoughts at bay; on the other hand, it proves how responsible he is. Before reaching down into the stream to touch a trout resting on the bottom, Nick conscientiously wets his hand, "so that he would not disturb the delicate mucus that covered him. If a trout was touched with a dry hand, a white fungus attacked the unprotected spot." The author who would cry out to his mother that his work was nothing to be ashamed of, and that the day would come when she would be proud of him, could not have continued writing if he had not believed himself to be, in his own way, a moralist. He had incorporated into himself too much of her personality to have embraced the nihilism with which his interpreters have been so eager to associate him.

The question of why the author elected not to specify the nature of the malaise that underlies Nick's happiness in "Big Two-Hearted River" can never be answered with certainty. But the most plausible answer is that, unlike "The Doctor and the Doctor's Wife" and "Soldier's Home," in which sons are clearly unhappy in the homes of their mothers, "Big Two-Hearted River" takes place in the woods. If Nick Adams had been revealed as a man so angry at his mother that he could not even forget her when he was off on a fishing trip, readers might simply have concluded that Nick was an emotional adolescent. The only way to avoid such a judgment would have been to show Nick using his time in the woods to sort out his feelings about his mother and come to an understanding of the tension between them. Writing that kind of story, however, would have required of Hemingway a degree of self-understanding that he would never achieve.

"I had a wonderful novel to write about Oak Park," he told the literary critic Charles Fenton in 1952, but "would never do it because I did not want to hurt liveing [sic] people." The excuse rings false. Neither as a man nor as a writer had Hemingway ever hesitated to hurt living people, and furthermore both of his parents were dead when he wrote to Fenton. If pangs of conscience had previously stayed his hand, why did he not write the Oak Park novel at some point during the ten years of life that remained to him after his mother's death in 1951? Clearly, it was not a concern for protecting his parents that forever prevented him from writing the book, but rather his own failure to master its materials. A novel-length exploration of the experience of growing up in Oak Park would have led Hemingway into a swamp filled with deep water and overgrown with trees, in which big trout might be hooked but not landed.

Having failed to work out his relationship with his mother, Hemingway went on to marriages that mostly did not work and to fictional commentaries upon them that are either as brutally direct as "The Doctor and the Doctor's Wife" and "Soldier's Home" are about his mother, or as brilliantly evasive as "Big Two-Hearted River." Three of his four marriages were important to him personally, the first, the second, and the fourth, but in terms of their fictional consequences, the first was by far the most significant.

Hadley Richardson was eight years older than Hemingway. She was raised in a roomy, comfortable house in the suburban West End of Saint Louis, where the oak trees and fine lawns recalled Oak Park's. Her mother's overriding interest was in varieties of religious experience, from theosophy to mental science to psychic phenomena. "A woman of strong personality and convictions," says Hadley's biographer, Alice Hunt Sokoloff, "she was the dominant influence in the Richardson family." Mr. Richardson ran a pharmaceutical business and was a heavy drinker, a habit of which his wife severely disapproved, and when Hadley was twelve years old, he committed suicide. The similarities in their backgrounds helped to make Ernest and Hadley feel that they belonged together, and so did their dreams of escape. When Hadley wrote to Ernest during their engagement that "The world's a jail and we're going to break it together," she knew she spoke for him as well as for herself.

"She's a wonderful tennis player, best pianist I ever heard and a sort of terribly fine article," Hemingway wrote to Grace Quinlan in the summer of 1921, a month and half before he and Hadley were married. Under his tutelage, Hadley also learned to fish as well as he could, and in the first two years of their marriage she kept right up with him as he walked over the Saint Bernard pass into Italy, played tennis at Rapallo, hiked through the Black Forest, spent three months skiing in Switzerland, handicapped the horses at San Siro and Auteuil, went to all the bullfights at Pamplona, and dined out every night in Milan at the Cova or Campari's. Despite the considerable difference in their ages—which for unstated psychological reasons must have played its part, too, in his attraction to her—Hadley was wonderfully youthful, a gutsy companion, a perfect pal.

In August, 1923, the endless honeymoon abruptly came to an end, as the Hemingways left Paris for Toronto. Hadley was pregnant, and they both wanted the baby to be born in a hospital on North American soil. (In Europe, it was still not the general practice to give anesthetics to women in labor.) On September 10, Hemingway reported for work at the Toronto *Daily Star.* He expected to be kept on local assignments but was told he might be sent out of town as well. A month later, he was in New York, covering the arrival of the British prime minister, David Lloyd George, when the news reached him that Hadley had gone into the hospital. The long train ride back to Toronto gave him ample time to worry about all sorts of things. Upon reaching the hospital the next morning he looked broken down "from fatigue and strain," as Hadley subsequently described him to Isabel Simmons, an old friend of Ernest's from Oak Park.

By the end of January, 1924, the Hemingways were back in

Paris, where because of Bumby, their baby boy, they now settled in a somewhat larger apartment than they had previously occupied. Soon, Hemingway's letters to his friends were bubbling with descriptions of where he and Hadley had just been and of where they were planning to go next. "We have more fun together all the time," he wrote to Howell Jenkins. "She is the best guy on a trip you ever saw. She is keeping her piano up and runs the house and the baby damned smooth and is always ready to go out and eat oysters at the café and drink a bottle of Pouilly before supper." The endless honeymoon had seemingly resumed—except that it hadn't. "It is just about morning," Hemingway wrote to the publisher Robert McAlmon in the predawn darkness of November 15, 1924, "Bumby had a night when he didn't sleep and Hadley and I've been up with him alternatively and together." Baby-sitter problems forced them to come home in the evening before Hemingway was ready to do so, and when they left Bumby with a sitter and went to the six-day bike races at the Vélodrome d'Hiver, Hadley's energies would give out in the hours after midnight, forcing her to curl up on the bench and nap, as her indefatigable husband went on cheering the riders.

In his immaturity, Hemingway was no more ready to accept the restrictions on his freedom that fatherhood had imposed than he had been to live by the rules of conduct laid down by his mother. The letters he sent to friends during 1924 had only praise for lovely, gallant Hadley, but in several of the stories he wrote for *In Our Time,* he revealed how deeply conflicted his feelings about her had become.

Of the six stories in the collection that reflect one facet or another of the author's angry, guilty, depressed state of mind, the most blatantly autobiographical is "Cross Country Snow." Nick Adams and his friend George are having such fun skiing by themselves in Switzerland that they both wish they could go on sampling the slopes indefinitely and "not give a damn" about anything else. Nick, though, is married to Helen, and Helen is going to have a baby. "Will you go back to the States?" George inquires. "I guess so," Nick replies. "Do you want to ?" George asks. "No," says Nick.

In "Cat in the Rain" and "Out of Season," the author extended his examination of the problems of young American couples in postwar Europe. But in the other three stories about

Hadley and himself, Hemingway projected his sense of foreboding backward in time, into stories of boyhood in Michigan before the war. He wrote "The Three-Day Blow," he later recalled in his memoir of the twenties, *A Moveable Feast,* while sitting in a café on the Place St-Michel on "a wild, cold, blowing day," and so he made it "that sort of day in the story." A marital weather as well got into the story, and into "Indian Camp" and "The End of Something."

Carlos Baker's biography tells us that Hemingway once knew a girl from Petoskey, Michigan, named Marjorie Bump, and that he "romanticized their friendship" in "The End of Something." Nick's girlfriend in the story is, to be sure, named Marjorie, but the fact that she fishes as well as he can, is very much of a pal to Nick, and yet is deeply in love with him, strongly suggests she is Hadley. Furthermore, the story does not "romanticize" Nick's friendship with Marjorie, it portrays the swift and ruthless destruction of their relationship. For Hemingway was testing out, through the composition of "The End of Something," the idea of divorce. In the mid-1930s he would do the same thing in "The Snows of Kilimanjaro" by portraying his second wife, Pauline Pfeiffer, as the rich-bitch spouse of a dying writer, even though at the time of writing the story Hemingway was assuring such correspondents as Max Perkins that "Pauline is fine," just as he had written only sweet words about Hadley in his correspondence of 1924.

As Hemingway conjured up Nick and Marjorie building a fire on a sandy point and watching it get dark, he was rehearsing a scene he would shortly play in his own life. "There's going to be a moon tonight," Nick says. "I know it,' Marjorie replies happily. Without warning, Nick turns on her. "You know everything," he says sarcastically. "I've taught you everything," he goes on angrily, "and now it isn't fun any more." Stunned, Marjorie asks, "Isn't love any fun?" "No," says Nick, his head in his hands. The feeling of emptiness that one can sense in Nick's laconic answers to George in "Cross Country Snow" is again evident in the wake of his anger at the end of "The End of Something."

The mood of depression in the follow-up story, in which Nick and his friend Bill get drunk on a cold and blowy afternoon and talk about Marjorie, is considerably deeper. If you hadn't broken off with Marge, Bill says, "you'd be back home working trying to get enough money to get married." Nick says nothing, so Bill resumes his effort to comfort him. "Once a man's married he's absolutely bitched.... He hasn't got anything more. Nothing. Not a damn thing. He's done for." Once again, Nick says nothing. Depression has reduced him from laconicisms to silence.

And sometimes silence is the prelude to suicide, as "Indian Camp" demonstrates. Through the wide eyes of a very young Nick Adams, we watch his doctor-father enter an Indian shanty one night and perform a Caesarean section on a young woman, using a jackknife to make the incision and tapered gut leader from a fishing kit to sew it up. Only after the operation has been successfully concluded does Dr. Adams discover that the woman's seemingly stoic husband, unable to bear his wife's screams, has slit his throat while lying in the upper bunk.

For years, incautious critics claimed that "Indian Camp" was based on the author's memory of an incident he had witnessed as a little boy. Thanks to Carlos Baker, the claim no longer has any credibility. Yet Baker's own belief that the "melodramatic circumstances" of the story were entirely an "invention" is equally misleading. Behind the grisly tale lay the circumstance of Hemingway's anxiety-ridden train trip back to Toronto on the night Hadley went into labor. Did Hemingway, on that long night, out of fear of being entrapped once again in family life, consider deserting his wife? Out of a sense of guilt at being absent from Hadley's side to help her through an ordeal which he himself had caused, did the train rider contemplate suicide? All we know is that he arrived at the hospital looking broken down with strain and fatigue. Yet eventually he did desert his wife and, as the Baker edition of his letters shows, by the time that "Indian Camp" and the rest of the *In Our Time* stories were published in October, 1925, the author was openly talking of killing himself. "Indian Camp" is even more eerily predictive than "The End of Something."

Like Hemingway on the train, who in his imagination could see his wife in the hospital even though he was hundreds of miles away from her, the Indian husband is there in the room, listening to the screams, yet is so unconnected to what is going on that it is as if he were somewhere else. He does not speak to his wife, he does nothing to assist the doctor, he displays no interest in watching the birth of his son. Instead, he lies silently on his bunk, smoking a pipe, and then rolls toward the wall. Why his will to live has been overmastered remains mysterious. Throughout the story he has said not a word, and Nick Adams is so young that his father has to reply to the boy's question about the tragedy on a very simple level. "Why did he kill himself, Daddy?" "I don't know, Nick. He couldn't stand things, I guess." Reading that exchange, one feels that the author has brilliantly finessed a situation which virtually demanded perceptive comment because he was at a loss to explain his own vulnerability to thoughts of self-destruction. If Nick had been sixteen or seventeen years old, he and his father conceivably could have had a probing discussion of why a man might be moved to kill himself on the night he became a father; by making Nick a young boy, the author precluded the possibility.

"Perfectly calmly and not bluffingly," so he later reminded Pauline Pfeiffer, Hemingway declared in the fall of 1925 that if his emotional split between Pauline and Hadley "wasn't cleared up by christmas I would kill myself." His flight from family life had led him into a love affair that had become more serious than he had bargained on.

If the recollections of the dying writer in "The Snows of Kilimanjaro" may be trusted as autobiographical confession, Hemingway was already consorting with other women as early as the fall of 1922, barely more than a year after his wedding to Hadley. "To me," he confessed to F. Scott Fitzgerald on July 1, 1925, "heaven would be . . . two lovely houses in town; one where I would have my wife and children and be monogamous and love them truly and well and the other where I would have my nine beautiful mistresses on 9 different floors." Not too many weeks after writing that letter, Hemingway sent Hadley and Pauline off to the Loire Valley together so that he could finish the first draft of *The Sun Also Rises* at full throttle. "I did not want to lose my speed making love," he explained a quarter of a century later to the art historian Bernard Berenson. But after the manuscript was completed, he told Berenson, he felt "hollow and lonely and needed a girl very badly. So I was in bed with a no good girl when my wife came home and had to get the girl out onto the roof . . . and change the sheets and come down to open the door." Having fornicated into a "state of absolute clear-headedness," he then went off with Hadley and Bumby to Schruns in the Vorarlberg, where they had "a wonderful, healthy, happy life," and he twice rewrote his novel. Pauline joined them at Christmas.

All very jolly, except that the hollow feeling he referred to in the letter to Berenson was depression. In the fall, he had threatened to kill himself if his love life were not cleared up by Christmas, but by then it was more agonizingly complicated than ever. A Christmas eve note to Scott Fitzgerald spoke of nights of sleeplessness and of all the "sons of bitching things I've done," and in another letter to Fitzgerald he admitted that he had been "in hell" since Christmas, "with plenty of insomnia to light the way around so I could study the terrain." Ever since he had met Hadley, he had regarded her as "the best and truest and loveliest person that I have ever known." He could not have written *In Our Time, The Torrents of Spring,* and *The Sun Also Rises* if he had not had her "loyal and self-sacrificing and always stimulating and loving . . . support," as well as the financial backing of her small inheritance. Bumby, he exclaimed, was so lucky to have her as a mother. Yet he was sexually enchanted and intellectually beguiled by Pauline. Besides being four years younger than Hadley, she was handsomer, wealthier, better dressed (she worked for the Paris *Vogue*), and far more willing to cater to Hemingway's dependency on female flattery. Most people, including Hadley, were embarrassed by Hemingway's vicious parody of Sherwood Anderson in *The Torrents of Spring,* but Pauline predictably adored it. The writer who put his new novel through two more drafts at Schruns was a man torn in half between wife and mistress.

Jake Barnes, the hero of *The Sun Also Rises,* has always been the prize exhibit of the war-victim interpretation of Hemingway. For Jake is sexually impotent as a result of a wound received in World War I, and he has trouble sleeping at night. But Jake's wound is not only the thematic preoccupation of the novelist, as Mark Schorer would have it; it is also a cover-up for artistic failure, a simplistic, sensationalistic, self-exonerating means of accounting for the hero's depressed condition. Jake's insomnia, the Baker edition of Hemingway's letters makes clear, was inspired by the sleeplessness of a married man at Schruns, and Jake's inability to make love to the woman he is in love with was inspired by Hemingway's inability to find sexual contentment in the arms of the "best and truest and loveliest person" he had ever known. In *The Sun Also Rises*, the author let a war wound stand for a more subtle and complicated disability which he was afraid to deal with directly.

But if Hemingway is the impotent Jake, who is the nymphomaniacal Lady Brett Ashley? This compulsive creature, who claims to be deeply in love with Jake, has generally been identified by the critics as the fictional counterpart of Lady Duff Twysden, whom Hemingway had sometimes encountered in the bars of Montparnasse (and may, just possibly, have bedded). Yet while Lady Brett's boyish hairdo and clipped-speech mannerisms were in all likelihood modeled on Lady Duff's, the real-life lady's sexual liberation fell considerably short of the fictional lady's insatiability.

In her raging need to fornicate, Lady Brett is Hemingway himself, as the novelist came close to acknowledging in a letter to the poet Archibald MacLeish in 1943. Each of his novels, he told MacLeish, contained one new thing he had personally learned in the course of his life, and the realization that *The Sun Also Rises* had been based on was, "Promiscuity no solution." To the considerable distress of the poet Allen Tate, who reviewed *The Sun Also Rises* in the *Nation* in 1926, the novel not only makes its wayward heroine an attractive person, it condones her incontinent behavior. The letter to MacLeish explains why. Hemingway never thought of not condoning Lady Brett's sexual self-indulgence because he never thought of not condoning his own. Hemingway's only objection to promiscuity was that it had led him into hell, not heaven. Instead of solving his emotional problems, it had multiplied them.

Hemingway has not rounded out his people, Allen Tate further complained in his review, he has created caricatures based on one or two traits; his vision of character is "singularly oblique." Singularly oblique indeed. The novelist had based both the principal female character and the principal male character on aspects of himself and had then depicted these representatives of his divided self as being desperately in love with one another. In the back seats of taxicabs, they hold hands and kiss and exchange endearments. Kinkiness, though, was utterly foreign to the spirit of Hemingway, in Hemingway's opinion. Never in my life have I "felt a 'malajust,'" he boasted to a friend in 1932. Kinkiness was a disease that afflicted only other writers, like F. Scott Fitzgerald, who was eternally worried, Hemingway jeered, about the size of his penis, or Gertrude Stein, who was a queer. Stein in particular became an object of his derision and contempt, for in addition to being a lesbian, she was a Jew. But Stein's worst sin of all in the eyes of the author of *The Sun Also Rises* was that although he had thought of her as a mother he could count on, she had failed to give him her unstinting approval.

"Mrs. Stein" was one of his nicknames for his real mother. No sooner had he fled from her authority to Paris than he placed himself under the wing of Miss Stein, at 27 rue de Fleurus. At first, it was marvelous. She gave him the "run of the house." She encouraged him in his writing. And when he eventually asked her to become Bumby's godmother, she agreed. Yet if he basked in her love and understanding, this enormously gifted, deeply damaged man was no more able to tolerate her authoritarianism than he had been his mother's. An exasperated remark she made about the irresponsibility of the generation to which Hemingway belonged may very well have marked the moment at which his increasing irritation with her began to fester into an uglier feeling. For in front of the text of *The Sun Also Rises* he placed her remark about his generation being lost in juxtaposition with a quotation from Ecclesiastes to the effect that one generation passeth and another cometh, but the earth abideth forever—and the juxtaposition was no more intended as a compliment to his surrogate mother than the ensuing novel was intended as a bow to the literary taste of his real mother.

To Max Perkins in 1926, he confessed that while he himself did not think "a hell of a lot" of his generation, he had resented Gertrude Stein's "bombast." "Nobody knows about the generation that follows them and certainly has no right to judge." In 1932, he told another friend that the purpose of the two quotations had been "to show the superiority of the earlier Hebrew writers over the later." In 1934, his accumulating anger finally exploded into hatred. Gertrude Stein "was a damned pleasant woman," he wrote to Arnold Gingrich of *Esquire*,

> before she had the menopause and it goes against my digestion to take shots at anyone who's ever been a friend no matter how lousey [sic] they get to be finally. Besides, I've got the gun and it's loaded and I know where the vital spots are and friendship aside there's a certain damned fine feeling of

> superiority in knowing you can finish anybody off whenever you want to and still not doing it.

The words seethe with the primitive rage of the child who drew beads on his father's head with a shotgun.

After Hadley and Ernest had come to a parting of the ways, Hadley insisted that he and Pauline also part; if, after a considerable number of months had passed, they still found that they loved one another, Hadley would agree to a divorce. Hemingway's letters to Pauline during the period of their separation are filled with allusions to "horrors at night" and to "black depression." When two people love one another terribly much and then go away from each other, he told her, "it works almost as bad as abortion." All you can do is lie awake at night and "pray and pray and pray you won't go crazy."

Yet within a few weeks of his marriage to Pauline on May 10, 1927, the presumably happy bridegroom wrote "Hills Like White Elephants," an emotionally urgent story in which a man like Hemingway pleads with a woman like Hadley that if only she will consent to an abortion, "We can have everything. . . . We can have the whole world." And three months later, the bridegroom wrote to his father and admitted that "After we were divorced if Hadley would have wanted me I would have gone back to her." Another era, in short, had begun in Hemingway's life and work, in which fantasies of what-might-have-been would loom very large.

Across the entire length of his adult life, Hemingway kept a double record of his feelings by writing stories and by writing letters. In contrast to the appalling frankness of the letters, the stories suppress information, conflate memories, play tricks with time frames, speak in symbols. But with the help of the letters, they can at long last be fully understood. In the light of this understanding, the interpretation of Hemingway's fiction that originated forty years ago in Edmund Wilson's misreading of "Big Two-Hearted River," and that was then magnified by Malcolm Cowley into a misreading of the entire *oeuvre,* can also be recognized for what it really is: the exploitation of an author's work for ideological purposes.

Taken together, the letters and the stories show that what happened to Hemingway on July 8, 1918, did not give him nightmares for the rest of his life. If World War I played hob with his future, it was not because of a wound but because it suddenly propelled a rebellious youth who was barely out of high school into a very much bigger and more exciting world than the one he was slowly getting to know as a newspaperman in Kansas City.

Perhaps his separation from his mother and the values she stood for could never have been accomplished in the spirit of mutual understanding and love that Sherwood Anderson describes so delicately in his account of the relationship between young George Willard and his mother in *Winesburg, Ohio*. Perhaps, like figures in an O'Neill tragedy, Hemingway and his mother were doomed to claw and slash at one another, no matter what. The high-gear acceleration in his development that resulted from the war, however, certainly did not enhance the chances of establishing peace on the home front. Hemingway came back to Oak Park in 1919 spoiling for a fight, and his mother was waiting for him.

10
More Facts!

Aided by the coeditors and research assistants he has assembled around him on the campus of the University of South Carolina, Matthew J. Bruccoli has spent the past quarter of a century battening on the literary reputations of Ring Lardner, F. Scott Fitzgerald, Ernest Hemingway, John O'Hara, Raymond Chandler, James Gould Cozzens, and Ross Macdonald. An anthology of Hemingway's deservedly forgotten cub reportage and a grossly overblown assessment of O'Hara's literary achievement are typical of the tawdry books that the Bruccoli cottage industry is forever foisting on the world in the name of discriminating scholarship.

But it is the glamorous author of *The Great Gatsby* whose life and work have been most frequently exploited by the self-promoting professor from South Carolina. On the first printed page of *Some Sort of Epic Grandeur,* his recent biography of the novelist, Bruccoli lists fifteen other books on Fitzgerald that bear his name—and the list is by no means complete. Whether out of modesty, which is unlike him, or out of carelessness, which is, Bruccoli fails to mention his inconsequential additions to bibliographical lore in *F. Scott Fitzgerald: Collector's Handlist* (1964) and *The Merrill Checklist of F. Scott Fitzgerald* (1970), or his microscopic contribution to literary appreciation in *Apparatus for a Definitive Edition: F. Scott Fitzgerald's The Last Tycoon* (1976), or his totally inexcusable reprint, in 1978, of the screenplay of Erich Maria Remarque's mediocre novel *Three Comrades,* which the badly demoralized Fitzgerald forced himself to write for Hollywood money in 1937.

Of the earlier books on Fitzgerald for which Bruccoli does take credit, his 1973 edition of the novelist's previously unpublished ledger is without question a fascinating document. For in its two hundred legal-sized pages, Fitzgerald set down a remarkably candid outline of his life from his fourteenth to his fortieth year, as well as a statement of his annual earnings from 1919 through 1936 and a meticulous history of all his published fiction through June 1937. Although Fitzgerald did not live to write his autobiography, in the ledger he at least made important preparations for doing so. By relieving interested readers of the necessity of consulting the original handwritten manuscript in the archives of the Fitzgerald Collection of the Princeton University Library, Bruccoli performed a real service.

Perhaps as many as four of the other Fitzgerald books of which Bruccoli is presumably proud were also worth publishing. The remaining ten, however, are extremely dubious pieces of work, and it is significant that the most dubious of the lot is the only one that required something more of the cottage-industry captain than mere clerical skills. In *Scott and Ernest: The Authority of Failure and the Authority of Success* (1978), Bruccoli abandoned his usual role as a cultural junkman specializing in superfluous anthologies, coffee-table picture books, Princeton Triangle Club cassettes, and assorted knickknacks, and took on the more demanding assignment of writing a history of the friendship between Fitzgerald and Hemingway. But the only way that Bruccoli was able to come to grips with his subject was by relying on the hoariest of received opinions. From first to last, the author of *Scott and Ernest* had nothing worthwhile to say about either Fitzgerald or Hemingway that had not long since been said by other critics. His dependence on clichés did not bother Bruccoli, however. As he called his work force to order and charged forward into the composition of a full-scale biography of Fitzgerald, he did so in the confidence that he possessed something that more than made up for his lack of fresh ideas.

Whenever he was asked to say what was new in the biography he had undertaken, Bruccoli tells us in the preface to *Some Sort of Epic Grandeur,* he always replied, "More facts." This little story then leads him to proclaim that "A biographer's first duty is to get things right." Twenty years have passed since the appearance of Andrew Turnbull's *Scott Fitzgerald,* we are reminded, but at long last "I have corrected and augmented the record."

On inspection, most of Bruccoli's vaunted corrections and augmentations turn out to be the most sterile fact-mongering imaginable. In relating, for instance, the circumstances of Fitzgerald's death, he not only insists on our knowing that the novelist was pronounced dead by a doctor named Nelson, but he goes on to provide us with the even more unwanted information that "the body was removed to the Pierce Brothers Mortuary, 720 West Washington Boulevard, in Los Angeles."

There are times, moreover, when Bruccoli's delight in identifying a negligible mistake in some other biography or memoir of Fitzgerald is made to look ridiculous by his concomitant failure to recognize the really serious flaws in the account in question. Thus he has a fine time demonstrating that Hemingway erred in saying in his memoir of the 1920s, *A Moveable Feast,* that the first time he ever laid eyes on Fitzgerald was in the spring of 1925, when the novelist walked into the Dingo Bar in Paris in the company of a fellow Princetonian named Duncan Chaplin. But it couldn't have been Chaplin who was with Fitzgerald, Bruccoli announces, because Chaplin was not even in Europe in the spring of 1925, let alone in the Dingo Bar, and Bruccoli has a letter from Chaplin to prove it! The discovery is scarcely earthshaking, but at least it could have served to alert the biographer to the possibility that every story that Hemingway tells about Fitzgerald in *A Moveable Feast* has been somewhat embroidered, if not made up completely.

Alas, Bruccoli soon proceeds to repeat without the slightest display of skepticism the most suspicious of all the memoir's eyebrow-raising tales about Hemingway's literary contemporaries. Out of "respect for Hemingway's expertise in masculine matters," says the biographer, paraphrasing the memoirist, Fitzgerald turned to him for counsel when his wife, Zelda, complained that "his penis was too small to satisfy her." After checking him in a men's room, Hemingway contemptuously informed his friend that he was "normal." In his naiveté, Bruccoli fails to assess the credibility of this terrible story in the light of Hemingway's own sexual anxieties and of his obsessive effort over many decades to persuade the world that his all-around expertise in matters masculine was no myth. Nor does the biographer reflect on the fact that *A Moveable Feast* was written toward the end of Hemingway's life, when a great many things were driving him crazy, including the horrifying realization that Fitzgerald's literary prestige had overtaken his own. What better way to pull the plug on the resurgent popularity of his rival than by depicting Fitzgerald in a men's room with his pants down, beseeching a self-confident Hemingway for reassurance?

For all his fetishism about getting things right, then, Bruccoli gets a lot of things wrong. But even if *Epic Grandeur* contained no errors of any kind it would still be an awful book, because it is built on the impoverishing assumption that the heaping up of facts is what biographical writing is all about, and that historical scene-setting, literary interpretation, evaluation of personality, and every other sort of analytical activity are dispensable extras. Historically speaking, Bruccoli has so little interest in, or understanding of, the period with which Fitzgerald's career will be forever identified that he is unembarrassed to sum it up in five paragraphs consisting entirely of such vapid sentences as "The Roaring Twenties were typified by the bull market and Prohibition." As for literary interpretation, *Epic Grandeur* ends with the assertion that "Fitzgerald is now permanently placed with the greatest writers who ever lived"; but the statement is nothing but hot air, for nowhere in the book can one find a comparison of Fitzgerald's achievements with those of other writers. And for all its documentation of the events in Fitzgerald's life, *Epic Grandeur* draws its evaluations of his personality exclusively from the comments of other observers; in the pages of Bruccoli's book we do not meet a man whom we have never understood quite so well before, we merely encounter the familiar beautiful-and-damned figure of the "lost generation" myth.

In addition to being an intellectual dud, Bruccoli's book is an aesthetic disaster. *Epic Grandeur* may contain more documentation than Turnbull's *Scott Fitzgerald,* but the charm of Turnbull's book is that it shadows forth the Princeton that Fitzgerald knew as an undergraduate and makes an army lieutenant's romance with the reigning belle of Montgomery, Alabama, live again in our minds. *Epic Grandeur,* in contrast, is poetically barren. Instead of shaping his materials into evocative designs, Bruccoli just keeps deluging us with more and more facts, as if they had the power to speak for themselves. Among other indigestible lumps, his biography contains complete listings of the tables of contents of various volumes of Fitzgerald's short stories; two pages of uninterrupted quotation from a memo by Fitzgerald to Hemingway about ways to improve *A Farewell to Arms*; four and a half pages of uninterrupted quotation from the stenographic transcript of a discussion between Fitzgerald and Zelda about their nightmarish marriage; and a ten-page sequence of documents beginning with two and a half pages of uninterrupted quotation from a letter by Fitzgerald to Zelda about their nightmarish marriage, followed by two sentences by Bruccoli, followed by five and a half pages of uninterrupted quotation from a letter by Zelda to Fitzgerald about their nightmarish marriage, followed by three sentences by Bruccoli, followed by a half page of uninterrupted quotation from a memo by a psychiatrist named Forel about Zelda's mental condition, followed by three paragraphs by Bruccoli, and ending with half a page of uninterrupted quotation from a self-justifying letter by Fitzgerald to Forel.

In a sense, *Epic Grandeur* is not a biography at all, but just another cottage-industry anthology of Fitzgeraldiana. Documentation, in Bruccoli's book, does the biographer's work for him. Yet the interesting and ironic fact is that the documentation also undoes the biographer's work. For although Bruccoli is unaware of it, his extended quotations do not always support his romantic ideas about Fitzgerald's life and work.

Epic Grandeur's appreciative discussion of *The Great Gatsby,* for instance, resounds with critical clichés about Fitzgerald's emotional loyalty to a vanished American dream.

The novelist once defined the essence of America as "a willingness of the heart," we are told, and it is this vision of historical innocence and generosity that furnished him with the moral yardstick by which he measured the corruption of "the second-rate people" who, on summer nights, used Gatsby's Long Island estate as an amusement park—Maurice A. Flink, the Hammerheads, Beluga the tobacco importer, and all the rest of the rotten lot. Yet, seventy pages earlier in the biography, in a chapter describing Fitzgerald's visit to Rome in the summer of 1921, we find the text of a letter to Edmund Wilson that reveals that the critical animus that would inspire him to write *Gatsby* might more accurately be described as an unwillingness of the heart:

> God damn the continent of Europe. It is of merely antiquarian interest. Rome is only a few years behind Tyre + Babylon. The negroid streak creeps northward to defile the nordic race. Already the Italians have the souls of blackamoors. Raise the bars of immigration and permit only Scandinavians, Teutons, Anglo Saxons and Celts to enter.... I think its [sic] a shame that England and America didn't let Germany conquor [sic] Europe. Its [sic] the only thing that would have saved the fleet of tottering old wrecks. My reactions were all philistine, anti-socialistic, provincial + racially snobbish. I believe at last in the white man's burden. We are as far above the modern frenchman [sic] as he is above the negro [sic].

The brilliantly satirical notation of the guests who exploited Gatsby's hospitality was the work of a writer who wanted to prevent people with names like Beluga and Flink from entering the United States. No wonder T. S. Eliot was excited about *Gatsby*; like his own early poetry, it raised xenophobia to high art.

In his remarks on *Gatsby* Bruccoli also quotes—characteristically without comment—Fitzgerald's admission that the major flaw in the novel is that "I gave no account of (and had no feeling about or knowledge of) the emotional relations between Gatsby and Daisy from the time of their reunion to [Gatsby's death]." Why is it that Fitzgerald had the imaginative power to depict paradise lost but not paradise regained? The question ought to interest a biographer, one would think—if one did not know Bruccoli, that is. As he makes clear in a cop-out phrase in the preface to *Epic Grandeur*, "I do not practice psychiatry." Thus while he eagerly endorses Hemingway's tall story about the short-arm inspection in the men's room, he does not allow it to become the occasion for a discussion of Fitzgerald's sexual imagination. All Bruccoli is interested in is the facts, man. Was or was not Fitzgerald's penis of sufficient size to satisfy his wife? Hemingway was sure that it was, and furthermore, says Bruccoli, in what may very well be the most inane exhibition of fact-mongering in his entire career, two other commentators on Fitzgerald's intromittent organ, "Arnold Gingrich, who once saw Fitzgerald with his bathrobe open, and Sheilah Graham, who slept with him," have also "attested that it was normal."

There is no evidence that supports Zelda's accusation that Fitzgerald was a homosexual. Yet at the root of her insane suspicions lay the quite accurate realization that the feminine component in her husband's personality was extraordinarily strong. Just how strong may be seen in the letter that Fitzgerald wrote to his younger sister Annabel during his junior year at Princeton, in which he offered her astonishingly detailed advice about how to dress, how to walk, how to take care of her skin, and so on. "A girl should always be careful," Fitzgerald warned, "about such things as underskirt showing, long drawers showing under stocking, bad breath, mussy eyebrows (with such splendid eyebrows as yours you should brush them or wet them and train them every morning and night as I advised you to do long ago. They oughtn't to have a hair out of place)."

The degree of imaginative involvement in the problems of feminine appearance that is revealed in this letter is further defined by Fitzgerald's smash-hit success in a Princeton Triangle Club show. He was so convincingly alluring in the part that the New York *Times* ran a photo of him in drag. That publicity in turn brought him fan letters from a number of men who wanted to meet him, as well as an offer from a vaudeville agent to book him as a female impersonator. Although he turned down the offer, Fitzgerald did attend a Psi U dance at the University of Minnesota dressed as a girl.

"I didn't have the two top things—great animal magnetism or money," Fitzgerald once observed with regret in his notebooks. Animal magnetism in his novels and stories, however, is possessed only by highly sexed brutes whom he clearly despises, like Daisy Buchanan's husband, Tom; the men in his work with whom the novelist identifies are passive, pleading creatures like Gatsby, who display no interest in sexual fulfillment. It is his collection of gaudily colored shirts, not Daisy, that Gatsby flings down in his bedroom. The "lost generation" myth may assert that the war-haunted young men of the twenties enacted a revolution in morals, but the most famous suitor in the literature of the period is as inhibited as any Puritan.

11
Only Yesterday

Frederick Lewis Allen was a journalist by profession, a political liberal by conviction, a Puritan by inheritance. In a time of national crisis, these varied elements of personal outlook fused into a view of history, and a remarkable book was born. Half a century has passed since *Only Yesterday* bestrode the best-seller lists of 1931, but Allen's portrayal of the 1920s as the age of jazz babies, speakeasies, sports worship, sex crimes, xenophobic politics, and governmental graft continues to dominate our sense of the period, as well as to lend credibility to the increasingly fashionable notion that the story of twentieth-century America divides neatly into decades, each with a character peculiarly its own.

To Allen's Calvinist forebears, several of whom arrived in New England aboard the *Mayflower*, crop failures and other setbacks to settlement were not cosmic accidents, but deliberate punishments meted out by a God made angry by lapses from rectitude among his people. In the wake of such chastise-

Reprinted from *The American Scholar*, Volume 49, Number 4 (Autumn 1980).

ments, penitent believers sought to discover how they had fallen into error through sober reflections on their recent behavior. Although later generations of Allens turned away from Calvinism as a creed, its obsession with self-scrutiny and sin stayed with them. Thus in 1878, the Reverend Frederick Baylies Allen was so alarmed by what he regarded as the moral disorder of modern Boston that he devised a system of ridding the city of sexually explicit books and other iniquities. Calling together a group of reform-minded citizens, he persuaded them to join him in founding the New England Watch and Ward Society. Until his death in 1925, the Reverend Allen was the organization's most zealous member. Four years later, his son and namesake demonstrated that he, too, in his way, was a child of Puritanism. Frederick Lewis Allen's virtually automatic reaction to the Great Crash of the New York stock market was to begin reflecting on all the changes in American behavior that had occurred since the end of the war with Germany.

By the winter of 1930, a book on the twenties was already taking shape in his mind. The people of the period had not known that the future held catastrophe in store for them, but Allen nevertheless intended to judge them in the light of it. Just as some of his bibulous friends in journalism were wont to measure the degree of their self-indulgence the night before by the size of their hangovers on the morning after, so Allen concluded—on the basis of America's fragile condition after the Crash—that the twenties must have been a ten-year-long bout of riotous excess and wanton irresponsibility. That present suffering implied prior guilt was one of Allen's cardinal assumptions as he set out to recapture the past.

Only a few years earlier, his opinion of American life in the twenties had been much more benign. In 1927, for instance, he had published a pair of magazine articles in which he attacked H. L. Mencken and Sinclair Lewis for their "fantastic picture" of the contemporary scene. These "highbrows" would have us believe, Allen had written, that their fellow Americans are "vulgar, depraved, and uncivilized," whereas an impartial examination would almost certainly reveal that the average citizen is "rather a good fellow, after all." The author of *Only Yesterday,* however, wished to forget those words. Denunciations of American depravity and vulgarity seemed to him to be quite justified, and in the chapter entitled "The Revolt of the Highbrows" he summarized the jeremiads of Mencken and Lewis with unqualified respect.

The Puritan moral presuppositions that Allen brought to the task of writing history were reinforced by the political prejudices of a liberal Democrat. In the course of the twenties, Allen had not voted for any of the Republican candidates for the presidency, and the onset of the Depression did nothing to improve his opinion of the GOP.

To Calvin Coolidge, in consequence, *Only Yesterday* vouchsafes a mere half-dozen pages, all of them scornful. "Neither he nor his intellect had ever ventured far abroad," runs a typical sentence, even though Coolidge's ownership of Latin, Greek, French, German, and Italian lexicons and grammars was only one of many signs of this Amherst graduate's wide-ranging curiosity. To Herbert Hoover the book gives even shorter shrift. From its brief and contemptuous account of his administration one comes away with the impression that Hoover drew most of his ideas about crisis management from Dr. Coué's *Self-Mastery through Conscious Auto-Suggestion.* Only to Warren G. Harding was Allen generous—in terms of space—lavishing an entire chapter, thirty-six pages, on his life and times. All to the purpose, however, of savaging Harding's presidency and of clinching the author's case that the twenties were an era of national decay. Robert K. Murray, in his excellent study *The Harding Era* (1969), accuses Allen of misleading "tens of thousands of young readers whose total exposure to the twenties [has come] through the pages of his *Only Yesterday,*" and Murray's ensuing analysis of Allen's mythmaking is devastating.

Among other canards, *Only Yesterday* would have us believe that Harding's ambitious wife had "tailored and groomed him into outward respectability"; that from the beginning of his career in politics he had served as "the majestic Doric false front" behind which a definable group of lobbyists, fixers, and purchasers of privilege called the Ohio Gang put over its "little deals"; that party bosses decided to nominate Harding for the presidency well in advance of the 1920 Republican convention and later sealed their bargain in a smoke-filled hotel room; that during the Harding years the nation's capital was infested with "blowsy gentlemen with cigars stuck in their cheeks and rolls of very useful hundred-dollar bills in their pockets"; that Charles Evans Hughes and Herbert Hoover were appointed to the Cabinet merely as window dressing; that Harding gave away offices "like a benevolent Santa Claus"; that he had an inferior intellect which could not cope with the intricate problems that came across his desk; that he was more interested in affairs of the heart than in affairs of state; and that his death may very well have been suicide.

Distortions of this magnitude suggest malice, except that Allen was not a malicious man. While his inaccurate statements about Harding bespoke a left-of-center willingness to believe the worst about conservative Republicans, they were also grounded in what he was convinced was the reliable testimony of contemporary newspapers and magazines. If he devoted fewer than four pages of *Only Yesterday* to the positive accomplishments of the dead president and approximately twenty pages to the scandalous conduct of a few of his friends and acquaintances, it was because a hundred headlines about Teapot Dome had fixed an image of overwhelming corruption in his mind. If he spoke unfairly about Harding's intelligence or made dark reference to a supposedly conspiratorial organization called the Ohio Gang, it was because the distinguished journalists William Allen White and Bruce Bliven had previously done so. Allen's misreadings of the twenties—of its social history no less than its political history—are ultimately traceable to an inadequately critical attitude toward the gargoyle journalism of the era.

Throughout the twenties Allen was himself a journalist. After a brief stint as a press-bureau propagandist during World War I, he went to work for Harvard University as its first director of publicity. New York, however, was where he wanted to be, and when he was offered a job on *Harper's* magazine, he took it. These experiences prepared him to write *Only Yesterday* by teaching him what the general reader wanted. All of the book's most engaging qualities—its breezy, informal prose style, its attention to the worship of Jack Dempsey and other popular heroes whom more orthodox historians refused to take seriously, above all its deft re-creation of various routines of daily life such as the rather alarming problem of starting up a Model T Ford—are journalistic in the best sense of the word. So, too, is the book's clever orchestration of song titles, advertising slogans, and the names of movie stars as a means of recapturing a bygone mood. For while Allen sat in judgment on the hedonism of the twenties, he also felt a nostalgia for the period's vanished pleasures. His wife, Dorothy, to whom he was very close, died while he was working on the book, and the completed volume is dedicated to her memory in more ways than one.

Yet if Allen's involvement in journalism helped to make him an imaginative historian, it also robbed him of a detachment toward the materials on which he most heavily depended. Too close to the trees to see very much of the woods, he never quite grasped the fact that the newspapers and magazines of the twenties illustrated developments in journalism with far greater fidelity than they mirrored events in the world. Thus in *Only Yesterday*'s most famous chapter, "The Revolution in Manners and Morals"—which has enthralled historians of our own time who ought to know better (see, for instance, the chapter called "The Revolution in Morals" in William E. Leuchtenburg's *The Perils of Prosperity*)—Allen insists that the Jazz Age overthrew traditional standards of American morality and that "one of the most striking results of the revolution was a widely pervasive obsession with sex." The most tangible piece of evidence he offers in substantiation of this claim is the vast amount of space that newspapers of the period gave to juicy scandals like the Hall-Mills murder case, the Snyder-Gray murder case, and the exigent demands imposed by the aging Daddy Browning upon his nubile Peaches. Having satisfied himself that the twenties had indeed gone crazy about sex, Allen ascribed the phenomenon to the following factors: the eat-drink-and-be-merry-for-tomorrow-we-die spirit with which "a whole generation" of young men had been infected by the war with Germany; the effect that flaming youth's example had upon middle-aged Americans—"they saw their juniors exploring the approaches to the forbidden land of sex, and presently they began to play with the idea of doing a little experimenting of their own"; the spread of the Freudian vision of the sex drive as "the central and pervasive force which moved mankind"; the sharp increase in the use of the automobile and its speedy transformation into a "house of prostitution on wheels"; and the movies' incessant emphasis on suggestive themes, as evidenced by the film advertisement which promised patrons "brilliant men, beautiful jazz babies, champagne baths, midnight revels, petting parties in the purple dawn, all ending in one terrific climax that makes you gasp."

In a gesture that was reminiscent of his father's investigative techniques, Allen made no effort to determine whether the film in question actually resembled the hype for it. Nowhere in his argument, indeed, did he pause to consider the possibility that he had grossly exaggerated the dimensions of the moral breakdown he was seeking to explain and that the "obsessive" newspaper coverage of certain scandals was symptomatic of a journalistic revolution, not a sexual revolution.

Hard information on what did or did not happen in the back seats of automobiles parked on dark streets half a century ago is, to be sure, not easily come by, but it would appear from the evidence of American literature that the changes in the sexual conduct of American men and women between, say, 1905 and 1925 were far less significant than the continuities. F. Scott Fitzgerald, of course, kicked off the twenties with the rather breathless announcement in *This Side of Paradise* that "Victorian mothers" had no idea "how casually their daughters were accustomed to be kissed," and *Only Yesterday* repeats that line. But Fitzgerald mainly had in mind the rather special daughters whom he had encountered at sophisticated parties in Saint Paul, Chicago, and New York. His fellow Princetonian Booth Tarkington, on the other hand, set down in the fiction he published in the twenties a much more encompassing account of American society than *This Side of Paradise* offers, and there is no question that most of the young women he depicted were much less venturesome, sexually speaking, than Fitzgerald's high-society flappers. The middle-class heroine of *Alice Adams*, for instance, equates sexual looseness with self-destruction, just as her mother does. *Only Yesterday*, however, overlooks *Alice Adams*, even though it is literarily of greater interest than *This Side of Paradise* and was far more popular with readers of the period.

On the question of whether postwar American males were given more to extramarital sexual adventures than their prewar counterparts, Allen once again skirted the best literary evidence by failing to point out that whereas George F. Babbitt's best friend sometimes cheated on his wife, so did the businessmen whom Dreiser had written about ten or twenty years earlier; and that Hemingway's Nick Adams not only lost his virginity well before a wartime spirit of eat, drink, and be merry allegedly infected the sex habits of America's young men, but had not required the help of an automobile to accomplish the feat. As for Babbitt himself, that quintessential man of the twenties drew back from the temptation of sexual dalliance, but *Only Yesterday* does not note this either. The sexual rectitude with which Jay Gatsby pursues Daisy Buchanan also goes unacknowledged.

Only Yesterday is a history that was inspired by journalism, yet Allen did not pay much attention to journalism as a historical phenomenon. If he had, he might never have written "The Revolution in Manners and Morals," for the careers of such men as Captain Patterson of the New York *Daily News* and Kent Cooper of the Associated Press conceivably could have taught him what the sensational newspaper stories on which his chapter relied really meant. Cooper's career in particular would have been instructive, because Cooper did more than any other single individual in the twenties to alter the content of the nation's newspapers. From the early years of the century, he had worked for the AP as a reporter and editor, but not until he became general manager in 1925 was he able to transform the nature of the news that the service sent out on its wire. Once in control, he immediately enlarged the scope of the AP's coverage to include information, pictures, and news features of wide human appeal that were of interest to "everybody," as he grandly says in his autobiography. Some of that human-interest news had to do with the theories of Einstein and Michelson and other scientific prodigies, but a larger share was devoted to manners and morals. If readers across the nation in the latter half of the twenties were more conscious of their countrymen's conduct than ever before, this was at least in part because of the executive orders of Kent Cooper.

Behind Cooper's decision to enlarge the AP's definition of the news lay the same consideration which had already prompted many individual publications to broaden their coverage of events; there were yawning holes to fill in the postwar American newspaper. From the moment the war with Germany ended, the size of newspapers had begun to increase. Spurred on by the demands of advertisers for more and more space, they steadily upped the number of pages per issue. The New York *Times* is a case in point. At the end of the war, the *Times* generally printed twenty-four pages daily. By 1921, issues of thirty-two, thirty-six, or even forty pages were the weekday rule, while the Sunday edition was more appropriately measured in pounds. An advertising linage that was ten times what it had been in the 1890s took up a good many of these extra pages, but not all of them. Into the emptiness of its newly created news columns, the *Times* poured sports stories, crime stories, and sex stories in revolutionary quantities. During the three weeks of the Hall-Mills trial, the *Times* saw fit to print more than half a million words about the case (as compared with the New York *Daily News*'s quarter of a million words). For the first Dempsey-Tunney fight in 1926, as Silas Bent has pointed out in an interesting book called *Ballyhoo*, the paper used the same size banner headline with which it had announced the Armistice.

Readers also pressured the publishers to put out thicker newspapers. As early as 1911, the journalist Will Irwin had described twentieth-century America's increasing demand for news as "a crying primal want of the mind, like hunger of the body." The sensational events of the war in Europe accelerated the growth of that demand, and as the newspapers feverishly expanded their staffs and stepped up the tempo of their reporting, the demand perversely became more insistent. A condition of something like insatiability had been achieved, in which the hunger for news was further inflamed by every improvement in the delivery of it or expansion in the supply. While this development was certainly astonishing, more astonishing still was the craving that Americans in the twenties began to display for frequent repetitions of the very same items of news. Thus radio coverage of sports events did not at all threaten the popularity of the newly expanded sports sections of newspapers, as some publishers had feared it would. Instead, the vocal accounts by Graham McNamee and other broadcasters inspired listeners to buy more newspapers, morning and evening, than ever before. Between 1919 and 1929, the purchasers of daily newspapers in the United States increased from 33 million to 42 million, even though newsreels and radio broadcasts were simultaneously becoming familiar elements of the cultural scene. That familiarity with the news did not diminish the nation's eagerness to take it in was also attested to by the success of *Time* magazine, which in its early years was nothing much more than a rehash of the newspapers to which its two young editors subscribed. In the 1920s, enlarged versions of the news drummed on the national consciousness in a rapidly intensifying tattoo. Not surprisingly, some Americans occasionally confused the panoramas of the media with the panorama of reality. One of them was the author of *Only Yesterday*.

The great press lords of the twenties—Joseph Medill Patterson, who launched the tabloid *Daily News* in 1919 and built the biggest newspaper circulation in New York in less than twenty-four months, the imperious Robert Rutherford McCormick of the Chicago *Tribune*, Roy Howard of the Scripps-Howard chain, Adolph Ochs of the New York *Times*, the aging but still active William Randolph Hearst—were all fascinated by mass living and eager to understand and use it. Yet with the exception of Hearst, none of these powerful men acquired the kind of celebrity that attached to certain reporters, editors, and magazine writers of the period. As the authors of *The Front Page* (1928) knew, the glamour of American journalism was to be found in the newsroom, not the boardroom. Whenever the columnist Heywood Broun walked into a Greenwich Village restaurant or hailed a taxi outside Madison Square Garden, witnesses to the event stirred with recognition of his burly figure. In the opinion of many Americans, the nation's most exciting writers were neither novelists nor poets, but sports reporters like Grantland Rice. The political gibes of William Allen White and H. L. Mencken were not merely reactions to the news, they *were* news. Commanding an attention unprecedented in the history of their profession, the famous journalists of the twenties imposed personal interpretations of events upon the minds of millions.

Of all the influential newsmen of the decade, the one destined to exert the profoundest influence upon subsequent historians was Frederick Lewis Allen's great friend, Walter Lippmann of the New York *World*. In *Only Yesterday*, in Leuchtenburg's *The Perils of Prosperity*, in Arthur M. Schlesinger, Jr.'s *The Crisis of the Old Order*, in Samuel Lubell's *The Future of American Politics*, in dozens of biographies and other sorts of books which have contributed to our consciousness of the twenties in America, Lippmann's journalistic observations are at work. His essays covered a wide range of subjects, but in his most ambitious pieces he developed a general theory of American society in the twenties. To

Lippmann the nation was really two nations. On one side of the fault line was the "old" America of small towns and farms, peopled by Protestants of native stock and dedicated to defending America's traditional values and beliefs. On the other side was the "new" America of the cities, alive with immigrants and enlightened by intellectuals. The "old" America had embraced the Prohibition movement and the anti-Catholic Ku Klux Klan; the "new" had taken Governor Al Smith to its bosom. These allegiances could be only partially explained in terms of religious affiliation or of contrasting attitudes toward drink; on their profoundest level of meaning, they were symbols of cultural difference. "The Governor's more hasty friends show an intolerance when they believe Al Smith is the victim of purely religious prejudice," Lippmann insisted. "Quite apart from the severe opposition of the prohibitionists, the objection to Tammany, the sectional objection to New York, there is an opposition to Smith which is as authentic, and, it seems to me, as poignant as his support. It is inspired by the feeling that the clamorous life of the city should not be acknowledged as the American ideal."

Of the many historians who ultimately made this argument their own, none took into account the newspaper and magazine contexts in which Lippmann propounded it. As a result, none of them understood that, in its own pontifical way, Lippmann's analysis of the city-country split in American society was no less characteristic an example of the gargoyle journalism of the twenties than Grantland Rice's likening of the Notre Dame backfield to the Four Horsemen of the Apocalypse, or Bruce Bliven's sensational descriptions of the Ohio Gang, or the oft-repeated comparison of Bartolomeo Vanzetti to Jesus Christ, or the assertion of the entire nation's press that Lindbergh's flight to Paris in 1927 was "the greatest feat of a solitary man in the records of the human race," as Lippmann's New York *World* put it. Although Lippmann's book *Public Opinion* (1922) contains a justly famous discussion of journalistic stereotypes, his consciousness of them did not mean that he was always able to erase their imprint from his mind. Lippmann was a city boy, born and bred, and his exclusive association of Prohibition and the Klan with rural America was the product of long exposure to the antiprovincial stereotypes of the New York press. In fact, Prohibition engaged the energies of political reformers on

Manhattan Island as well as of religious fundamentalists in Manhattan, Kansas, while the recrudescent Klan burned crosses in Chicago and Indianapolis neighborhoods no less often than in the countryside between them. Even the Hoover-Smith presidential campaign of 1928 did not vindicate Lippmann's analysis. For as the historian Allan J. Lichtman has decisively demonstrated in *Prejudice and the Old Politics: The Presidential Election of 1928*, only one variable counted in that election: religion. Catholics shifted into the Smith camp and Protestants shifted into the Hoover camp no matter whether they lived in the old America or the new.

Lippmann's view of America in the twenties as two cultures divided along demographic lines tells us more about his own prejudices than about his countrymen's. Moreover, he ignored the emergence of the suburbs. Were new communities like Shaker Heights culturally a part of the city or of the countryside? Lippmann's categories simply had no room in them for the suburban phenomenon. Instead of thinking about the complexities and contradictions of American culture in the twenties, Lippmann projected a desperate struggle between the forces of light and the forces of darkness, in which the forces of darkness were still prevailing—for had not the retrogressive countryside been successful in keeping the clamorous life of the cities from being acknowledged as the American ideal? This analysis was miserably misconceived, yet it lives today in the work of New Deal–oriented historians who have a political stake in the idea that the Republican-dominated twenties were a shameful time. For all its ideological appeal, however, Lippmann's commentary might not have been so readily accepted if it had not been for his friend Allen's ensuing portrait of the decade. *Only Yesterday* made it easier than ever to believe in the decadence of the twenties.

Only Yesterday also launched the myth of the moral health of the thirties. Interested as always in sexual matters, Allen spoke in his closing pages of the long skirts and draperies and white gloves of 1930 and 1931 as "the outward sign of a subtle change in the relations between the sexes." The revolution in manners and morals, he announced with puritanical triumph, "had at last reached an armistice." Instead of being laughed out of court, this totally unsubstantiated argument was taken up and elaborated upon by hundreds of commentators on the American scene. Soon it became a commonplace for them to say that although Depression-era America had a terrible hangover, at least the nation was sober once again. As Malcolm Cowley put it in *Exile's Return*, in a chapter called "New Year's Eve," the twenties had been "an easy, quick, adventurous age, good to be young in; and yet on coming out of it one felt a sense of relief, as on coming out of a room too full of talk and people into the sunlight of winter streets." Neither Cowley nor any other devotee of this sort of analysis has ever stopped to consider that Prohibition was in force in the twenties and that Repeal occurred in the thirties. For the writers who believe that America's moral character changed significantly after the Crash are more interested in pursuing alcoholic metaphors than in thinking about alcoholic facts.

12
The First Lady's Lady Friend

Lorena Hickok, who as a child was beaten and raped by her father and who as a young woman came to love Eleanor Roosevelt with a passionate intensity, was often jealous and resentful of the young men whom Mrs. Roosevelt gathered around her in the later years of her life. Miss Hickok seems to have particularly disliked the writer Joseph P. Lash. Thus when Mrs. Roosevelt died in 1962 and Lash undertook to write the story of her partnership with her husband, Miss Hickok denied him access to the letters she had exchanged with Mrs. Roosevelt. "Good old Joe," she vowed, is not "going to get his hot little hands into my papers."

And now, from beyond the grave, Miss Hickok has succeeded in totally demolishing the credibility of Lash's argument in *Eleanor and Franklin* (1971) that in the wake of FDR's love affair with her own social secretary in the summer of 1917 Mrs. Roosevelt realized "she could not achieve fulfillment through someone else," but that in the 1930s this "woman of sorrow" found a substitute satisfaction in rendering "a service of love to her stricken country." In the process of reducing Lash to trash,

Reprinted by permission from *The Times Literary Supplement*, July 11, 1980.

Miss Hickok has also disposed of Arthur M. Schlesinger, Jr.'s contention that Mrs. Roosevelt ultimately triumphed over her debilitating self-doubts through "a terrifying exertion of self-discipline" and an "incomparable and incessant self-control." For the Hickok-Roosevelt correspondence makes it clear that Mrs. Roosevelt shed the low self-esteem which had afflicted her all of her life at precisely the moment in the early 1930s when she was at last receiving the unqualified love of another human being.

The intermediary through whom Miss Hickok has posthumously discredited the work of uncomprehending male historians is a former reporter for the New York *Times*, Doris Faber, who in the spring of 1978 accepted an assignment to write a brief life of Mrs. Roosevelt. Arriving in Hyde Park, New York, to do research at the Franklin D. Roosevelt Library, Mrs. Faber discovered that only a few days before, as luck would have it, the papers of the late Lorena Hickok had at last been made available to scholars. The papers did not contain the full run of the Hickok-Roosevelt correspondence. Miss Hickok had attempted to reclaim from Mrs. Roosevelt all of the letters she had written to her, but hundreds of them had apparently not been saved. Moreover, fifteen letters by Mrs. Roosevelt which originally had been deposited with the papers had subsequently been removed and burned by Miss Hickok, after she had decided on second thought that they were too indiscreet to be seen by others. Additional letters by Mrs. Roosevelt which were found in Miss Hickok's apartment after her death by a member of her family had also been destroyed, for reasons that remain unclear. Yet for all their lacunae, the papers included the impressive total of 3,360 letters, of which 2,336 were by Mrs. Roosevelt. The bulk of the letters had been written in the 1930s, and the first of them dated from the autumn of 1932, shortly before the presidential election which would thrust a painfully insecure and ungainly woman into a role she contemplated with horror.

The sheer bulk of the Hickok-Roosevelt correspondence startled Mrs. Faber, especially after it became apparent to her that the two women had supplemented their torrential letter-writing with almost nightly telephone calls. But what was far more startling to Mrs. Faber was the gushily romantic language of the letters. Her first reaction to the nature of the relationship which that language implied was to attempt to have the Hickok papers sealed up again until at least the year 2000. When this proved impossible, she decided that she simply could not walk away from a biographical discovery of such magnitude. She would turn the papers into a book. If Miss Hickok had had foreknowledge of the fact that the time bomb she had placed in the FDR Library would eventually be detonated by another woman, it surely would have warmed her lonely heart.

The relationship of Mrs. Roosevelt and Miss Hickok began on a summer morning in 1932. While waiting to learn whether the Democratic convention in Chicago had nominated her husband for president, the wife of the governor of New York invited two reporters from the Associated Press to have breakfast with her in the Executive Mansion in Albany. As they left the mansion a short time later, one of the reporters turned to the other and said, "That woman is unhappy about something." The speaker was Lorena Hickok, who knew something about unhappiness herself.

As a child in the upper Middle West, Miss Hickok had conceived a bitter scorn for her mother and an implacable hatred of her father. "I kept wondering all through those childhood years," she later recalled, "why my mother, who was ... just as big as my father, let him do the things he did." A man of maniacal temper, Hickok was incapable of holding on to any sort of job for long, and as he hauled his family from one scruffy town to the next in quest of new employment, he took out his rage in extraordinary acts of aggression against the members of his household. One day, for instance, he became angry at the sight of his small daughter biting her fingernails. Grabbing Lorena's hand, "he thrust the tips of my fingers into my mouth, and made me bite on them, holding my jaws together with his big, strong hands, until the tears rolled down my cheeks." Soon, he began to whip and beat her, sometimes going after her with a stave out of a butter keg. On one occasion when Mrs. Hickok protested that he might kill Lorena, he hurled a chair at his spouse by way of reply. By the time Lorena was fourteen, her father had sexually violated her and her mother was dead. That the woman with whom Mr. Hickok had taken up shortly decided to send Lorena out into the world as a hired girl in a succession of other people's homes was in one sense another act of cruelty; yet it was also a great blessing for the child to be free at last of her father's sadistic grip. Years later, when Miss Hickok was informed that he had committed suicide and she was asked to contribute money for funeral expenses, her reply was, "Send him to the glue factory!"

In 1918, eleven years after starting work as a maid, Lorena Hickok had metamorphosed into a star reporter for the Minneapolis *Tribune.* A big, bluff, and hearty woman, she was very much "one of the boys" in the newspaper's city room. While continuing to work for the *Tribune,* Lorena also enrolled as a freshman at the University of Minnesota, where her powerhouse manner and appearance soon caught the attention of a small-statured, extremely shy, superlatively wealthy young woman, two years her senior, named Ella Morse, who was dabbling with English courses at the university and trying to write poetry. Almost immediately the two young women decided to take an apartment together in the swank Leamington Hotel, Ella having offered to pay the bills. For eight years they were inseparable. Then in 1926 they moved to San Francisco, where Lorena intended to write novels. But while Lorena sat at home, cursing her lack of imagination and crumpling page after page, Ella renewed her acquaintance with a widower whom she had known years before. They eloped to Arizona, and Lorena was crushed. When she renewed her newspaper career in New York a short time later, she had no expectation of ever falling in love again.

Eleanor Roosevelt's mother, like Lorena Hickok's mother, was named Anna. That fact may have been the only exact similarity between their lives which the two women discovered during their long talks together in the fall of 1932, talks which had been made possible by Miss Hickok's suggestion to the Associated Press that she should be allowed to cover the activities of the wife of the Democratic candidate for president. Yet if Mrs. Roosevelt's experiences had been very different from Miss Hickok's, she, too, had known heartbreak, early and late. In its own genteel way, the marriage of her parents had been as thoroughgoing a disaster as the union of Mr. and Mrs. Hickok. Eleanor's father was an attractive but indolent man whose excessive drinking so offended his coldly proper wife that after several tense years she all but banished him from her sight. Only sporadically did Eleanor see the father whom she adored after she grew beyond infancy, and when she did see him, his attention to her was so erratic that she felt even more unsure of his love. Before her tenth birthday he was dead: the fantasy that he would some day desert her forever was now fulfilled. In her grief the child was unable to turn to anyone, for her mother, too, was dead, while the grandmother into whose care she had been delivered was a woman of storybook strictness who had no interest in consolation. The orphan, to be sure, had aunts, but their idea of establishing rapport with their niece was to call her "the ugly duckling."

From the day of her wedding to Franklin Roosevelt, Eleanor received further disparagement from a domineering and possessive mother-in-law, whose side was often taken by her son. In the course of the next dozen years, Eleanor found further reason for distrusting herself in her manifest ineptitude as a mother. Then in 1918 she learned of her husband's romance with Lucy Mercer. Once again, Eleanor Roosevelt had not been able to hold the attention of a man she loved. During the 1920s, Mrs. Roosevelt increasingly sought out the company of women friends, two of whom were probably lesbians. Whether consciously or unconsciously, she seemed to be looking for a new kind of love life, but in any event she did not find it, and her sense of inadequacy did not abate. In contrast to the tough and self-assured Lorena Hickok, who in spite of her emotional wounds rebuilt her journalistic career to the point where she was considered one of the top wire-service reporters in the country, Mrs. Roosevelt was so shy and nervous that she even doubted her ability to discharge the ceremonial duties of a politician's wife. Thus on the day of the presidential nomination speeches at the Democratic convention in 1932, she sent a letter to two friends, in which she poured out her anguish. She simply "could not live" in the White House, she exclaimed. Shortly thereafter, she had breakfast with two reporters from the Associated Press, one of whom spotted her unhappiness. Because the reporter was herself unhappy, she felt drawn to Mrs. Roosevelt and resolved to rearrange her journalistic schedule so as to see her again. The transformation of a doubt-scarred ugly duckling into the most admired woman of her time was about to begin.

By the time Franklin Roosevelt was inaugurated president on March 4, 1933, his wife and Miss Hickok were deliriously in love. "Hick darling, All day I've thought of you & another birthday I *will* be with you.... Oh! I want to put my arms around you, I ache to hold you close. Your ring is a great comfort. I look at it & I think she does love me or I wouldn't be wearing it!" (ER to LH, March 7, 1933). "Just telephoned you. Oh! it is good to hear your voice, when it sounds right no one can make me so happy" (ER to LH, March 8, 1933). "My pictures are nearly all up & I have you in my sitting room where I can look at you most of my waking hours! I can't kiss you so I kiss your picture good-night and good morning!" (ER to LH, March 9, 1933). "I've been trying today to bring back your face—to remember just *how* you look.... Most closely I remember your eyes, with a kind of teasing smile in them, and the feeling of that soft spot just northeast of the corner of your mouth against my lips: I wonder what we'll do when we meet—what we'll say. Well—I'm rather proud of us, aren't you? I think we've done rather well" (LH to ER, December 5, 1933). "I wish I could lie down beside you tonight — take you in my arms" (ER to LH, September 1, 1934).

Did Lorena Hickok initiate Eleanor Roosevelt into the pleasures of Sapphic sex? As the two women lay entwined in one another's arms, were orifices penetrated, were orgasms achieved? In *The Life of Lorena Hickok, E.R.'s Friend,* Doris Faber cannot bring herself to formulate these questions explicitly; nevertheless, she is mesmerized by them, and with many a blush and embarrassed gulp she keeps returning to euphemistic versions of them throughout her book. Whether out of honest conviction or out of fear of angering the priestly guardians of Rooseveltian memory, she repeatedly rejects the idea that the answer to these questions could possibly be yes. Yet almost every time she does, she tacks on a highly ambivalent afterthought, as if she were trying to take the curse off a misrepresentation of what she really believes. What was the relationship, she asks, in her typically roundabout fashion, that was symbolized by the sapphire ring belonging to Lorena Hickok that Eleanor Roosevelt proudly wore? Until recently, Mrs. Faber answers,

> it would have been all but unthinkable to raise such a question involving a woman of Eleanor Roosevelt's stature. Indeed that word—*unthinkable*!—was the reaction of the senior archivists at Hyde Park when they first scanned the Papers of

> Lorena Hickok. To them, the effusively affectionate passages in numerous letters were the expression of just an intense, if unusually belated schoolgirl crush. At least with regard to E.R. herself, this verdict is, I believe, essentially justified. The preponderance of the evidence, and the total context of her life, does support it. Nevertheless, there undoubtedly were nuances of less naiveté in her relationship with Hick; their correspondence contains dozens of passages that offer some grounds for such an assumption.

Strikingly absent from this tortuous piece of analysis is any acknowledgment of how passionate the letters are, or any consideration of the question of whether Lorena Hickok was sexually importunate. Mrs. Faber says that the archivists' verdict of schoolgirlish innocence is justified "with regard to E.R. herself" and leaves it to the reader to wonder whether LH would have been satisfied with exploring the soft spot northeast of her lover's mouth.

What is most unfortunate, however, about Mrs. Faber's obsessive concern with "Did they or didn't they?" is not her unwillingness to pursue the question as hard as she might have, but rather her certainty that no other issue is more important. Only fleetingly does she give evidence of realizing that the great interest of the Hickok-Roosevelt correspondence consists in its revelation of how Eleanor Roosevelt broke free of a lifetime of self-doubt. In the aftermath of her husband's electoral victory in November, 1932, Mrs. Roosevelt quietly observed in an interview with the woman reporter with whom she had recently established a clandestine relationship: "For him I am deeply and sincerely glad. I would not have had it go otherwise. And now I shall start to work on my own salvation." In those softly spoken words, one can already hear a new sound of confidence and determination, and if one pays attention to the tone of Mrs. Roosevelt's voice in the letters written to Miss Hickok across the next two years, one can hear an ever stronger note of self-confidence, swelling triumphantly out of her odes to joy. The more pages Mrs. Roosevelt fills with protestations of how much her secret private life has come to mean to her, the more pages she devotes to telling Miss Hickok about her rapidly expanding public life. The Hickok-Roosevelt correspondence not only chronicles a love affair, it traces the emergence of the most active First Lady in American history.

Mrs. Roosevelt focused her newly developed political assurance on the alleviation of human misery. That development, too, has a vital connection to her relationship with Miss Hickok. As Henry James demonstrated in *The Bostonians* almost a century ago, the political reformer and the sexual deviant can sometimes be found at the same address. Olive Chancellor, the lesbian protagonist of the novel, looks at the world from the point of view of a psychic outcast; her fierce opposition to the social status quo is the logical complement of her personal sense of marginality and alienation. That both Mrs. Roosevelt and Miss Hickok were extraordinarily concerned with the suffering of poor Americans in the 1930s can be partially explained by the fact that Miss Hickok was forced to give up her newspaper career in order to continue her romance with Mrs. Roosevelt, that she thereupon went to work for Harry Hopkins's Federal Emergency Relief Administration—which gave her detailed knowledge of the poor—and that she passed on everything she learned to Mrs. Roosevelt. Their exchanges on this subject, however, did not take place in a vacuum. They took place in the context of a love affair which the participants had to keep secret lest they be disgraced and which had been built upon mutual confessions of victimization and despair. For reasons which Henry James would have had no trouble in understanding, the special nature of their relationship caused these women to be particularly attuned to the plight of helpless victims of the Depression.

Because Mrs. Faber did not develop the significant implications of her subject, her book must be rated a failure. She does deserve appreciation, though, for a responsible presentation of the evidence she stumbled upon. Thanks to her, future historians will be able to write vastly more believable appraisals of Eleanor Roosevelt than those we now have. Unfortunately, the most influential American reviewers of *E. R.'s Friend* have not acknowledged this fact. Indeed, the most influential of them all, Arthur Schlesinger, Jr., has done his best to bury the story of Lorena Hickok in an unmarked grave—as Miss Hickok, I suspect, knew long ago that he would.

For Schlesinger is the blindly loyal guardian of a pantheon of political heroes whose human failings he is prepared to defend at no matter what sacrifice of factual or psychological plausibility. As a historian, Schlesinger can be impressive. His description, for instance, in *The Age of Roosevelt* of the permutations of New Deal policy makes sense of the subject at the same time that it does justice to its well-nigh fantastic complexity, whereas other New Deal historians have been defeated by the task.

But whenever Schlesinger feels called upon to defend his heroes, he is apt to say very foolish things. One of his worst moments occurred in 1966, shortly after Jonathan Daniels published a memoir called *The Time between the Wars,* which blew open the story of Franklin Roosevelt's relationship with Lucy Mercer. In an article he at once dashed off for the *Ladies' Home Journal,* Schlesinger did his best to hose down and wash away this blemish on the Rooseveltian escutcheon. If Lorena Hickok happened to read the article, it must have given her several minutes of bitter merriment.

In Schlesinger's judgment, the story told by Daniels had "been wrested terribly out of proportion" by the press. We must remember, he said, that Franklin Roosevelt and Lucy Mercer were "reared in the last years of the Victorian era." Theirs was a "Henry Jamesian drama of renunciation" which "reflects credit on everyone involved." Now, even if we ignore the fact that a good many of Henry James's novels and stories deal with extremely sordid examples of secret sex, this argument is nonsense. The romance itself certainly did not reflect credit on Franklin Roosevelt and Lucy Mercer, and while they shortly gave up seeing one another, there is no evidence that they did so for moral reasons which demand our admiration.

The idea that Franklin Roosevelt and Lucy Mercer were governed in their maturity by the moral code of their Victorian childhoods also makes no sense; their romance was a product of the very different atmosphere of the First World War.

Schlesinger looks even more foolish in the paragraphs in which he discusses Eleanor Roosevelt—or rather, in the paragraphs in which he avoids discussing Eleanor Roosevelt. Jonathan Daniels had maintained that Franklin's love affair "almost broke his marriage to Eleanor," and the tone of voice in which Schlesinger conveys Daniels's contention to his readers makes it plain that he does not agree with it. Schlesinger acknowledges that when Franklin Roosevelt began to exhibit delight in having Lucy Mercer around, this "no doubt . . . worried Eleanor Roosevelt, as it would any wife." Having got that minimizing admission off his chest, Schlesinger then proceeds to ignore

Eleanor Roosevelt. The question of whether Franklin was going to divorce Eleanor and marry Lucy is examined by Schlesinger from Franklin's point of view and from Lucy's, but not from Eleanor's. The fact that Franklin and Lucy kept in touch over the years, that she was an invited guest at his first inauguration, is acknowledged—and morally justified—by Schlesinger without regard to how Eleanor might have felt. ("Oh, Arthur," I seem to hear Lorena Hickok saying, as she looks up from her copy of the *Ladies' Home Journal*, "if only you knew what Eleanor and I were doing during those inaugural days when Franklin had the audacity to have Lucy Mercer at his side!")

Only toward the end of the article does Schlesinger take up Daniels's assertion that Eleanor was "bitter and jealous of Lucy" through all the years when Lucy was apt to be Franklin's guest in the White House or at Bernard Baruch's South Carolina plantation. Schlesinger's reply to Daniels is the part of the article that Lorena Hickok would have liked best, I think. As to Eleanor's feelings, Schlesinger says: "How can anyone possibly know?"

> Mrs. Roosevelt certainly retained all her life a suspicion of stylish and, as she thought, frivolous ladies. But she was a woman of immense discipline, perception and wisdom. She understood that other women could supply something—some instinct for the gaiety and fun of life—which her husband needed and she could not give him.

Fun for Franklin, discipline for Eleanor.

But what is even more distressing than Schlesinger's total blindness to Eleanor Roosevelt's emotional needs is his failure to comprehend that the story of Franklin Roosevelt's betrayal of his wife casts light on his political behavior. Instead of seeking to play down the story, Schlesinger should have used it to reach a fuller understanding than he has thus far displayed in his *Age of Roosevelt* volumes of the dark side of FDR's conduct in the White House. An airy duplicity, a brazen hypocrisy, were hallmarks of the Rooseveltian presidency. Dangers at home and abroad may have necessitated such conduct, but the point is that FDR was an instinctive deceiver and always had been. One also has to wonder whether the president, with his uncanny capacity for sensing what other people were thinking, came to suspect Eleanor of deceiving him with Lorena Hickok. A man in a wheelchair might have had a particularly urgent desire to know for sure. Can it be that FDR's complicated relations with the FBI began with a request to J. Edgar Hoover to place his own wife under surveillance?

When the New York *Times* broke the news story that a biography of Lorena Hickok was about to be published, the indefatigable Schlesinger sprang to his typewriter once again. Forty-eight hours later, the Washington *Post* carried his byline above a special article. I could not care less, he began, what Eleanor Roosevelt's sex life was like—but the very alacrity with which he had written showed that he cared very deeply. We have to remember, he continued, that Mrs. Roosevelt was reared in the last years of the Victorian era, when women were apt to talk in a way that modern interpreters can easily misunderstand. It was the same sort of argument he had made in the *Ladies' Home Journal* piece. A few months later, Schlesinger reviewed *E. R.'s Friend* on the front page of the *New York Times Book Review*. I could not care less, he protested, what Mrs. Roosevelt's sex life was like, but we have to remember that she was reared in the last years of the Victorian era.

13
Malcolm Cowley Forgets

Almost fifty years ago, Malcolm Cowley remarked in regard to *Exile's Return,* his forthcoming memoir of the 1920s, that "There is always the temptation, in writing about your own past, to interpret the facts discreetly with the purpose of showing what a wholly likeable fellow you were." In *The Dream of the Golden Mountains,* his recently published memoir of the 1930s, Cowley has succumbed to that temptation even more blatantly than he did in *Exile's Return.* Supposedly, the book is based on the articles and reviews he regularly contributed to the *New Republic* during the Depression years, but the image of himself he presents to us in *The Golden Mountains* is rather different from the man of the *New Republic* pieces. Although Cowley finally forswore his political fellow traveling in 1940, he still has not acquired an adequate respect for historical truth. Just as he once ignored the patent falsity of the defendants' confessions at the Moscow purge trials in order to argue that the trials had been eminently just, so in *The Golden Mountains* he has not hesitated to consign unpleasant facts about what he said and did in the thirties to an Orwellian memory hole. Cowley is

Reprinted by permission from *The American Spectator,* October 1980.

now in his eighties, and he has posterity very much in mind. If he has his way, history will not remember him as the man whom Eugene Lyons described in *The Red Decade* (1941) as "the Number One literary executioner for Stalin in America."

What the author of *The Golden Mountains* wants us to find most likeable about him is his honesty. One man is always representative of an age, he says of himself in the preface, "when he gives honest testimony about what he has felt and observed." On page 82, he recalls the nature of his literary ambitions in the thirties—"I wanted to write honestly." On page 228, he reminds us that in *Exile's Return* "I had taken the risk of speaking candidly about my own life." But Cowley's campaign to persuade us of his honesty is not merely carried out by bald assertion. Through the details he chooses to emphasize about his personality, he also seeks to convince us that he is a man to be trusted. "And that author, that observer who is trying to be candid about himself," Cowley writes, "what sort of person was he in 1930?" From a Harvard man who had spent most of the 1920s in Europe, we might expect an answer emphasizing his cosmopolitanism. But, as Benjamin Franklin discovered long ago, a cosmopolite can often enhance his credibility by pretending to be a rustic, and this lesson has apparently not been lost on the author of *The Golden Mountains*. Without qualification, Cowley insists that

> he was still a country boy after spending most of his life in cities; he had a farmer's blunt hands . . . . He never forgot that he came of people without pretensions, not quite members of the respectable middle class. He was slow of speech and had a farmer's large silences, though he was not slow-witted; people were fooled sometimes.

Along with his trustworthiness, Cowley would have us admire his benignity. Other historians have stressed the combativeness of American intellectual life in the early 1930s, but Cowley remembers the battles of those days as "good fun," and he plunged into them, he says, with the exhilaration of a college halfback diving into a scrimmage. Only gradually did he realize that "real blows were being exchanged by others." Did this realization then cause Cowley himself to turn nasty? *The Golden Mountains* offers no evidence that it did. Thus Cowley repeatedly praises John Dos Passos and Edmund Wilson without ever once suggesting that his earlier opinions of these writers had sometimes been less than complimentary. And while he freely admits that William Phillips, Philip Rahv, James T. Farrell, and other leftists sometimes "bludgeoned or shillelaghed me," as he ruefully says about Farrell's attacks, we get only the faintest sense of why they were so angry at him, and no sense at all that he ever replied to them in kind. In the confrontation he cites with Phillips and Rahv, for instance, Cowley asserts that, in the face of their comments, "not many [of which] were eulogistic," he was simply "amused and polite."

Yet while Cowley does not want us to fail to notice the contrast he alleges between his own manner and that of his critics, the principal business of his memoir is not to snipe at ancient adversaries. Indeed, more often than not Cowley is at pains to evade the issue of sectarian differences on the Left. Thus in his discussion of the Communist-front League of American Writers, the impression is created that anti-fascist intellectuals were indiscriminately welcomed into the organization and that no one was ever excluded or condemned for criticizing the Communist party or the USSR, whereas the reverse was true. For the overriding purpose of *The Golden Mountains* is to rehabilitate the myth that the 1930s was an era of revolutionary brotherhood. What Cowley wants us to remember above all else about the thirties is that it was a time when hundreds of writers were caught up in a dream of a new social order—a dream of the golden mountains. "Our right fists raised in the Red Front salute," says Cowley, we marched forward toward "a classless society." The Soviet Union had "shown us the way."

The vision of a marching band of brothers so dominates Cowley's book that vitally important individuals frequently get lost in the shuffle, including, not least, the author. Repeatedly, the narrative "I" gives way to "we," or "they," or "the writers," or "the members," or "the delegates." And as the decade progresses and the bickering of the brotherhood intensifies to the point where it can no longer be ignored, Cowley is still apt to speak of anonymous groupings rather than of specific people.

> As for the Russian purges, . . . there would never be unanimity about them, except in respect to the general uneasiness they created among left-wing intellectuals. Even those who believed that the defendants were guilty of the crimes to which they confessed couldn't help feeling that the evidence

> revealed a disheartening state of affairs in Russia. As one trial followed another, more and more persons rejected the confessions, and soon they would also reject the Communist Party. But there was no unanimity even among the rejecters.

This passage does not even make clear where Cowley himself stood on the issue of the purges, but it does make clear why the author of an ostensibly personal book should have found it convenient to speak as often as he does in an impersonal vein. What better way, after all, for Cowley to avoid taking responsibility for certain positions he once held than to hide himself in a crowd?

Readers who are eager to meet the historical Malcolm Cowley will have to turn from *The Golden Mountains* to the relevant volumes of the *New Republic*. But readers who are concerned with the more interesting question of how a man goes about creating a historical myth about himself will want to read memoir and magazine in conjunction. The first of the many discrepancies between the two involves an obscure writer named Ralph Borsodi. On page 6 of *The Golden Mountains*, Cowley genially recalls him as one of the many visitors who came to the offices of the *New Republic* in the early years of the Depression to describe their schemes for remaking America. Borsodi's idea was to resettle millions of urban families on five-acre subsistence homesteads. The difficulty with the project, Cowley observes with wry good humor, is that it required capital, a part-time job in the city, and a cooperative wife like Mrs. Borsodi.

When we turn to Cowley's assessment of Borsodi in the *New Republic*, we find a different point of view. The writer's crackpot scheme did not strike Cowley as at all funny, it infuriated him. With the sort of rhetorical overkill which at the end of the thirties would belatedly prompt Edmund Wilson to castigate him for practicing "Stalinist character assassination of the most reckless and libelous sort," Cowley tore into the harmless crank as "a dangerous messiah." The reason for his fury was that as a back-to-the-land enthusiast Borsodi regarded the Soviet Union's titanic effort to industrialize as a terrible mistake. "He speaks with contempt and hatred," said Cowley, his voice quivering with contempt and hatred, "of everything done in Russia."

But of all the false impressions about himself that Cowley

creates in *The Golden Mountains*, the most audacious is the proposition that he was fully committed to the Communist cause for only a few years. By 1935, he asserts, he had developed "doubts about what the party was doing in America and in Russia too." His *New Republic* pieces, however, demonstrate a continuing and unqualified adoration of Stalin. On April 24, 1935, for instance, Cowley drew a sneering contrast between the socialist H. G. Wells's utopian fixation on the "golden future" and the Soviet dictator's awesomely impressive concentration on the "iron present." (If as a memoirist Cowley had been more true to the man he used to be, he would not have employed a golden metaphor in the title of his book, inasmuch as his imagination in the thirties was enthralled by a baser metal.)

One week later, Cowley celebrated May Day with a review of the Communist Anna Louise Strong's *I Change Worlds*. With glowing approval, the literary editor of the *New Republic* recapitulated Miss Strong's account of a high-level conference held in Moscow on the problem of what to do about the *Moscow News*, a somewhat unsuccessful illustrated weekly for American engineers and tourists, of which Miss Strong was the managing editor. Among those present at the conference was Stalin. "Stalin did not frown or pound his fist on the table," wrote Cowley, eagerly paraphrasing Miss Strong,

> he gave no commands; he scarcely made suggestions. He merely listened, asked people what they wanted, what they thought, but his questions went straight to the heart of things. Suddenly all the difficulties had vanished. It was decided to transform The Moscow News into a bigger and livelier paper.... These were not Stalin's orders. The decisions seemed to come from everybody and to express a common will.... [Thus was Miss Strong] given a sudden and lasting insight into the whole soviet system of administration.... A system like this—which Miss Strong describes more intelligently than any other writer on Russia—seems tyrannical to people on the outside, whereas, to those millions who help to formulate policies, it seems the most democratic system that ever existed.

On September 11, 1935, Cowley dismissed George Kitchin's *Prisoner of the OGPU* as one of the myriad anti-Soviet books currently being published because "Messrs. Hitler, Hearst and their allies" are "frantic" that Western labor movements will take heart from the Soviet experiment. "Liars are paid by them at the best space rates. Old manuscripts are taken out of trunks, dusted off, peppered with atrocities and published as the latest news from Moscow." The real news, according to Cowley, was that "Yes, thank you, our Russian neighbors are doing quite well." With some of their major industrial and agricultural problems at last out of the way, the Soviet leaders were now "turning their attention to minor products—flower beds, jazz bands, joy, light wines and the secret ballot."

Cowley's whitewash of legal murder in Moscow appeared on April 7, 1937, in a review of *The Case of the Anti-Soviet Trotskyite Center,* issued by the USSR's Commissariat of Justice. That the defendants had displayed a Dostoevskian eagerness to confess to the most outlandish crimes was an idea without merit, in Cowley's opinion. "The behavior of the prisoners on the witness stand . . . was certainly that of guilty men lacking popular support and ashamed of the deeds that had brought them there." Far from being Dostoevskian, their behavior was "normal under the circumstances." It was only "their actions before arrest that belong in a Dostoevsky novel." The confessions, Cowley reiterated, were "undoubtedly sincere." As for the indictment, the major part of it was "proved beyond much possibility of doubting it." A year later, in a review of another volume of stenographic evidence about another trial, Cowley again was impressed by the "enormous accumulation of evidence" against the defendants, and again was contemptuous of the forced-confession theory. "There were no Tibetan drugs, no subtle Chinese tortures." The real question, he opined, "is not why the conspirators pleaded guilty, but why they conspired."

During the remaining months of 1938, Cowley demonstrated his unwavering devotion to Stalinism with a defense of the political censorship of literature and a scathing critique of the anti-Stalinist *Partisan Review,* which its editors quite rightly termed "a malicious and politically motivated attack."

Throughout 1939, Cowley still kept the faith, despite the announcement of the Nazi-Soviet Pact. Thus in October of that year he described Stalin's embrace of Hitler not as the final betrayal of a revolution but as the "experiment" of a realist. The most shameful exhibition, however, of what Cowley was prepared to do for Stalin in 1939 was his participation in the literary execution of John Dos Passos.

When the second volume of *U.S.A.* was published in 1932, Cowley had praised the book as "a landmark in American fiction"; Dos Passos's writing, he said, had "conviction, power, and a sense of depth, of striking through surfaces to the real forces beneath them." The reviewer also had warm words for the third volume of the trilogy when it appeared in 1936. On February 9, 1938, Cowley again took space in the *New Republic* to express his admiration for *U.S.A.* Sixteen months later, however, he and a number of other reviewers came down on Dos Passos's latest book, *Adventures of a Young Man,* like the knife blades of a rank of guillotines. As James T. Farrell shortly thereafter pointed out in an indignant essay in the *American Mercury,* Dos Passos had been judged on political, not literary, grounds. Having become disillusioned with the Communist party's cynical manipulation of causes and issues, Dos Passos had written a novel to say farewell to the Left. *Adventures of a Young Man* had both the strengths and the weaknesses of all of Dos Passos's social fiction. While its portraits of people were crude, the narrative had power and conviction and it struck through surfaces to the real forces beneath them. But because the book was much too strongly anti-Communist for prevailing Popular-Front tastes, it was condemned as a weak and inferior work. Cowley and company's reception of the novel, said Farrell, "reads like a warning to writers not to stray off the reservation of the Stalinist-controlled League of American Writers."

The thirties, in W. H. Auden's phrase, was "a low dishonest decade." One of the representative men of that era was the literary editor of the *New Republic,* but unlike Whittaker Chambers and other erstwhile servants of tyranny, he has not sought to redeem himself by coming clean about his former activities. His memoir of the thirties is a cover-up. To the multiple dishonesties of Cowley's career we must also add the leading reviews of *The Golden Mountains,* all of which praised it for precisely the quality it most conspicuously lacks. In the *New Republic,* R. W. B. Lewis spoke of the "cogency" of the memoir. In the New York *Times,* Alfred Kazin saluted the author as an "honest writer." In the Washington *Post,* Daniel Aaron asserted that "among the memorialists of the 1930s, Malcolm Cowley is one of the most reliable and informative."

Moreover, Aaron added, Cowley has "never confused literary standards with political loyalties." The memoirist's "easy idiomatic prose," said Aaron, "perfectly conveys his air of speculative detachment."

What in the world could have possessed these reviewers to make such irresponsible statements? The case of R. W. B. Lewis can be quickly dismissed. He simply does not know what he is talking about. The dishonesty of his review of Cowley's book consists of a pretension to an expertise about American intellectual life in the 1930s that he does not possess. The cases of Kazin and Aaron, however, are more complicated. There can be no doubt that both men are familiar with every piece of journalism that Cowley published in the period. They were certainly in a position, therefore, to detect the disingenuousness of *The Golden Mountains*.

But in order to expose Cowley, Kazin would have been obliged to acknowledge certain unflattering truths about his own reviewing in the thirties, including his participation in the literary execution of Dos Passos, and as Kazin's autobiographies amply demonstrate, he is a man with no taste for self-criticism. The facts about this starry-eyed opportunist are these. In the late thirties and early forties, he was a close associate of Cowley's. Then during the Cold War he claimed to have broken with Cowley over the Moscow trials, although there is no public record of such a break. Now that Cowley in his old age has become an object of veneration in many quarters (like Lillian Hellman, he has been greeted at public gatherings with standing ovations), Kazin can think of only complimentary things to say about him.

Twenty years ago, Aaron interviewed or corresponded with almost every famous literary radical in the country, in the course of working on a book called *Writers on the Left*. The experience of becoming acquainted with these legendary creatures was apparently so thrilling to Aaron that it permanently disabled his critical faculties. In a severely disapproving review of *Writers on the Left*, William Phillips of the *Partisan Review* called attention to Aaron's failure to offer any sort of judgmatic evaluation of the people he had written about. "Aaron's seeming lack of bias actually produces a biased view of the 30s," Phillips pointed out, "the bias coming from the assumption that something called the 'record' is identical with the history." Clearly troubled by Phillips's review, Aaron published a long and defensive essay a few years later in which he announced that his attitude toward critical scholarship was the same as that of the ancient lady who owns the Aspern Papers in Henry James's story: "The truth is God's, it isn't man's; we had better leave it alone. Who can judge of it?—who can say?" If Malcolm Cowley says he has tried to write about the 1930s as candidly as he could, what right does a mere reviewer have to say that he has not?

14

Versions of Walter Lippmann

When a military conscription bill finally cleared the U.S. Congress in May, 1917, one of the measure's earliest and warmest advocates in the world of journalism suddenly realized that he himself might very well be called to the colors. The superbly healthy twenty-seven-year-old bachelor thereupon wrote to Secretary of War Newton D. Baker asking for an exemption. After searching his soul as candidly as he knew how, said Walter Lippmann, he had decided that he could better serve the nation in some other way than as a soldier. Worry about his parents—in whose New York City home he still lived—also affected his decision. "My father is dying," he informed the secretary, "and my mother is absolutely alone in the world. She does not know what his condition is, and I cannot tell anyone for fear it would become known."

In *Walter Lippmann and the American Century,* Ronald Steel adds to his account of this episode the passing observation that Lippmann's father "was not to die for another ten years." As if unaware of the disturbing implications of this tidbit, Steel

Reprinted by permission from *Commentary,* Volume 70, Number 4 (October 1980).

then drops the subject of Lippmann's letter to Baker and hastens on to the next item of business on his rapidly unfolding agenda. It apparently did not occur to him that readers interested in the moral history of a moralist might be curious to know the nature of the ailment that Lippmann's father was suffering from in the spring of 1917, and whether the sick man really did appear to be at death's door. Why Lippmann wanted Baker to know that he had not told anyone else about his father's condition is another suspicious point that Steel glides blithely past. As for Lippmann's expressed compassion for his mother's loneliness, it, too, raises a question, for Daisy Lippmann was an extremely imperious woman. While her only child had always been comforted by his mother's announced belief that he could accomplish anything he set his mind to do, he also felt threatened, as he grew out of early boyhood, by her dominating personality. From adolescence onward he had therefore contrived to put an emotional distance between them. Was the concern about his mother that Lippmann voiced to Baker the product of a belated guilt feeling, or did it represent a further effort to manipulate the sympathies of the secretary of war? Our ability to answer this question would certainly be improved if we knew what, if anything, Lippmann did to ease his mother's loneliness in 1927 when she finally did lose her husband, but unfortunately Steel has not bothered to investigate this matter either.

It also seems not to have occurred to him to keep reminding us about the letter to Baker in the course of describing the events immediately following. If Lippmann had allowed himself to be drafted, he might have been able to stay on with his parents for several months before his number came up. But the price of his successful attempt to dodge the draft was that he leave home without delay, and he paid it without a qualm. Three days after sending the letter to Baker, he joyfully accepted the secretary's answering invitation to join his staff in a civilian capacity. Less than three weeks later, Lippmann was on the train for Washington.

Steel's failure to deal analytically with the letter to Baker is altogether characteristic of his lack of biographical imagination. Time and again, he misses the chance to confront the complexities of the man he is writing about. No other journalist in our history has ever written more thoughtfully or more beautifully about democracy in America than Lippmann did in such books as *Public Opinion* and *The Public Philosophy*. At the same time, however, that he dedicated his mind to democratic problems, he defined himself as a superior being to whom the democratic obligations of ordinary citizens did not apply. A similar contradiction marked his career as a moralist. Not content with the authority that accrued to him as the most well-known political commentator of the twentieth century, Lippmann sought to be recognized as the conscience of mankind. Yet while he held the conduct of other people to a very high standard indeed, mankind's self-appointed conscience was himself guilty of conscienceless acts.

Because Steel has been unwilling—or unable—to think about these contradictions, he has very little sense of the personality pattern they help to describe. The strength, such as it is, of his biography lies in its command of the purely external facts of Lippmann's life.

From the time that he entered Harvard with the famous class of 1910—the class to which T. S. Eliot, John Reed, Robert Edmond Jones, H. V. Kaltenborn, Bronson Cutting, Heywood Broun, and Alan Seeger also belonged—it was clear that Lippmann was one of the most amazing young men in the world. Before he was old enough to vote, the brilliant and the powerful had begun to beat a path to his door, as they would keep on doing for the rest of his life. A literary career that would eventually be marked by a dozen major books, several hundred articles, and several thousand editorials and columns was launched with a series of essays in the *Harvard Monthly*, one of which so enthralled Professor William James that he sought out Lippmann in his dormitory and congratulated him. The visiting British lecturer Graham Wallas felt so indebted to the ideas of this *Wunderkind* that after his return to Britain he dedicated a book to him. Professor George Santayana was so impressed by Lippmann's promise as a philosopher that he invited him to stay on at Harvard as his assistant. When Lincoln Steffens appeared in Cambridge in search of a bright young man to help him with the muckraking pieces he was writing for *Everybody's*, everyone he talked to told him to hire Lippmann.

In 1912, the Socialist mayor of Schenectady, George Lunn, succeeded in persuading Lippmann to become his administrative assistant. A year later, Herbert Croly invited him to join the staff of the newly formed *New Republic*. After the war, Herbert Bayard Swope lured him onto the New York *World*, and in 1924 Lippmann assumed command of the *World's* editorial page. When the *World* was bought by Scripps-Howard in 1931 and merged with the *Telegram*, Lippmann chose from the multitudinous offers that cascaded in on him to become a syndicated columnist for the New York *Herald-Tribune*. For the next thirty-five years, the column brought him a degree of power that no other newspaper pundit has ever matched. On his trips abroad, potentates and sages alike vied for the chance to see him. In Washington, his journalistic influence was in a class by itself.

But what was Lippmann like as a person? *Walter Lippmann and the American Century* conspicuously fails to deal with that vital question. Even though Steel is familiar with thousands of details about Lippmann's career, Lippmann has remained a stranger to him. As a result, he repeatedly gets caught off guard in his narrative by things that Lippmann says or does, and in his confusion all he can think to do is doggedly record them, make a brief statement that pretends to understanding, and move on. Thus when Lippmann decries in his second book, *Drift and Mastery*, the very mode of analysis that informs his first, *A Preface to Politics*, Steel weakly says, "If nothing else, *Drift and Mastery* showed Lippmann's intellectual flexibility, his willingness to jettison old ideas as soon as new ones were at hand." But what was it in Lippmann's makeup that made him so willing to be so flexible—and that would lead him to forswear a staggering number of other enthusiasms in the course of his career? To ascribe his changeableness to intellectual flexibility is simply to restate the problem.

Steel is equally at a loss to account for Lippmann's attitude toward the Jews in Germany in the 1930s. This attitude first appeared in a column written in the spring of 1933, not long after the Nazis began making bonfires out of books written by Jews and "liberals." Hitler is preparing for war, Lippmann warned, and only two factors are holding him in check: fear of the French army and the psychic satisfactions afforded by the pogrom against the Jews. The peculiar implication of the column was that Jewish suffering was protecting the peace of Europe. A week later, Lippmann again addressed himself to events in Germany, this time hailing a speech by Hitler, in which the dictator surprisingly promised that Germany would not seek to settle its political claims by force, as a genuinely statesmanlike address. There will be some who say, wrote Lippmann, that the speech was insincere. "I do not take this view. The truer explanation, I believe, is that we have heard once more, through the fog and the din, the hysteria and the animal passions of a great revolution, the authentic voice of a genuinely civilized people." Uncivilized deeds were being committed every day in Germany, he admitted, but these atrocities did not reflect the whole nature of the German people:

> Who that has studied history and cares for the truth would judge the French people by what went on during the Terror? Or the British people by what happened in Ireland? Or the American people by the hideous record of lynchings? Or the Catholic Church by the Spanish Inquisition? Or Protestantism by the Ku Klux Klan? Or the Jews by their parvenus?

The brutishness of the Nazis, in other words, was a blot on the fair face of civilization, but so was the vulgarity of upstart Jews. Lippmann's placement of the two phenomena on the same moral plane was outrageous, and so was the accompanying innuendo that some of the Jews in Germany had been so pushy that they had brought their persecution upon themselves. In this column, says his plainly shocked biographer, Lippmann went beyond the "celebrated disinterestedness" of most of his work into a "tortured analysis" that was "deeply revealing." Presumably Steel means that the column had revealed something about Lippmann himself. But what was it that was revealed? Steel does not say. Earlier in his book he had called attention to Lippmann's choice of Gentile women as marital partners, to his membership in exclusionistic clubs, and to his steadfast refusal to identify himself with Jewish groups of any kind, so perhaps we are supposed to guess that the self-revelation in question is that Lippmann was ashamed of being Jewish. But shame does not account for the brutal callousness of Lippmann's remarks, any more than intellectual flexibility does for his fickle habit of repudiating his previous opinions. Furthermore, the biographer does not ask himself whether the callousness and the fickleness might somehow have been related.

The Lippmannesque figure who is the central character in Louis Auchincloss's novel, *The House of the Prophet,* observes that in order to write a successful biography a writer must know how to pick and choose among the available materials. Having been Lippmann's lawyer, Auchincloss may very well be in command of as much information about the columnist's life as Steel possesses. But unlike Steel, Auchincloss has known how to pick and choose, for he has a profound understanding of the man he is writing about. As a result, *The House of the Prophet* gives us more insight into Lippmann in 275 pages than *Walter Lippmann and the American Century* does in 600. That comparison, however, is too faint a way to praise Auchincloss's achievement. In the lights and darks of Lippmann's life, Auchincloss has at last found a subject that fully challenges his imaginative gifts. The powerful literary portrait he produced not quite two decades ago in *The Rector of Justin* has now been surpassed both in psychological subtlety and moral significance.

Like *The Rector of Justin, The House of the Prophet* is a fictional biography, told from several different points of view. The biographer who has solicited recollections of Felix Leitner, the famous columnist, from a number of his admirers and detractors, and who is himself the principal narrator, is the great man's long-time and utterly adoring research assistant, Roger Cutter. Through the multiple perspectives of its various narratives, the biography asks us to consider whether Leitner was a sort of intellectual saint, whose exalted mission it was to tell the world the political and moral truth, or a monster of self who had pursued what he thought of as the good things in life—public glory, the joy of writing, the ease of wealth—at no matter what cost to others, so long as their pain did not show enough to spoil his fun. On occasions that range from summer walks on Mount Desert Island to Georgetown dinner parties to a barge trip through the south of France, these polar interpretations of the protagonist's life are expanded and qualified by dramatic illustration and explicit formulation. Perhaps the most penetrating of the many attempts to sum up what made Leitner tick is put forward by his former law partner, Grant Stowe. (Before turning to column writing, Leitner had briefly been a Wall Street lawyer.) Still bitter that his former associate had quickly betrayed the best interests of the firm, Stowe asserts that

> the man was an egotist, pure and simple. He was incapable of conforming to any pattern, noble or ignoble. Sooner or later he was bound to separate himself from the team, whatever team it might be, and redefine himself in relation to it in less than complimentary terms. The reason he was so dangerous was that the pleasure that he derived in separating himself from the team was greater than any material or even moral advantage that he might possibly derive from staying with it.

Although Stowe's analysis is by no means the last word about Leitner, it carries us a long way toward understanding why the columnist was so willing to sever any sort of tie—familial, religious, patriotic, intellectual—that bound him to other people, or even to his own earlier self as expressed in his writings: his extraordinarily self-centered, emotionally stunted personality got a big kick out of betrayals.

Leitner's dissociation of himself from his Jewish heritage is certainly better explained by this appraisal than by the familiar explanation of Lippmann as a social-climbing snob who was ashamed of being Jewish. Leitner himself is witheringly sarcastic about the snob theory. Appalled by the thought that some day a biographer might be so uncomprehending as to write about "my being ashamed of my Jewish heritage, my denial of my past, my cultivation of Wasp society," he exclaims, "Oh, it's too nauseating to think of! Why, in an America that is rapidly approaching classlessness, are our historians and sociologists so obsessed with class distinctions?" Proud Felix Leitner had never been ashamed of anything in his life; if he had decided not to keep up his identity as a Jew, it was for intellectual and spiritual reasons. Yet if the columnist's scorn is sufficient to demolish the charge that his decision to distance himself from Jewish groups and Jewish causes was governed by shame, it is significant that he does not address himself to the possibility that it was governed by pleasure.

His egotistical aversion to team play again seems evident in his successful attempt to avoid army service in 1917. And only a man who found a twisted delight in hurting people who were counting on him could have behaved as Leitner does in the central episode of *The House of the Prophet*, the episode that Leitner's biographer, Roger Cutter, describes as "the single most important emotional and moral event" of the columnist's life, the episode in which two marriages are destroyed and a long-term male friendship ends in devastating humiliation.

Steel's treatment of the parallel episode in Lippmann's life seems much more fictional, in a sense, than Auchincloss's, for the romantic details he chooses to play up, and his lack of a critical attitude toward the "hero" and the "heroine," are the soggy stuff of which stories in magazines like *Woman's Home Companion* and *Good Housekeeping* are made. Walter Lippmann and Hamilton Fish Armstrong, the editor of *Foreign Affairs,* were as close as Damon and Pythias, Steel tells us, except that the friendship was not equal, for Armstrong worshipped the ground that Lippmann walked on. The two men lunched together once or twice a week at the Century Club; they sat together at meetings of the Council on Foreign Relations; they spoke on the phone nearly every day. Moreover, the two friends and their wives, Faye Albertson Lippmann and Helen Byrne Armstrong, often dined *à quatre* in New York and visited each other's country homes, and in 1934 they went off together for a tour of Egypt and the Mediterranean. Then one afternoon in May, 1937, Armstrong phoned Lippmann to say that he was held up at the office. Would Walter mind taking Helen to dinner? Lippmann took her to the Rainbow Room in the newly constructed tower of Rockefeller Center. Over drinks, he began to tell Helen how lonely he felt in his marriage. "She listened gravely, asked questions delicately, softly laid her hand on his. They drank more wine than they were used to. They danced on the crowded floor, holding each other closer than they ever had before."

Onward the narrative oozes. Lippmann and Helen "plunged wildly" into an affair. Armstrong soon found out about it, but was "willing to forgive all." The lovers then discovered that they could not give one another up, and so Lippmann wrote Faye a letter, informing her that he wanted a divorce. "I do not know," the letter began, "whether this will seem to you an indirect way of dealing with the affair." In the one sentence in his account of the scandal that has a critical bite to it, Steel calls the beginning of that letter "a gem of an understatement." In November, 1937, with his own divorce almost final and Helen preparing to go to Reno, Lippmann also wrote a letter to Armstrong. His former friend refused to read it, however, and in the thirty-five years that remained to him as editor of *Foreign*

Affairs he never again permitted Lippmann's name to appear in the magazine.

The characters in *The House of the Prophet* who comment on the affair between Leitner and Gladys Satterlee, the wife of Leitner's closest friend, the stockbroker Heyward Satterlee, are as impatient with the clichés of romantic love as Steel is content with them. Thus Fiona Satterlee, the daughter of Heyward and Gladys, would have hooted at any account of the affair that did not acknowledge her mother's manipulativeness. Right from the start, in Fiona's opinion, Leitner had been "largely Mother's victim," a man more to be "deplored . . . for weakness than condemned for housebreaking." Gladys was an independently wealthy, socially ambitious woman who was willing enough to maintain her first marriage until an internationally famous intellectual came into her lion-hunting sights. Unlike Steel's book, Auchincloss's permits us to glimpse the cold calculations that lay beneath a middle-aged woman's seemingly reckless passion.

But the most searing condemnation of Gladys comes from Roger Cutter, who is horrified by the psychological damage she inflicted on her first husband when she selected his best friend as her lover, whereas Steel lets what Helen Armstrong did to her first husband when she took up with Lippmann go completely unjudged. While Heyward Satterlee has had a much less interesting career than Hamilton Armstrong did, Cutter's words catch the agony of both men equally well:

> Felix's friendship represented to Heyward the distinguished aspect of a life otherwise banal, the proof that there could be in a poor stockbroker's soul something that a genius could, not only recognize, but value, like the deep red glow that the observer at last begins to make out in the somber grays and black of a Rothko canvas. Heyward could have forgiven Gladys any lover but Felix. For her to take his friend was not simply an act of adultery, it was a kind of murder.

Only Cutter's uncritical devotion to Leitner prevents him from being able to admit that Leitner was a partner to that crime. There will always be "a relentless few," Cutter uncomprehendingly complains, who will speak of Felix Leitner as "the man who had betrayed his best friend and then tried to explain it in a beautiful letter."

The House of the Prophet, then, does not blink at any of Felix Leitner's terrible faults. Yet the novel also insists on his greatness. Walking with the columnist through the Carnavalet Museum in Paris, young Fiona Satterlee rejoices in his great personal gift of "making each chapter, even each paragraph, of life complete and interesting in itself." Once you let his extraordinary intellect encompass your problem, Fiona says on another occasion, he will "bathe you in the sparkling stream of an understanding that is greater than any kindness." And in contrast to Steel's life of Lippmann, which never comes close to doing justice to the literary artistry of Lippmann's columns, *The House of the Prophet* pays exquisite tribute to Leitner's journalism. His columns were all the same length, says Roger Cutter,

> almost to a word count. They usually fell into three sections: the statement of theme, a marvel of conciseness; the basic discussion, which contained the essential literary part, sometimes dramatic, sometimes rhetorical, sometimes almost poetic, a brief but exhaustive exercise in alternative arguments and points of view; and finally the conclusion, usually framed in a Leitner paradox. Felix dealt ordinarily with foreign affairs or government news, but he also noticed great events, such as the moon landing or the cure for polio, or the obituaries of famous men, and every six months he would compose a piece on what he once described with a dry smile as the "eternal verities." There was something of La Rochefoucauld in his method; as the great Frenchman strove to catch life in epigrams, so did Felix seek to hammer his columns into reflections of the essence of the political scene.

On the one hand he was an emotional monster; on the other hand, he was an intellectual saint. The dichotomy is instructive, but the novel finally goes beyond it. A woman named Julie Pryor, who had acted as Leitner's hostess in the years after his second divorce, insists in the closing pages of the book that saints—"except perhaps Saint Francis of Assisi, and the tales about him were probably made up, anyway"—*are* monsters. Leitner's singleminded devotion to his craft and the celebrated disinterestedness of his judgments were the flip side of his heartlessness.

Through its reconciliation of the light and the dark sides of Leitner, the novel once again deepens our understanding of

the historical personality on whom he is modeled. The man who did not hesitate to break the heart of Hamilton Fish Armstrong was also impervious to the blandishments of the most adroit political flatterers of our time. Franklin D. Roosevelt, John F. Kennedy, and Lyndon B. Johnson were very charming men in their various ways, and they all did their damnedest to put America's premier columnist in their pockets. They did not succeed. At times, Lippmann's expressions of disappointment in their political leadership seemed merely willful, as, for example, when he said of Kennedy in the summer of 1961 that he had failed in the role of "popular teacher." For what was Kennedy if he was not a rhetorical president? The initial failures of his incumbency had much more to do with his lack of attention to the cloakrooms of Capitol Hill than with any inability to communicate with the people. But far more often than not, Lippmann's analytical detachment worked in impressive combination with a powerful factual grasp.

Inasmuch as Ronald Steel's previous work as a writer has been in the realm of political analysis, one would expect that he would be at his best in demonstrating how remarkably well Lippmann's newspaper columns have stood the test of time, especially in view of the deadline pressures under which they were produced. Unfortunately, Steel's approach to the political issues of twentieth-century America is as predetermined as Lippmann's was exploratory. Thus whenever one of Lippmann's independent-minded opinions conflicts with one of Steel's historical pieties, the biographer never pauses to consider whether the columnist might have had a point. Instead, Steel takes him to task, sometimes openly, more often by more subtle—and cowardly—means. This opinion of Lippmann's, he is wont to say, was certainly a disappointment at the time to the men of good will among his readers. In instances where a more dispassionate biographer might have found cause to praise Lippmann, Steel is repeatedly moved to disparage him.

In 1927, for instance, the glory of Lippmann's editorials on the Sacco-Vanzetti case was that he tried to figure out the facts for himself and refused to hunt with the liberal wolf pack headed by Felix Frankfurter and his college classmate Heywood Broun. When the three-man review panel appointed by Governor Fuller of Massachusetts and headed by President Lowell of Harvard confirmed the jury's verdict of guilty and

refused to recommend a new trial, the liberal outcry was ferocious. Lippmann, however, bravely hailed the panel's report for its "fairness, consideration, shrewdness, and coolness." Shortly thereafter, he beat a partial retreat from this position and demanded that the panel show why the prejudice of the trial judge should not require a new trial, but he continued to resist the virtually unanimous opinion of the liberal intelligentsia that Sacco and Vanzetti were such gentle souls that they could not possibly have committed murder. After the execution, Lippmann again sought a middle ground. While praising Frankfurter and the defense committee for their readiness to uphold the rights of the humblest and most despised members of society, he also congratulated the Lowell panel for suffering a disagreeable duty and for its resolute pursuit of the truth. When Steel informs us that some of Lippmann's liberal friends were "puzzled" by this opinion and that others were "openly contemptuous," he is in effect letting us know how he himself feels. If, however, Steel had bothered to acquaint himself with the Sacco-Vanzetti scholarship of the last twenty years, he would know that there is increasing support for the view that Sacco and Vanzetti did not deserve a new trial and that they were guilty of the crime for which they were executed.

But as the antiquated citations in his footnotes attest, Steel is not acquainted with recent Sacco-Vanzetti scholarship. Indeed, he is not even conversant with the undisputed facts of the case. The two men, he says, "were picked up in 1920 for distributing anarchist literature and accused of murdering a payroll clerk." But a guard as well as a paymaster was murdered in the holdup, and Sacco and Vanzetti were not picked up by the police for distributing anarchist literature. They were arrested while riding on a streetcar and they had no such literature in their possession. What caught the attention of the police was that the men were heavily armed.

In addition to admonishing Lippmann for his departures from left-liberal orthodoxy, Steel also tries to make him over, in the final years of his column writing, into a left-liberal hero. Perhaps the columnist's "finest hour," he proclaims, was his opposition to the Viet Nam War. But by what criterion was this a finer hour than his refusal to join in the excoriation of the Lowell review panel? Or than his willingness in 1936 to brave the jeers of his intellectual friends and vote for Landon, on the grounds that another Democratic landslide at the polls would be bad for the country and bad for FDR? Even if Lippmann had gone on to prophesy that in the wake of smashing victory a power-intoxicated president would attempt to pack the Supreme Court, I am quite sure that Steel would still have given his finest-hour award to Lippmann's columns on Viet Nam. For as a writer Steel is a creature of the 1960s. No other era in American history bulks as large in his mind as that turbulent decade. His statement about Lippmann's finest hour merely illuminates his own badly delimited and highly partisan view of history.

Clearly, a proper biography of Walter Lippmann remains to be written, but it will be a long time, I suspect, before anyone undertakes the task. Although Ronald Steel has not done enough work to do justice to his subject, he has done enough to spoil it for other writers. Which is all the more reason to be grateful to Louis Auchincloss for his remarkable novel.

15
The Regressive Historians

Richard Hofstadter demonstrated in *The Progressive Historians* (1968) that the criticism of historical writing can be as interesting as literary criticism at its best. His assessments of Charles A. Beard's *An Economic Interpretation of the Constitution of the United States*, V. L. Parrington's *Main Currents in American Thought*, and Frederick Jackson Turner's *The Significance of the Frontier in American History* combine rigorous historiographical analysis with a keen attention to the historical setting in which these works emerged. "The Regressive Historians" is a title with several layers of meaning, but as a pun it expresses my desire to bring Hofstadter's textual-contextual method to bear upon a later phase of American historical scholarship.

This essay is about three historians of the 1960s and early 1970s who resemble Hofstadter's Progressives, at least in their range of interests. Bernard Bailyn achieved fame, as Beard did, with a book about late eighteenth-century politics. Like Parrington, Leo Marx is an interpreter of the historical significance

Reprinted from *The American Scholar*, Volume 47, Number 4 (Autumn 1978).

of American literature. Eugene D. Genovese is a sectional historian, although the Old South, not Turner's West, is his special concern. The main reason, however, for my singling out Bailyn, Marx, and Genovese is not that they roughly match Hofstadter's threesome but rather that their most ambitious books have been widely read. "My criterion was, above all, influence," says Hofstadter; it has been my criterion as well.

The Progressive historians took their cues from the intellectual and political ferment of the period from 1890 to 1915. The regressive historians became prominent during a far darker era. Except for the Civil War years, the Republic did more damage to itself in the 1960s and early 1970s than in any other moment of our history. Inevitably Bailyn, Marx, and Genovese were affected by the time in which they wrote, and so were their many admirers. Although very different from one another, all three of these historians were acclaimed for what I regard as their regressive interpretations of the American past.

The Ordeal of Bernard Bailyn

In the early 1960s, at the invitation of Howard Mumford Jones, Bernard Bailyn agreed to edit the political pamphlets of the American Revolution for the Harvard University Press. The editing of the pamphlets was a considerable undertaking. Even the compilation of a bibliography was a wearying task. When completed, it included more than four hundred examples of "all sorts of writings—treatises on political theory, essays on history, political arguments, sermons, correspondence, poems." Each of the texts selected for republication had to be painstakingly annotated. When he finally sat down to write a general introduction to the first (and thus far the only) volume of *Pamphlets of the American Revolution* (1965), it was natural that Bailyn felt an urge to justify his labors by saying something significant about them. Any scholar would have felt that way.

Bailyn's introductory effort was served by a delicately tuned literary sensibility. What he sensed in the language of the pamphlets was pulsating conviction. An earlier generation of historians had interpreted the references to "corruption" and "conspiracy," which saturate the literature, as propagandistic devices deliberately employed by the pamphleteers to whip up an otherwise indifferent public opinion. Bailyn, however, realized that to the pamphleteers those words were serious. They were not merely propagandistic; they were the hallmarks of an ideology. Radical journalists and other opposition groups in early eighteenth-century England had suspected that men in high office had become corrupted by power and were conspiring to aggrandize and perpetuate their authority by subverting the constitutional liberty of their countrymen. The oppositionists built their suspicions into the very structure of British politics, and eventually they affected American politics as well. In the years after 1760, when the British took steps to make the management of their empire more efficient, many Americans interpreted such measures as the Stamp Act as proof that the conspiracy was finally hatching and that they were its intended victims. It was not so much the new intrusions of British authority into their lives as the American interpretations thereof that propelled the colonists into rebellion.

Only one problem remained. Had a long-familiar ideology magnified and distorted the colonists' grievances against the British, or had it clarified them? Had a received rhetoric of corruption and conspiracy caused the Americans to make molehills of genuine grievance into mountains of unfounded suspicion, or had it helped them to describe a new and dangerous threat to their liberty? Did the new rules of the imperial game objectively deserve to be described as "Intolerable Acts," or did they not? In short, were the rebels fantasts or realists?

Unfortunately, Bailyn never allowed himself to realize he had two options. Not for a fleeting moment did he pause to consider that there were two sharply different ways of reading the corruption-and-conspiracy ideology. For Bailyn was extremely eager to get his introductory essay into print. If he chose option one—if he elected to argue that the whole explanation of the American Revolution was contained within a rhetoric—he would not have to go beyond the evidence of the pamphlets. If, however, he chose option two—or even took the time to discuss its historical merits before discarding it—he would have to take into consideration all sorts of evidence not contained in the pamphlets. Like many intellectuals before him, Bailyn found it convenient to reduce the study of American history to an analysis of abstractions.

Leftist historians like L. Jesse Lemisch (pronounced Polemisch by nonadmirers of his harangues), who openly taunt Bailyn at historical meetings and caricature his ideas in magazines like *Radical History Review,* are wont to characterize him as a politically reactionary snob whose historical sympathies lie with the Tories. There is a rough justice in the first part of that charge, but it needs to be more carefully defined. Like many of the Harvard admirers of John F. Kennedy, the editor of the pamphlets of the American Revolution was an elitist liberal who believed that only a happy few knew what was best for the people. Yet if Bailyn was a political snob, he was no Tory. What Lemisch and company have failed to appreciate is that the Toryism of Bailyn's scholarship was inadvertent. Confident that he had read the pamphlets correctly, he rushed into print with a series of inadequately thought-out and increasingly overstated arguments that inexorably forced him to traduce the patriots' cause. Having chosen option one, he was stuck with it, and the more he talked about it, the deeper he sank into difficulty. In the most important passage of *The Ideological Origins of the American Revolution* (1967), which is his best-known book, Bailyn summed up what a magnifying and distorting ideology finally did to the minds of "the majority of American leaders."

> This peculiar configuration of ideas constituted in effect an intellectual switchboard wired so that certain combinations of events would activate a distinct set of signals—danger signals, indicating hidden impulses and the likely trajectory of events impelled by them. Well before 1776 the signals registered on this switchboard led to a single, unmistakable conclusion—a conclusion that had long been feared and to which there could be only one rational response.

No loyal subject of George III ever spoke more elegantly about the alarmist propensities of the rebel mind.

In addition to its evasion of the fundamentally important question of whether the rebels' "unmistakable conclusion" about the perfidy of Albion might have been correct, the quotation is marked by deception, misconception, and inconsistency. That preliminary business, for instance, about "the majority of American leaders," is *poudre aux yeux.* Were town selectmen or militia company officers on his list of leaders, or did they have to be elected to provincial legislatures or rise to high rank in the Continental Army before they qualified? What were the reasons that governed the author's choice of a selective principle? To these questions Bailyn provided no answers, for the simple reason that he had never bothered to define what he meant by "leaders" and had never compiled a list. His statistical "majority" was plucked from thin air.

Beneath the deceptiveness of his numbers game lay a far graver deception. Americans who remained loyal to their king in 1776 were as familiar with the corruption-and-conspiracy ideology as were those who vowed to overthrow him. Bailyn's vague reference to "American leaders" enabled him to circumvent this embarrassing fact, because otherwise he would have been compelled to admit that he could not explain why the light signals and alarm bells in the loyalists' switchboards had not been activated by the events that had turned on the rebels'. Bailyn triumphantly presented his argument as the reason why the American Revolution occurred. The loyalists, however, were the ghosts at his victory banquet. He had not accounted for their deviant behavior. And his inability to say why some Americans continued to resist the idea of revolution threw into doubt his contention that he had explained why others had been overwhelmed by it.

His description of the rebel mind also displays an astonishing obliviousness of the twentieth century's acceptance of the principles of dynamic psychology. Bailyn is not only a psychological determinist, he is an old-fashioned psychological determinist. The metaphor that controls his description of the way in which colonial Americans came to the decision to make a revolution reads like a cross between Ivan Pavlov's reports on his conditioned-reflex experiments and the inventive dreams of Alexander Graham Bell. By any standard of modern psychology, Bailyn's switchboard metaphor is rigid, mechanistic, and absurd.

Even more bizarre is his last-second reference to the rebels's decision to declare their independence as a "rational response." The switchboard metaphor asks us to believe that incessant ideological bombardment had programmed the rebels' minds, so that they reacted with automatic suspicion and hostility to every British move. Such reactions, however, have nothing to do with rationality, so why did Bailyn describe the final link in the chain of rebel responses as rational? The answer is that the author of *The Ideological Origins* was deeply discomfited by the Tory position into which he was being driven by the iron logic of option one. In talking of the rebels as if they were switchboards and nothing more, he had stripped them of their temperaments, their judgmental powers, their relationships with parents and friends, their political and economic associations, their individuality; he had reduced them to the level of automatons, governed by some sort of equivalent of Ohm's Law. The British had been wont to refer to the rebellious colonists as children, but in Bailyn's far more regressive vision the rebels were scarcely human. Yet he did not intend to be this insulting; indeed, he wanted it known that his sympathies were Whiggish. At the sacrifice, then, of psychological consistency, he rounded off the key passage in *The Ideological Origins* by characterizing the break with Britain as rational. Most reviewers, however, paid little heed to Bailyn's puzzling and maladroit effort to prove that he was no Tory. What they brought away from *The Ideological Origins* was the memory of how a magnifying and distorting ideology had precipitated the American Revolution.

The rush of events in the late 1960s also contributed to an interpretation of Bailyn's book that the author had not counted on. *The Ideological Origins* appeared at roughly the same time that student attacks on the universities were starting to escalate into mob violence. Bailyn found that in spite of himself he had written just the sort of critique of the revolutionary impulse that many professors over the age of thirty wanted to read. In the sort of wacky interplay between the Left and the Right that has often characterized the American mind, Bailyn was launched into orbit as a Tory apologist by romantic revolutionaries like Mark Rudd.

The leading American historian at Mark Rudd's university was Richard Hofstadter, and the shift in Hofstadter's point of view in the course of the 1960s explains why he and a number of other left liberals in the New York intelligentsia were particularly taken with Bailyn's book.

In the 1950s and early 1960s, Hofstadter wrote a number of essays about various individuals and groups in American history whose political views were dominated by what he called "the paranoid style." The most striking fact about these essays is that they all deal with Americans whom he either disliked or feared. In defense of this curious historical practice, Hofstadter naively asserted that "of course, paranoid style has a greater affinity for bad causes than good." He might just as well have said, "a total affinity for bad causes," inasmuch as he resolutely passed up every golden chance American history offered him to write about the paranoid style of "good" Americans, such as Andrew Jackson's maniacal campaign against that corrupting, tentacular "Monster," the Bank of the United States—not to mention the paranoid style of professors who wrote about paranoid style, or the ceaseless suspicions of poets like Delmore Schwartz, author of the plaintive epigram, "Even paranoids have real enemies."

In 1965, however, the year Hofstadter collected and published his essays as a book, his sensibilities were unavoidably affronted by the paranoid style of a good American cause. Lyndon B. Johnson, having triumphed at the polls the previous November, now began to carry out the foreign policy of Barry Goldwater, and the reaction of college students was galvanic. Protests against the conspiracy of "the best and the brightest" erupted on a hundred campuses; before too long, the universities were also linked to the conspiracy. Thus did a good cause tip over into indiscriminate paranoia, one of the targets of which was the American institution Hofstadter cherished above all others. In an interview with a *Newsweek* reporter in July, 1970, Hofstadter dubbed the current era "the Age of Rubbish," and summed up his disgust with New Left activists by remarking sardonically, "I was raised on a more severe brand of Marxism."

By the time, then, that Hofstadter read *The Ideological Origins,* he was prepared to believe that fears of conspiracy and feelings of persecution had attended another good cause—the birth of the Republic. In early 1968, Hofstadter's horrified fascination with the parallelism between the revolutionary present and the Revolutionary past must have grown even stronger, because tension had begun to build in an ominous way on the Columbia campus. In April—the month that makes Americans think of Lexington and Concord—the dispute about the construction of a new gym boiled over into "the battle at Morningside Heights." *The Ideological Origins* was being reenacted right before Hofstadter's eyes. His admiration for the book became known throughout the university and beyond, and when the winners of the Bancroft Prize and the Pulitzer Prize for history were announced that spring, the awards were interpreted by some observers as a demonstration of Hofstadter's influence. For both prizes went to Bailyn.

Having already achieved recognition at the outset of his career for his impressively solid work in entrepreneurial history, Bailyn now enjoyed fame for his questionable work in political history. From both the Left and the Right he was perceived as a historian who believed that the American Revolution was an example of the paranoid style, even though he himself eschewed the depth-psychology terminology. His depiction of rebel alarmism was denounced by radicals, but praised by disillusioned liberals. Wherever he went, Bailyn aroused polarized responses. He had become, in sum, a sixties writer, whether he liked it or not. A terrible uneasiness still assailed him from time to time about the nature of his fame, but at least one thing was clear: after the Harvard "bust" of 1969, Bailyn had no further desire to call revolutions rational. At long last, paranoia and its verbal variants entered his working vocabulary.

The Ordeal of Thomas Hutchinson (1974), a biography of the last civilian royal governor of Massachusetts and a bitter-end loyalist who ended his days in England sorrowing for his beloved homeland, is a deeply ambivalent book. Mixing arrogance and guilt, it records Bailyn's ordeal as painfully as it does Hutchinson's. The book opens with the author's prefatory insistence that he is writing out of an Olympian detachment. From high above the tree line of Tory-Whig partisanship, he sees and understands and sympathizes with everyone who played a part in the Revolution, the winners and the losers alike; his view of the whole drama is "tragic." Of course, "it would be foolish to deny that I have been influenced in writing [this biography] by the events of the late 1960s . . . . I am quite certain, in fact, that my understanding of Thomas Hutchinson's dilemma in using troops to quell public disorders . . . has undoubtedly been sharpened by the course of American politics in the late 1960s and early 1970s." We should not, however, misconstrue his consciousness of these events: "This is a book about the eighteenth century." The long disclaimer ends, though, on a revealingly wistful note, as if Bailyn knew that his biography would not be perceived as the work of a nonpartisan, any more than his earlier books had been perceived as the work of a Whig. "When one looks at the record of what historians have said about the American loyalists, the likelihood of escaping partisanship of some distorting kind seems extremely small, and the effort I am making to do precisely that seems doomed to failure from the start."

Finally, the preface tells us what the story of Hutchinson's life will accomplish. Bailyn does not acknowledge that his inability to explain the deviation of the loyalists was the reason above all other reasons why *The Ideological Origins* failed to live up to its title; he says that he will now make clear why some Americans chose to remain loyal to their king. The story of "the American loyalists . . . will allow us to see the Revolutionary movement from the other side around, and to grasp the wholeness of the struggle and hence in the end to understand more fully than we have before why a revolution took place and why it succeeded." Through the case history of Thomas Hutchinson, "the most important loyalist of all," we will be shown "the origins of the Revolution as experienced by the losers."

Alas, Hutchinson's sad story casts no historical shadow. *The Ordeal* signally fails to show us why we should conclude that the life of the unusually well-to-do, unusually well-connected man it centers on was representative in any way of the lives of loyalists in general, most of whom did not enjoy anything like Hutchinson's worldly advantages. *The Ordeal* confirms beyond a shadow of a doubt the impression left by *The Ideological Origins:* Bailyn has not the slightest idea of what sorts of characteristics and experiences the loyalists shared in common and therefore has no understanding of them as a group. Yet if Bailyn's biography miserably fails as a general explanation of loyalism, it does help to explain the loyalism of Thomas Hutchinson. Bailyn, as he indicates in his preface, learned a great deal from his experience of the Harvard "bust." He learned what it felt like to be an establishment insider who knows that the social order he is fighting for has made grave mistakes, but whose first duty is to preserve its integrity against the onslaught of anarchy. That experience informs and illuminates his analysis of Hutchinson's political conduct.

The Ordeal also shows, for the first time in Bailyn's career, that he has a talent for writing narrative history. On its allegorical level—that is, the level on which Bailyn recapitulates the violent incidents in the Harvard Yard in 1969 and their reverberating consequences—his book is continuously exciting and satisfying. The students who stormed University Hall, in the center of the Harvard Yard, headed at once for the Dean of the Faculty's confidential files, and at their leisure desecrated the Faculty Room. It is of this scene that Bailyn invites us to think as he tells the story of the sacking of Hutchinson's house in the summer of 1765. No matter how often I read chapter 2, "The Face of Revolution," I am at once swept up by Bailyn's surging and compelling narrative. Maddened by its "morbid, pathological, paranoiac" hatred of Hutchinson, the most violent mob yet seen in American history,

> more violent indeed than any that would be seen in the entire course of the Revolution, attacked the Boston mansion of Thomas Hutchinson, chief justice and lieutenant governor of Massachusetts. Hardly giving Hutchinson and his family time to flee from the supper table into the streets, the rioters smashed in the doors with axes, swarmed through the rooms, ripped off wainscotting and hangings, splintered the furniture, beat down the inner walls, tore up the garden, and carried off into the night, besides £900 sterling in cash, all the plate, decorations, and clothes that had survived, and destroyed or scattered in the mud all of Hutchinson's books and papers, including the manuscript of volume I of his *History*, and the collection of historical papers that he had been gathering for years as the basis for a public archive.

Yet when I stop reading and realize that an allegorical lens is coloring my view of the tumultuous events leading up to the Revolution, my simple pleasure in Bailyn's prose turns into a more complex response. The "bust" gave Bailyn an unforgettable insight into the wild, anarchic passion that characterizes the mood of mobs, and in re-creating that passion in his book he deepens our understanding of Revolutionary politics and earns our gratitude. In the final analysis, though, I find his allegorizing outrageous. Through deliberately evoked associations, he equates the awesomely tough, incontestably impressive men of 1765 with the adolescent myrmidons of the New Left. While the equation has less regressive implications than the switchboard metaphor, it is somehow more insulting.

Beyond the conscious allegory in *The Ordeal* lies an unconscious one, which completes our sense of the author's ordeal.

Bailyn's portrait of Hutchinson's personality does not add up. On the one hand, we are told that he was pragmatic, profit-conscious, self-serving, and devious. On the other hand, we are encouraged to believe that he was highly intelligent, principled, broad-visioned, and misunderstood. What prompts these contradictory statements, and why is Bailyn unable to resolve them into a coherent summation of the man? The key that unlocks these riddles lies hidden in the fact that Hutchinson, besides being a politician, was a Massachusetts historian. Upon his eighteenth-century protagonist, a twentieth-century historian of Massachusetts unconsciously projected his divided, irresolute sense of himself as a scholar who had been driven toward a political position in which he did not believe by the ineluctable logic of a badly chosen argument. In the anguishing ordeal of his schizoid hero we can sense the pain which Bailyn's ambiguous position in Revolutionary scholarship has caused him for almost twenty years. The role of a Tory historian made him famous, but it has never made him comfortable.

The Literary Parables of Leo Marx

What made Leo Marx such a charismatic figure for the undergraduates at Amherst College in the 1960s, and why did his book *The Machine in the Garden* (1964) immediately become one of the holy texts in American studies programs across the nation? The answers to both questions have more to do with ideology than with critical acumen. Marx had an impact on the consciousness of the sixties because his literary parables meshed with the psychic consequences of an unparalleled American affluence.

To many high school and college students whose comfortable lives had known neither the Depression nor World War II, the overblown rhetoric in which Lyndon B. Johnson described his Great Society was as unbelievable as it was boring, while his commitment of American troops to South Viet Nam struck them as the act of an international criminal. In their disillusionment with the president, they turned to alternative gurus, who dispensed wisdom through filthy speech, free sex, rock 'n' roll, communion with nature, and assorted drugs. Between trips, some of the students came back to politics—with a vengeance. The guru who told them they were right to think that the American system had to be destroyed was Herbert Marcuse.

In the course of working on *The Machine in the Garden,* Professor Marx also discovered Marcuse. It was an important moment for him. Without Marcuse I doubt that he ever would have pulled together a publishable manuscript, for the dialectical materialism in which he had believed since youth had created serious difficulties for him. In the book he was trying to write, he proposed to demonstrate that for many generations Americans had been torn between two sharply conflicting conceptions of their country. This life-of-the-mind equivalent of Karl Marx's class struggle was symbolized by two images: the image of America as a simple rural paradise versus the image of America as an urban industrial power. A green garden was the symbolic thesis in Professor Marx's dialectic, a railroad train the symbolic antithesis. Where, however, was the symbolic synthesis, which could give his readers a heart-lifting vision of the future? He found it hard to speak specifically about a successful resolution of the conflict between a nation of open fields and woods and a nation of smoking factories. Another difficulty was that Karl Marx's basic quarrel was not with machines per se; it was the ownership of the means of production that concerned him. Professor Marx's manuscript, by contrast, had cast machines in the role of the snake in the Garden of Eden. How could he possibly acknowledge that he fully shared *Das Kapital's* acceptance of modern machines when his praise of the principal American prose writers centered on what he was convinced were their horrifying descriptions of trains, steamboats, and automobiles?

Dr. Marcuse cured these problems in a jiffy. He taught Professor Marx that machines repressed instinctual drives, fostered psychic helplessness, and deserved to be depicted as horrid. He also showed Marx that he did not have to worry about not having a symbolic synthesis in mind. A vision of total destruction was all he needed to hold his book together, plus a subliminal suggestion or two that radical college students would certainly survive Apocalypse, even as Ishmael lived to tell the tale of Moby-Dick's annihilation of Captain Ahab and his crew.

Because of its bifurcated Marxist-Marcusean lineage, *The Machine in the Garden* is one of the few books of the sixties that spanned the generation gap between the Old Left and the New. The book's hatred of capitalism warmed the hearts of thirties radicals, while its condemnation of eros-blocking machines and celebration of greenness made it beloved among the flower children. On the bookshelves in student dormitories Marx's green-covered *Machine* took its place beside Charles Reich's *The Greening of America,* albeit Marx disagreed with Reich's contention that the peaceable kingdom could be achieved peaceably. "Ishmael is saved as Job's messengers had been saved, in order that he may deliver to us a warning of disasters to come." Marx, in the almost cheerful tone in which he predicts future disasters, and in his failure to specify what sort of value system he would like to see emerge on the other side of Apocalypse, reveals himself to be a far more regressive historian than either Bailyn or Genovese. Like Marcuse, who once shrugged his shoulders by way of reply to the British journalist Henry Brandon's question about what sort of civilization he hoped would sprout from the rubble of the present one, Marx is content to end his book with the altogether negativistic proposition that the values of greenness as defined by our very best writers "probably cannot . . . be embodied in our traditional institutions." It is bad enough to regress into a Tory attitude toward the American Revolution, or into a celebration of the master-and-slave society of the Old South. But to rest content with nihilism takes the prize.

The first chapter of *The Machine in the Garden* is entitled "Sleepy Hollow, 1844." The reference is not to Washington Irving but to Nathaniel Hawthorne, who sat down in a clearing in the woods near Concord, Massachusetts, one summer morning to await "such little events as may happen," so that he could record them in his notebook. The scene is peaceful, full of sunlight and shadow, and Hawthorne records his sense impressions in "that pleasant mood of mind where gaiety and pensiveness intermingle." Suddenly the sylvan silence is rent by a piercing noise.

> But, hark! there is the whistle of the locomotive—the long shriek, harsh, above all other harshness, for the space of a mile cannot mollify it into harmony. It tells a story of busy men, citizens, from the hot street, who have come to spend a day in a country village, men of business; in short of all unquietness; and no wonder that it gives such a startling shriek, since it brings the noisy world into the midst of our slumbrous peace.

What Marx does not tell us is that this passage is extrapolated from a recital of numerous interruptions, all of them trivial, which demonstrate that Hawthorne has extraordinarily sensitive ears. For example, one of his ears is somehow invaded by a fly—"the most impertinent and indelicate thing in creation." Then a mosquito dive-bombs him—"this incident has disturbed our tranquillity." Disagreeable words like "shriek" and "harsh" are used to describe the train's whistle, but they are also evident in his notations of the "sharp, shrill' chirrup of a squirrel, and the hum, "terrible to the ear," of that damned mosquito.

Marx ignores these comic details because he is determined to convert the scene into a solemn-serious paradigm of what he conceives to be the central drama of nineteenth-century American culture: the abrupt, frightening entrance of the engine of modern industrial technology into the pastoral tranquillity of nature's nation, and the registration of that epochal intrusion by one of the writers of "our first significant literary generation," who in the mid-1840s were just coming into full possession of their powers. Every detail of the quotation is loaded with meaning for Marx, but the date is the most significant of all. Repeatedly Marx comes back to 1844. It is the year Emerson delivered a lecture in which he discussed the relationship of machinery to Transcendentalism; the year in which the young Melville returned from the Pacific and began to feel his life unfold within him; the year before Thoreau went to live by Walden Pond; the year, roughly, in which Mark Twain retrospectively placed the adventures of Huck Finn. Eighteen forty-four was a year of "radical change." Indeed "the fact is that nothing quite like the event announced by the train in the woods had occurred before." He has introduced the "little event" of 1844, Marx explains, "to mark the shaping of a metaphor, or metaphoric design," which appears again and again in American literature after that date. With Vergil's *Eclogues* in mind—for Vergilian pastoral, says Marx, is the font from which American pastoral writing has flowed—"we can see that the episode in Concord woods does not represent the beginning so much as the decisive turning point of a long story."

The justification for Marx's insistence on the pivotal importance of 1844 can be found, he says, in W. W. Rostow's *The Stages of Economic Growth*, in which the period 1843–60 is defined as the "take-off" stage of American industrial growth.

The "take-off" period, Marx says, quoting Rostow, is "the great watershed in the life of modern societies," for it is then that the forces of economic progress "expand and come to dominate the society." In the United States, as in France, Germany, and Russia, the introduction of the railroad was the most powerful single initiator of growth. Hawthorne, in sum, had twitched in the woods at the first sound of take-off. Nothing more vividly illustrates Marx's eagerness to deceive himself, and his readers, than his truncation of Rostow's argument at this point. What Marx neglects to add is that nineteenth-century America was a big country, and that its regions—much more sharply differentiated then than now—advanced economically at strikingly different rates of speed. "If," says Rostow, "we are prepared to treat New England of the first half of the nineteenth century as a separable economy, its take-off into sustained growth can be allocated to the period, roughly, 1820–1850." Its take-off, moreover, was—like old England's—powered by a disproportionately large cotton-textile industry.

By 1844, therefore, those bred-in-the-bone Yankees, Hawthorne, Emerson, and Thoreau, had been living through take-off for most of their lives and could hardly have been surprised by it. Had Marx made a serious historical effort to begin his book at the moment when take-off first became a subject for discussion by New Englanders, he would have focused on what ministers and politicians had had to say about textile factories in the 1820s.

A further instance of Marx's misconception of take-off is provided by Rostow's critics, who have persuasively argued that take-off for the American economy as a whole ought not to be graphed as a steep vertical climb lasting only seventeen years, but as a much more gradual curve, beginning in 1815 or even earlier and terminating, as Rostow argued, in 1860. Rostow's critics place particular emphasis on the effect of the Erie Canal (completed in 1825) upon the growth of a market economy in the state of New York. What makes this statement of particular interest to historians of American culture is that New York in the 1820s was the one state in the Union which could boast that two of its native sons were major writers. Why did not Marx begin his book with Irving and Cooper, both of whom responded literarily to the take-off of New York's economy? I can only conclude that Marx deliberately avoided their interesting commentaries on economic change, because if he had not, he would have been forced to relate them to canal boats, which he had no interest in discussing. The canal boat has a pastoral aura, even though it had an urbanizing effect; it lacks the train's demonological attributes of fire, smoke, speed, iron, and noise that Marx was counting on to make his anticapitalist, antitechnological parables come alive in the minds of students and fellow teachers. Another reason why Marx cherished fire and smoke is that they have been associated with human society since prehistoric times. Whenever the American writers mentioned either word—which, like all writers through recorded history, they inevitably did all the time—Marx intended to claim the reference as a metaphorical allusion to trains and other technological monsters, and dare anyone to tell him he was wrong. Neither the canal boat nor water-powered textile factories offered such open-ended possibilities to the parable maker.

The noise of the train in Sleepy Hollow, says Marx, "is a cause of alienation in the root sense of the word"; it "estranges" Hawthorne from the "meaning and value" of nature; it is the "presentiment of history bearing down on the American asylum." But this is to suggest that Hawthorne lived in nature, which is not true. "Sleepy Hollow, 1844" is not an American version of Vergilian pastoral, which Marx claims it is, for it records the observations, not of a reclusive farmer, like Vergil's Tityrus, but of a resident of the Old Manse in Concord, who is merely a visitor to the sylvan glade. Because he is a visitor, he understands and is untroubled by his awareness that visitors from the "hot street"have come to spend the day in rural Concord. The train from which they alight is not an intruder from another world, but a technological invention that has emerged from within the context of republican values and was viewed by Hawthorne, no less than by his fellow citizens, as an extension of nature, not as its dire enemy and destroyer. Just as the train has brought city men to a country village, so many Americans—including Hawthorne—delighted in taking trains on even longer excursions into New England nature. "They annihilate the toil and dust of pilgrimage; they spiritualize travel!" Hawthorne wrote in *The House of the Seven Gables.*

The symbiotic relationship between nature and technology gave many Americans an exhilarating sense of fulfillment.

"Machinery and Transcendentalism agree well," trumpeted Emerson. "Get into the railroad car," he noted in his journal, "and the Ideal Philosophy takes place at once.... The very permanence of matter seems compromised & oaks, fields, hills, hitherto esteemed symbols of stability do absolutely dance by you." During such moments, he was thrillingly certain that matter was "phenomenal." In addition to its philosophical delights, Emerson found train travel marvelously convenient. As he pointed out in a letter to a friend in Newton, he and his brother Charles could easily reach Newton by train in time for tea and return home the next morning. The stage coach and the railroad between them, said Emerson, had created a transportation revolution that was bursting the old rules of American life "like green withes." By his association of trains with greenness, the essayist asserted how "natural" he believed them to be.

Yet many citizens of the Republic were troubled, as many citizens in other industrializing societies of the nineteenth century were, by the pollution of the environment that take-off produced. In the minds of many Americans, moreover, the triumph of civilization over the wilderness symbolized the death of the God-given uniqueness of America. With admirable skill, a number of writers endeavored to express both the dark and the bright sides of the national mood. While acknowledging that there was a conflict between nature and technology, they did so within larger affirmations of their complementarity. One of these writers was Thoreau, although you would never know it from Marx's interpretation of *Walden*.

On the shore of the pond we are once again in a threatened version of pastoral, according to Marx. "The whistle of the locomotive penetrates my woods summer and winter, sounding like the scream of a hawk sailing over some farmer's yard." The hawk, says Marx, is noted for its "rapacity," and in its scream we hear again the "discordant machine of the Sleepy Hollow notes." The statement misses the Transcendental significance of Thoreau's sentence. In likening the train's sound to the hawk's, Thoreau is proclaiming the naturalness of modern technology. The train is a welcome part of his environment, and as he warms to the task of praising it, even Marx is forced to give ground. Putting the best face he can on Thoreau's rhapsodic paragraphs, Marx grudgingly admits that the chapter called "Sounds" is a "sustained evocation of the ambiguous meaning of the machine and its relation to nature." Again Marx misses the point. The lash of Thoreau's satirical wit is mainly applied to the builders of the train, rather than to the train itself.

> When I meet the engine with its train of cars moving off with planetary motion, . . . as if this travelling demi-god, this cloud-compeller, would ere long take the sunset sky for the livery of his train; when I hear the iron horse make the hills echo with his snort like thunder, shaking the earth with his feet, and breathing fire and smoke from his nostrils (what kind of winged horse or fiery dragon they will put into the new Mythology I don't know), it seems as if the earth had got a race now worthy to inhabit it. If all were as it seems, and men made the elements their servants for noble ends! If the cloud that hangs over the engine were the perspiration of heroic deeds, or as beneficent as that which floats over the farmer's fields, then the elements and Nature herself would cheerfully accompany men on their errands and be their escort.

The one and only note of ambiguity about trains in this passage is contained in the invidious comparison of the engine's smoke to the beneficent cloud floating over the farmer's fields—and the note is so subordinate to Thoreau's enthrallment with the railroad "demi-god" as to be scarcely noticeable.

Is there any literarily trustworthy work in *The Machine in the Garden?* Yes, there is. The discussions of the eighteenth-century writers Jefferson, Crèvecoeur, and Robert Beverley are all quite believable. Once the machine enters the garden, though, the parable maker takes over and all is lost. Marx tries to make the steamboat that collides with the raft in *Huckleberry Finn* into another presentiment of history bearing down on the asylum, as if Sam Clemens's years in the pilothouse had not made him incurably nostalgic about side-wheelers, as his nom de plume implies; steamboats as well as rafts infallibly conjured up for him the vanished Eden of his youth. Frank Norris's description in *The Octopus* of a speeding train's slaughter of a flock of errant sheep, and of the dead animals' "black blood, winking in the starlight," is converted by Marx into yet another horrifying symbol of industrial capitalism, at the cost of ignoring the central fact about Norris's imagination: his love of killing and worship of force. Marx describes Nick Carraway's decision to go back to the Middle West after Gatsby's funeral as "a belated, ritualistic withdrawal in the direction of 'nature.'" But somehow Marx manages to overlook Nick's feelings about the mode of transportation that will take him there.

> One of my most vivid memories is of coming back West from prep school and later from college at Christmas time. Those who went farther than Chicago would gather in the old dim Union Station at six o'clock of a December evening, with a few holiday gayeties, to bid them a hasty good-by. I remember the fur coats of the girls . . . and the chatter of frozen breath and the hands waving overhead as we caught sight of old acquaintances. . . . And last the murky yellow cars of the Chicago, Milwaukee & St. Paul railroad looking cheerful as Christmas itself on the tracks beside the gate . . . . That's my Middle West—not the wheat or the prairies or the lost Swede towns, but the thrilling returning trains of my youth.

Nick's "nature" is a railroad train. A critic not dominated by ideological regressiveness would have made a great deal of that.

The centerfold in Marx's magazine of parables is his hallucinogenic rendition of *Moby-Dick.* To get us in the proper frame of mind, Marx begins by saying that the calamitous story Ishmael is going to tell us "is a portent of further trials to come: we too may expect our integrity and faith to be tested." This invitation to us to identify with Ishmael is immensely flattering, for Ishmael is an isolato, which is a nifty thing to be, morally speaking, because it means you have not been corrupted by the nasty institutions of American power. In addition to being flattering, the invitation also appeals to our instinct for survival. If we will only part company with American capitalism as decisively as Ishmael—according to Marx—disengages himself from the mad capitalist's pursuit of the white whale, we will morally qualify to come through Apocalypse unscathed. In the world of Marcusean fantasy, an act of conscience is a warranty of safety. "All are directed toward Ahab's goal . . . except Ishmael. In the end he alone is saved, a fact that comports with his success in establishing a position independent of Ahab and the fiery quest."

With that assurance in mind, we are well launched. The next matter to be cleared up is why an analysis of a whaling voyage belongs in a book about green fields and railroads. The effort of explanation requires all of Marx's ingenuity. It seems that *Moby-Dick* is an "oceanic pastoral" (you heard what the man said, Vergil), and that a little question asked by Ishmael at the outset of the novel is pregnant with implications. What Ishmael is asking in this question, we are informed, is whether it is possible "to mediate the claims of our collective, institutional life and the claims of nature." One could never guess from this gloss that Ishmael's question is an example of tall-tale American humor. In the first pages of the book, Ishmael delights us with a description of the sea-gazing habits of New Yorkers on Sunday afternoons. From Corlears Hook to Coenties Slip they stand, "thousands and thousands" of them, "fixed in ocean reveries." Why aren't they spending Sunday afternoon in the country, Melville asks in effect. "Are the green fields gone?" Marx takes this buoyant, charming, transparently rhetorical question utterly seriously; in fact, he would have us believe that it is nothing less than the overture to the symphony. Searching Melville's ensuing magniloquence for every scrap of botanical metaphor he can find, Marx turns the watery "meadows" of the South Pacific into wall-to-wall AstroTurf, and then announces that Ishmael has "rediscovered" the green fields—which certainly comes as a surprise to attentive readers, inasmuch as Ishmael never said they had disappeared in the first place.

Marx also introduces modern technology aboard the *Pequod* by means of metaphor. "Swerve me?" cries Ahab. "The path to my fixed purpose is laid with iron rails, whereon my soul is grooved to run." Marx concludes from such outbursts that Ahab is a mechanical man, made of cogs and wheels. The charge is untrue. The hunter of Moby-Dick deliberately abandons mechanical aids, such as his quadrant, in the course of his quest. Indeed the closer he comes to the white whale, the more aware we become of Ahab's humanity, as for example in the scene where he weeps.

The final major mistake Marx makes in his Marcusean rewrite is his assertion that Ishmael disengages from the mad capitalist's fiery quest. Chapter 96, according to Marx, "is at once a repudiation of the quest, a reaffirmation of reason, and a tribute to the man large enough to withstand the extremes of hope and fear." In support of that statement he points to the concluding paragraph:

> Give not thyself up, then, to fire, lest it invert thee, deaden thee; as for the time it did me. There is a wisdom that is woe; but there is a woe that is madness. And there is a Catskill eagle in some souls that can alike dive down into the blackest gorges, and soar out of them again and become invisible in the sunny spaces. And even if he for ever flies within the gorge, that gorge is in the mountains; so that even in his lowest swoop the mountain eagle is still higher than other birds upon the plain, even though they soar.

Once again, Marx's perception is skewed. This passage is presented to us, as indeed the entire story is, as the recollection of an aging man who asks that we call him Ishmael. When he warns us not to give ourselves up to fire, lest it invert us, "as for the time it did me," old Ishmael is referring to the entire voyage, not merely to a part of it. Furthermore, the acknowledgment that there is a woe that is madness is immediately followed by the assertion that the lowest, darkest moods of eagle-like madmen still range above the highest flights of mind of sane but ordinary men. Even though young Ishmael knew Ahab was mad, he revered him as a superior being and remained his faithful follower.

When Moby-Dick bursts into view on the second day of the climactic chase, "the triumphant halloo of thirty buckskin lungs" is heard—not twenty-nine, but the *Pequod*'s full complement of thirty. On the third and last day of the chase, Ishmael is the bowsman in Ahab's boat. Ishmael survives Apocalypse not because he was innocent, but because he was fantastically lucky. *Moby-Dick* offers neither flattery nor reassurance to Marcusean nihilists.

Smelling the Magnolias with Massa Gene

In an exchange of views a few years ago with "Comrades Foner, Greenberg, Perkins, and Siegel," Eugene D. Genovese momentarily indulged in personal confession. "While opposed to ideological history and presentism, I have never written a line that has not been, in [the historian] George Rawick's phrase, 'a political intervention.'" In *Roll, Jordan, Roll* (1974), Genovese does indeed intervene. For as the political scientist Harry V. Jaffa has observed, Genovese claims to have found in the "antagonistic cooperation" of slaves and masters far more of a sense of community than in the Yankee centers of early nineteenth-century capitalism, and by relentlessly insisting on that judgment he seeks to discredit late twentieth-century capitalism as well. Throughout Genovese's regressive fantasy, one is reminded of a comment by Marx and Engels in the *Communist Manifesto:* "The bourgeoisie, wherever it has got the upper hand, has put an end to all feudal, patriarchal, idyllic relations. It has pitilessly torn asunder the . . . feudal ties that bound man to his 'natural superior.'" Just as Marx and Engels paid tribute to a feudal past in order to arouse yearnings for a communist future, so for similar reasons does Genovese pay tribute to the Old South.

The social order and moral standards of the slaveholders "left . . . something to be desired," Genovese concedes in a breathtaking understatement in his earlier book, *The World the Slaveholders Made* (1969), but at least, he says, they were not dominated by capitalistic greed. "The values of the plantation, its way of thought and feeling, were antithetical to those of the bourgeois world. The relationship of master to slave, in itself an extension of the relationship of father to perpetual child, could be reconciled to the cash nexus only imperfectly." In part, this preposterous statement derives from the Southern historian U. B. Phillips's *American Negro Slavery* (1918), in which Phillips portrays slavery as a system of marvelously harmonious social relationships between patriarchal white masters and happy-go-luck darkies. The main source of Genovese's misconception of the master-slave relationship, however, is an ideologue from antebellum Virginia, George Fitzhugh. To Fitzhugh, the unrestricted exploitation of wage slaves in Northern factories was "little better than moral Cannibalism," and far more oppressive to the laborer than domestic slavery. In the North, increases in profits went solely to the owners, whereas in the South, Fitzhugh averred, increased profits raised the slave's standard of living as well as the master's, because the slave was a member of the plantation "family."

"I have come to think of him as an old friend," Genovese has written of Fitzhugh. "As my affection and admiration deepened, the task of rescuing him from detractors became something of a private mission." Yet in the long and admiring essay on Fitzhugh that takes up half of *The World the Slaveholders Made*, Genovese fails to mention one of the key facts about Fitzhugh's career. Throughout the most important years of his writing life, Fitzhugh was the personal friend and literary hireling of the South's most energetic advocate of capitalistic expansionism. As the founder-editor of *De Bow's Review* and sometime professor of political economy at Louisiana State University, James D. B. De Bow was in a position to influence Southern public opinion. As Superintendent of the United States Census, he was painfully aware of how far Northern industrial capitalism had outstripped Southern plantation capitalism. De Bow urged the Southern planters to modernize their business methods and force the reopening of the African slave trade. He also pleaded for a diversification of the region's economy. The South needed artisans, banks, textile factories, paper mills, and, above all, railroads. "No people on earth have the means of building railroads so economically, so speedily, and with such certainty of success, as we of the South," De Bow proclaimed, and one of the main reasons for this was "available cheap negro labor." De Bow did not regard slaves as members of a beneficent plantation "family." Rather, he saw them as one of the richest sources of Southern capitalism, and so did the planters for whom he spoke. De Bow, not Fitzhugh, represented the mainstream of antebellum Southern thinking about race relations.

De Bow spoke in statistics. Yet he was tolerant of other men who spoke in more imaginative terms—as long as they, too, advocated slavery. Thus he opened the columns of *De Bow's Review* to poets like William J. Grayson, author of a counterattack on *Uncle Tom's Cabin,* and to maverick polemicists like Fitzhugh. De Bow also had a weakness for racist anthropologists. His favorite was the ineffable Dr. Josiah Nott, co-author of *Types of Mankind,* which scientifically "proved" that Negroes were innately inferior, and editor of an English translation of Gobineau's *The Moral and Intellectual Diversity of Races,* which later meant so much to Hitler. Nott's ideas of Aryan superiority also dominated the mind of Genovese's old and admired friend Fitzhugh.

Roll, Jordan, Roll does not deny that the lot of the slaves was often harsh. Nevertheless, the benignity of plantation paternalism afforded the slaves sufficient "space" in which to lay the foundations for a separate black nation. At the heart of their achievement was their religion, which fused Christianity with African folk belief, including the belief in magic, into a distinctive black faith. Through this faith, the slaves shaped their "autonomous identity." Verification of this sweeping statement is offered in a chapter called "Origins of the Folk Religion." In three key paragraphs, Genovese sets out to demonstrate the inaccuracy of the traditional idea that the strength of "Africanisms" or of African religion per se among the blacks during the eighteenth century did not survive into the late antebellum period except in a few special places. The fact of the matter, says Genovese, is that "white as well as black sources attest to persistence all across the South even after slavery had passed." In the final sentence of the last of these paragraphs he declares that "the planters never doubted that their slaves' Christianity contained a good dose of African belief." In a book of 665 sprawling pages, this sentence is the most important assertion of Genovese's thesis that the slavocracy allowed the blacks to develop cultural independence, and Genovese duly footnotes it.

The footnote consists of four references: to the Laurence Family Papers at Nashville, to the Calvin Henderson Wiley Papers at Chapel Hill, to J. Carlyle Sitterson's *Sugar Country,* and to Charles Sackett Sydnor's *Slavery in Mississippi.* At first glance, the references are impressive; upon closer examination, they prove to be a hollow shell.

The citation from the Laurence Family Papers takes us to a reminiscence by a woman named Emily Donelson Walton, in which she recalls a slave named Uncle Guinea George, of whom she had been somewhat afraid during her childhood because of his claim that he had once been a cannibal. He boasted to everyone that he had had his teeth sharpened so that he could chew better, and "he would tell the boys in the family," Mrs. Walton recalled, "about being a cannibal in Africa, and sing weird songs in his own language when at work in the field at cotton picking time." Nowhere in Mrs. Walton's recollection of Uncle Guinea George is his religious faith even remotely alluded to, let alone broken down into its component parts. Genovese's citation from the Laurence Family Papers is a sham.

The same word applies to his citation from the Calvin Henderson Wiley Papers. For the subject that is under discussion in the document to which Genovese refers is the duty of the good Christian to preach the gospel to all peoples everywhere and to strive earnestly and constantly for their repentance and conversion. Unfortunately, says Wiley, many races which are "much the superior of the negro," and which have had many opportunities for repentance, "seem likely to fade away before the dawning of the Millennial era," whereas "poor, blind, servile Ethiopia"—that is to say, the Negro race—is not only "stretching forth her hands, & crying to be cast into the healing waters," but seems likely to be a "permanent occupant of the world." There is nothing in the passage to indicate that Wiley believed that the faith of Christian blacks differed in any way from the faith of Christian white men like himself. In the "Note on Sources" at the end of *Roll, Jordan, Roll,* Genovese says that "two decades of work" in the documents of Southern history have helped him to recognize "what is and is not typical—what does and does not ring false." One might more accurately say that in two decades of work he never learned a proper respect for historical truth.

The citation from J. Carlyle Sitterson's *Sugar Country* is somewhat less fraudulent than the citations from the two archival documents, for Sitterson does at least take up the question of residual African belief. Sitterson, however, does *not* assert that African religion was fused with Christianity into a distinctive black religion; rather, he says, it existed "underneath" the slaves' Christianity. "The 'Guinea' religion," Sitterson says in his precise way, "never completely died out in southern Louisiana. Through the ante bellum period it was replenished through the addition of Negroes smuggled in and taken through the bayous . . . and sold." Far from supporting Genovese's contention that the traditional view of the role of African religion in black American Christianity is wrong, Sitterson exemplifies that view. Only in very special places in the late antebellum South—like the bayou country of south Louisiana—did belief in African religion persist.

The passage to which we are led by the citation from Sydnor's *Slavery in Mississippi* also makes *Roll, Jordan, Roll* look sick:

> Few records of the superstitions of Mississippi slaves have been found. Whether the negro brought the following belief from Africa is not known; it may have been borrowed from the whites, for cases of this superstition can be found in European folklore. John, a slave, was accused of having

> committed murder in Hinds county. During the trial it was stated that he and another slave, Willis, together watched a crowd of people going toward the body of the murdered negro. Willis told John that a jury was being formed and that all the negroes who had been working near the scene of the crime would have to file past the body, each in turn placing his hands on it, and that blood would flow from the wounds as soon as the murderer touched the body. On hearing this John at once jumped the fence behind the place where he had been talking to Willis and started running away from the scene.

The contrast between Sydnor's honest confession that he cannot make a definite statement about the origins of this folk story and Genovese's declaration, delivered with all the boldness of a riverboat gambler who is sure that no one will bother to check his sleeves, that "the planters never doubted that their slaves' Christianity contained a good dose of African belief" could hardly be more damning. The Sydnor passage, morever, makes no reference to the alleged fusion of African folk belief and Christianity.

Circular arguments, slippery-slick non sequiturs, collapsing time frames, irrelevant quotations, and gloriously unfootnoted generalizations also contribute to the excitement of reading *Roll, Jordan, Roll.* If you happen to be interested in African history and want to know where Genovese learned so much about so many tribes that he can expansively say that "the slaves' standard of formal courtesy toward the whites arose not only from their servile condition but from a sense of justice inherited from Africa," you will just have to keep on guessing, because he does not reveal his sources. A paragraph on the slaves' gratitude to kindly masters is equally imaginative, even though it is backed up by two quotations, because the first is a reminiscence of the Danish statesman Bernstorff's relations with his serfs, while the second is an observation of twentieth-century Southern blacks by the sociologist Charles S. Johnson. The interesting statement that "married black women and their men did not take white sexual aggression lightly and resisted effectively enough to hold it to a minimum" is not footnoted, nor is the paragraph in "Wives and Mothers" about the greater equality between men and women in the slave family as opposed to the white family, nor the paragraph about the "remarkable number of [black] women [who] did everything possible to strengthen their men's self-esteem and to defer to their leadership."

The only fault Genovese finds with the slaves is that not enough of them rebelled. He is very quick, though, to explain away their failure. It was not a pathology induced by slavery that prevented the blacks from rebelling, but their religion—their grandest achievement. The slaves' Christianity tied them to their Christian white folks and therefore militated against a general uprising. Nevertheless, the slaves' religion prepared the way for "the struggle of subsequent generations of black Americans to fulfill that prophecy they have made their own":

> But that which ye have already hold
> fast till I come.
> And he that overcometh, and keepeth
> my works unto the end, to him will I
> give power over the nations . . . .
> I am the root and the offspring of
> David, and the bright and morning star.

"Power over the nations." The line is from Revelation, but as the words come rolling like Jordan out of Genovese's typewriter, they turn into a prophecy of social revolution.

16
Self and Society

Who lost America? It wasn't the Left's fault, replies Christopher Lasch in his apocalyptic book, *The Culture of Narcissism.* For more than fifty years, to be sure, radical intellectuals in this country have done their best to discredit "the authoritarian family, repressive sexual morality, literary censorship, the work ethic, and other foundations of bourgeois order." But if those foundations are now collapsing, and Lasch is quite sure that they are, the bourgeoisie has no one but itself to blame. It is not the triumph of cultural radicalism, the author assures us, but a stunning transformation in the character of bourgeois individualism that is the key to the cultural crisis of our time. The severely repressed, morally rigid "economic man" of yesteryear—that fervent defender of time-hallowed customs and institutions whom J. P. Marquand gently satirized in *The Late George Apley*—has given way to an anxiety-ridden character out of Joan Didion's *Play It As It Lays,* who "acts out" his impulses in a desperate quest for a meaningful life. Instead of enforcing restrictions on personal freedom, as his puritanical

Reprinted by permission from *Commentary,* Volume 67, Number 4 (April 1979).

ancestors did, the permissive American of today tries to get rid of them. The temple of bourgeois values is therefore being destroyed by the very class that built it. To the "psychological man" of contemporary America, immediate self-gratification is the only god worth serving.

According to Lasch, the shift toward "psychological man" originated in the gradual assumption of childrearing functions by surrogate authorities responsible to the state, to private industry, or to their own codes of professional ethics. "In the course of bringing culture to the masses, the advertising industry, the mass media, the health and welfare services, and other agencies of mass tuition took over many of the socializing functions of the home and brought the ones that remained under the direction of modern science and technology." These developments profoundly affected the patterns of familial intimacy, and the altered structure of parent-child relations eventually worked a change in the structure of American personality. "On the principle that pathology represents a heightened version of normality," Lasch argues that we can most clearly appreciate what has happened to us by reading through the growing literature on "pathological narcissism." In the symptom constellations and character disorders of certain kinds of mental patients we can see the image, as in a cracked glass, darkly, of an entire nation's narcissism. If our "way of life . . . is dying," it is not merely because of the objective contradictions of advanced capitalism—economic stagnation, the impending exhaustion of natural resources, and the like—but because we ourselves, as individuals, are sick.

Lasch brings to this argument a wide acquaintance with the very best authorities on narcissistic illness, from Freud to Melanie Klein to a host of more recent specialists, including Otto Kernberg, Heinz Kohut, Warren Brodey, and Peter Giovacchini. That Lasch understands what he has read is apparent in the mini-essays he gives us on such topics as "Narcissism, Schizophrenia, and the Family" and "Narcissism and the 'Absent Father.'" Popularizations in the best sense of the word, these lucid resumés of a difficult science remind us of what the magazine *Psychology Today* might have become had it not descended into sensationalism. Lasch's erudition also makes him a perceptive critic of other popularizers of psychiatric modes of thought, as well as a devastating commentator on such deplorable fads of the day as the "new consciousness movement," which in effect advises people not to make too large an investment in love and friendship, to avoid excessive dependence on others, and to live for the moment. In a passage which seems to me definitive, Lasch diagnoses this advice as simply a reinforcement of the emotional malaise which gave rise to the consciousness movement in the first place.

Yet at the same time that he has profitably gone to school to the psychiatrists, Lasch seems to have all but forgotten that he was formally trained as a historian. I am going to argue, he says, that changes in the patterns of domestic intimacy occurred over a period of several generations, but the argument he makes is far more a matter of assertion than demonstration. He does not take us into the lives of representative American families, or indeed into the life of any family, in the era prior to the appearance of surrogate authorities on childrearing, and prove to us by specific example that mothers and fathers used to have confidence in themselves as parents and that they communicated that self-confidence to their children. Nor does he take us into representative American homes one, two, and three generations later and show us how parent-child relations changed, as he claims they did, and how those changes enhanced the growth of narcissistic traits in their offspring. In lieu of family history, he gives us a series of random comments about social reformers of the late nineteenth and early twentieth centuries who were professionally interested in children's welfare. But the reformers' claims to expertise do not come close to being a proof that American parents were progressively devaluing themselves, or that their children's personality structures were changing.

Having failed to produce solid evidence, Lasch is finally forced to turn to a quotation from Geoffrey Gorer, whose book, *The American People* (1948), bears the same relation to the study of our national character as Velikovsky's *Worlds in Collision* does to astrophysical research. The American mother, declares Lasch, quoting Gorer, has come to depend so heavily on experts that she "can never have the easy, almost unconscious, self-assurance of the mother of more patterned societies, who is following ways she knows unquestioningly to be right." Like most of Gorer's airy assertions, the statement carries no ballast—which is why Lasch immediately calls on a supporting witness. According to this observer, the "immature, narcissistic" American mother "is so barren of spontaneous manifestation of maternal feelings" that she "studies vigilantly all the new methods of upbringing and reads treatises about physical and mental hygiene." She acts not on her own feelings or judgment, but on the "picture of what a good mother should be." Now, Lasch may not be a diligent historian, but he is not without cleverness, and he handles these remarks so as to make them appear to be another broad observation about modern American mothers and thus a confirmation of Gorer's generalization. But in fact, the remarks are narrowly targeted. Drawn from a 1949 article in the *American Journal of Orthopsychiatry*, they refer only to the mothers of a small cluster of children whose psychological development had not been typically American, as the very title of the article indicates—"Adaptation of the Psychoanalytical Technique for the Treatment of Young Children with Atypical Development."

Lasch also fails to point out that the mothers in what Gorer calls "more patterned societies" did not raise their babies without plenty of advice from members of their extended families. Whether they lived in medieval Europe or in the islands of the South Pacific in Margaret Mead's time, these mothers did not go it alone. Much the same thing may be said of the mothers of early nineteenth-century America, as the biographical literature of the period makes clear. In a society largely made up of towns and villages, American mothers relied on the readily accessible wisdom of relatives and neighbors, as well as of the family doctor.

Mothers who raised their children with the help of John B. Watson in the 1920s, or of Arnold Gesell in the 1930s, or of Benjamin Spock and T. Berry Brazelton in more recent decades, did so partly because urbanization had made traditional sources of know-how less available. Some of these mothers, we can be sure, were also haunted by a distrust of their own instincts, like the women described in the psychiatric journal article cited by Lasch, and their surrender to the dictates of the pediatric manuals may well have disabled them further. But how large a percentage of the total did they constitute? How many other mothers in the last sixty years have set just as high an evaluation on their maternal talents as their counterparts did a century ago? How many, indeed, have been so strengthened by their faith in the efficacy of modern medicine and the wisdom of pediatric science that their confidence in their childrearing ability has surpassed that of all previous generations of American mothers? Confronting and disposing of these questions are tasks that are absolutely essential to the credibility of *The Culture of Narcissism*, but the author acts as if they did not even exist. With a dogmatism so insistent that it comes across as anguish, Lasch proclaims that the habit of relying on outside experts can only be interpreted as destructive of "parents' confidence in their ability to perform the most elementary functions of childrearing," and hence destructive of the capacity of their children "to form strong psychological identifications with their parents."

Sifting through the "wreckage" of contemporary American civilization, Lasch sees one sign of a new and better life. A growing distrust of experts and governmental bureaucracies has led men and women "in small towns and crowded urban neighborhoods, even in suburbs," to initiate decentralized experiments in cooperation which possibly signify "the beginnings of a general political revolt." Most observers regard grass-roots disenchantment with big government as a conservative force in American politics, but Lasch prefers the ancient dream of the Left: deep down, "the people" of this nation really don't like capitalism, and eventually they will revolt against it.

The rest of Lasch's report on the current state of the Union consists entirely of denials that there is anything worthwhile going on. Thus he derides the idea that the rise of new religious cults and the swelling attendance at traditional churches augur another "Great Awakening" of piety. "The contemporary climate is therapeutic, not religious," he avers. "People today hunger not for personal salvation . . . but for the feeling, the momentary illusion, of personal well-being, health, and psychic security." But as the thinness of his footnotes reveals, Lasch has not earned the right to speak in a tone of authority on these matters. His scornful dismissal of the spiritual content of the religious revivalism of our time is simply an impertinence—an impertinence, I might add, which does not even have the saving grace of humor. Unlike H. L. Mencken, Lasch is an anticleric who never makes us laugh.

The chapters in *The Culture of Narcissism* on the "new illiteracy" in our schools and on the "degradation" of American sports are full of troubling facts. Yet the facts are as familiar to us as the news magazines and pop-sociology books from which the author seems to have gleaned them. What one wants from Lasch is not another rehearsal of current events, but an explanation of them. Once again, however, he is content to let polemicism substitute for serious analysis. To say, for instance, that our schools have been shaped in the image of narcissism is profitless when the charge that we are narcissistic has not been proved in the first place.

Throughout his book, Lasch expresses a vivid contempt for what he calls "the privileged classes." Thus in his discussion of American universities he observes that "Mass education, which began as a promising attempt to democratize the higher culture of the privileged classes, has ended by stupefying the privileged themselves." As an example, he cites a group of Ivy League undergraduates who had never heard of the Oedipus complex and did not know who Oedipus was. I, too, am concerned about those students. Yet *The Culture of Narcissism* contains other examples of the stupefaction of the privileged classes which bother me even more, namely, the sloppy mistakes of the middle-aged professor who wrote the book. He misquotes General Douglas MacArthur. He refers to T. S. Eliot's "The Waste Land" as *The Wasteland* and to Wagner's Bayreuth as Beyreuth. He garbles Vince Lombardi's famous remark about winning being the only thing and then describes it as "George Allen's dictum." Before giving the entire nation a sermon on its loss of intellectual self-discipline, Lasch should look to his own.

Index